Albania
Escaping the East, Aspiring for the West

Perparim Xhaferi

Albania
Escaping the East, Aspiring for the West

Perparim Xhaferi

Connor Court Publishing

Connor Court Publishing Pty Ltd

Copyright © Perparim Xhaferi 2020

ALL RIGHTS RESERVED. This book contains material protected under International and Federal Copyright Laws and Treaties. Any unauthorised reprint or use of this material is prohibited. No part of this book may be reproduced or transmitted in any form or by any means, electronic or mechanical, including photocopying, recording, or by any information storage and retrieval system without express written permission from the publisher.

PO Box 7257
Redland Bay QLD 4165

sales@connorcourt.com
www.connorcourt.com

ISBN: 9781922449436

Cover design by Maria Giordano. Upper photo: The Great Mosque of Tirana (courtesy of Skender Bushi). Lower photo: Berlaymont building of the EU Commission (Brussels)

Printed in Australia

Contents

Acknowledgement	ix
Preface	xi
List of Tables and Figures	xiii
1. Albania: The Space of Imagination	1
2. The Ottoman Rule (1385-1912)	33
3. Recognition, Survival and Collapse of Albania (1913-1990)	75
4. Modern Turkish and Albanian Identities in the post-Cold War Period	111
5. Albanian Identity and the Ottoman Culture in the Work of Ismail Kadare	141
6: Farewelling the East?	163
Bibliography	195
Appendix	223
Index	229

To Jona, Greta and all Albanians.

Acknowledgement

Escaping the East, Aspiring for the West is an attempt to void historical stereotypes and provide the English reader with challenges Albania is facing in the twenty-first century. This book is result of a decade of research by the author on the topic. The journey of researching as a newcomer to Australia and a former PhD student has been challenging, but joyful. This research, and indeed this book, could not have happened without the help of some special people, to whom I am indebted.

Firstly, I wish to thank my principal supervisor at the University of Sydney, Professor Peter Morgan for his support, persistence and trust, during this research. Peter is one of a few Albanian literature scholars in the West, and his review on this book means a lot to me.

Secondly, I would like to thank the people who participated in this journey; providing their opinions and reflections on the topic. A special person that I want to thank is Ismail Kadare who, despite his busy agenda, in August 2013, allocated some time to meet with me and discuss his thesis regarding Albanian identity. Special thanks to Ilir Yzeiri and Hajro Limaj for their electronic correspondence and support. I also can't thank enough two Albanian researchers and archaeologists, Dr Era Bushi-Xhaferaj and Dr Skender Bushi. They have provided some valuable and never seen before maps and photos, but also offered their research on late antiquity. I would like to thank my colleagues and friends Jacob, Elizabeth, Chiara, Marco, Biaggio and Maren for their support and suggestions. I have learned a lot from them, and I feel extremely privileged to have been part of a positive group of friends.

A special thanks to Professor Bruno Mascitelli for his help with this book. Not only has Bruno encouraged me to write the book, but he also patiently edited and proofread the manuscript.

Finally, I would like to thank my family for their constant support through the entire research. My wife, Anila, for being patient with my studies. I simply couldn't have done it without her moral support, but more importantly, being there for our kids, at times when I was challenged by this research. I only hope my daughters, Jona and Greta, will forgive me for failing to spend more time with them during this research. Similarly, I hope they know more about their Albanian heritage after reading this book.

Given the difficulty in working with Albanian names and translations, I am responsible for any error the book may contain.

Preface

This book on Albania's political destiny in the 21st century is a welcomed and possibly unrivalled contribution to a much unknown theme not only in Australia but in most English-speaking constituencies. The book brings a treasure of historic information, revelations and analysis on Albania's roots and legacies and focuses especially on the Ottoman historic rule, domination and connection. It is supported by some revealing figures rarely seen on this subject. The book makes the case that historically Albania has been a victim at the hands of Balkan neighbours such as Serbia and Greece in the quest for territorial control and plunder as well as the power plays of imperialist regional powers such as Turkey, Russia and Italy. In almost all cases Albania emerges as the loser – a status one could say continues to this very moment.

While the book shows that under the Hoxha rule which began in 1944, some sense of national security and legitimacy was finally attained but marred by the political peculiarities and insecurities evidenced by this regime. Albania collapsed in 1990 as did the rest of Yugoslavia and revived many of the power plays prior to the Second World War including the Turkish alliance and connection. The work of Dr. Xhaferi demonstrates clearly that Albania with all of its historic legacies with the Ottoman rule, is still searching for its preferred strategic direction. It has gravitated between seeing its interests furthered with an alliance with the West, or more specifically with Europe, or with the presence of modern Turkey and its greater level of influence in the region. Joining NATO in 2009 and now seeking membership of the European Union, are signs that a Western direction is possible.

What is clear from Xhaferi's work is that irrespective of whatever legacies there were with the Ottomans and today modern Turkey – Albania will seek out what is in its political and economic interests. It is a small nation with limited influence and in many cases has limited choices. The outcome of this decision and political choice is still at play. This book informs the reader of these pressures and ultimately of the potential political direction of this small and besieged nation. I commend Dr. Xhaferi for this excellent coverage which will stand as an important text in this space for years to come.

Bruno Mascitelli

31 October 2020

Tables and Figures

Table 1 Estimated number of Albanians living abroad
          in 2005   22

Figure 1 Illyrian tribes from V BC to II AD   24

Figure 2 God of fertility, Amantia, III to II BC   25

Figure 3 Map of Albanian sites of Amphorae of late antiquity
          (IV to VII AD)   27

Figure 4 Albanian-Christian monuments in the
          Middle Ages   37

Figure 5 Three Albanian proposals, London Conference
          (1912)   79

Figure 6 Albanian Provisional Government claims
          (1919)   85

Figure 7 Stages of Greece's expansion of territory   91

Figure 8 Albania and Epirus with names of Illyrian tribes   92

Figure 9 The theatre of Butrothon (modern Butrinti)   93

1
ALBANIA: THE SPACE OF IMAGINATION

This book is based on my research but also a reflection of my personal life. I have a long-standing interest in the perception of Albanian identity by the world outside Albania. As can be understood – I am myself Albanian. A year after the Albanian communist government collapsed, I found myself a migrant in Europe where I struggled to express and display my Albanian identity, which evidently was not compatible with the Italian-European identity of those around me. I migrated to Italy in a most unofficial manner and I was in the beginning not familiar with the Italian language. Nor was I familiar with aspects of Italian tradition such as the deep ingrained tradition of Catholicism, of Sunday mass and the religious celebrations, of the gestures while speaking and the expectations of social intercourse in this country.

Despite my best attempts to learn and communicate in Italian, difficulties abounded. Living as an "undocumented" migrant was challenging as it is for most migrants in Italy. However, I realised that my customs and traditions, while different from those of Northern Italy, where I tried to make a new beginning, did not prevent me from integrating into this new society. I also realised that while some elements of my culture and tradition, such as songs, ceremonies and the "Albanian way of life" were slipping away from me, I started to absorb elements of the Italian culture and identity. While I never doubted Italy's hospitality to millions of migrants across the region, the settlement and integration remained a constant challenge for me and many other Albanians. In my mind, the main reason was a lack of multiculturism structures and understanding by the Italian government. However, Mascitelli and De Lazzari argue that the issue was even bigger than the Italian government, as "multiculturalism did not fail in Italy…it simply never existed" (2016: 61). In fact, for some Italians, I remained an "Albanese", a loaded term that meant being a thief, a criminal, rough and backward. Notwithstanding the fact that, alongside Greece, Italy provided shelter for nearly one million Albanians, after the end of the Cold War, feelings towards Albanians in Italy, and indeed Europe, have been influenced by stereotypical perceptions.

The racist sentiments on social media are complemented by the Italian media which has played a pivotal role in painting Albanians as thieves and smugglers as evidenced in the television series *Commissario Montalbano*. Thus, my personal experience, representing a generic post-Cold War Albanian migrant experience, fleeing due to food shortages and political and economic instability, in search of a better life, may also be useful to understand contemporary Albanian national identity and the way it may develop in the future. I, as a researcher, am inside this story, and my own experience colours my interpretation.

As outlined above, my history can be seen as representative of a common Albanian migrant who was born in Albania under the rule of Enver Hoxha, left Albania after the Cold War and lived in the West. I am now a citizen of Australia. Therefore, I brought to Australia a sort of an "Albanian identity" that in reality was mixed with an "Italian identity", which then amalgamated again with the "Australian way of life".

Albanian identity is contested on many levels. In the domestic sphere, Albanians are still wrestling with poverty and meeting basic economic needs. Arguably, poverty and globalisation have had an impact on domestic Albanian cultural norms and behaviours. However, in the international arena, Albanians are still misunderstood.

Albanian identity misperception: ignorance, speculation and stereotypes

Since the Middle Ages, Albanian people have been perceived as "mysterious" and subject to other poorly informed perceptions. Albanian lands and Albanians entered the "European imagination as a place of adventure, romance, and exoticism" (Morgan 2010: 5). Information about Albania emerged from reports of a small number of Western travellers, who visited Albanian villages in the nineteenth and twentieth centuries, and who conveyed their impressions about the Albanian lands to the West. Schwandner-Sievers informs us of the different interpretations of Albanian identity by German and British travellers at the beginning of the twentieth century. While German "Schmidt-Neke has shown that ideal-type descriptions of Albanian customary law, noble masculinity and warrior's honour underpin German Wehrmacht autobiographies", the British view as expressed by Durham concentrated on the Ottoman occupation and displayed a "measure of sympathy with the emerging insurgencies against the 'Ottoman Yoke'" (Schwandner-Sievers 2008: 57).

In 1928, Durham requested the British King and government send troops to Albania, out of sympathy for local Albanians who were threatened by Slav, Teuton and Greek geostrategic ambitions. On the other hand, she emphasised that Albanians were subject to "the fierce violence of local customary laws" (Durham [1909], 1985). Other artwork reflected subjective opinions of travellers about the Balkans and Albanians. An example is the description by Karl Krumbacher, an archaeologist, philologist and founder of the German Byzantine studies, who visited the Balkans in the late nineteenth century; reporting that Albanians were street sweepers (Todorova 2009: 71-74). A further example—Todorova discusses—is Ami Boue's nineteenth century description of the Ottomans as "serious and good-natured", Greeks as "refined", Serbs as "militant", Bosnians as "rough" people, Herzegovinians as "cheerful", whereas

Albanians as "witty". Those narratives presented at best superficial descriptions of the Balkan people that poorly reflected the spectrum of Albanian culture.

Although stereotypes are common on the Balkan Peninsula, Albanians suffered more from them than other Balkan nations. Both externally and within the Balkans, Albanians are portrayed to be the worst. The attempt to stigmatise Albania is at best a misunderstanding of the facts in their historical context, and at worst, a systematic attempt to craft "Albanianism" as an association with Said's concept of "Orientalism" (Said 1995: 7-8). The overarching theme of Said's Orientalism is that of Western hegemony over the Orient. However, applying this approach to Albania is problematic as it was not only the West, but also the Oriental Ottoman domination, which had influence in re-shaping Albanian identity. In 1913, Serbian Prime Minister Vladan Djordjevic (1844-1930) as part of anti-Albanian nationalist propaganda created and distributed pamphlets portraying Albanians "as inferior and thus, little capable of nation-building themselves", to the point that Albanians were seen as "primeval", "gypsy like" and also the only "tailed" devil-like people; still quite undeveloped (Schwandner-Sievers 2008: 52).

Before and after the collapse of The Porte[1], along with being labelled "primitive", Albanians were considered to be Turks and thus, enemies to their neighbours. Being portrayed as a weak and frail existence, Muslim in a sea of Christianity, is the way the stereotype sought to be vindictive, provocative and demeaning. The Albanian support for the Ottomans was, and still is, used as the reason Albanians are portrayed as "Muslims" in the middle of the Balkans. Another example is Stalin's famous quote during a meeting with Tito's foreign affairs advisor Edward Kardelj in which he stated that Albanians "...seem to be rather backward and primitive people...

---

1 The Ottoman Empire was also called *The Sublime Porte*, or *The High Porte*, or simply *The Porte*.

they can be as faithful as a dog; that is one of the traits of the primitive..." (Vickers [1995] 2001: 171). These stereotypes have remained to the present day powerful and unchanged throughout the Balkans and the West.

Hence, the current perception of Albania and Albanians is a dark space, evil and dangerous world, as it is portrayed in JK Rowling's *Harry Potter and the Goblet of Fire* (Alpion 2011: 113), or in the movie *Taken*. Over the past decades various scholars have noted these stereotypes as Schwandner-Sievers reminds us:

> The power of such imagery cannot be ignored, not least because it supports the arguments of particular, often violent Albanian interest groups, while effectively forcing the average, non-violent Albanian, faced with the outside world, into everyday mimicry, self-denial or apology, to mention just a few of the symptoms of Albanianism at work (Schwandner-Sievers 2008: 61).

Schwandner-Sievers and Todorova agree that only during the decline of the Ottoman Empire, did the Balkan people start to appear to the Western European imagination as potential nation-states, while they were at the same time perceived as second-class citizens. However, within the Balkans another sub-hierarchy was created, and according to Pettifer, even today, "racial and religious" stereotypes depict Albanians as "dangerous, Muslim and criminal; and Serbs as democratic, Christian and European", which continues to "make [Albanians] a convenient scapegoat" (Pettifer 2001: 19). It can be argued that this judgment for Albanians did not change, even with the collapse of Yugoslavia in the early 1990s after Serbian atrocities in Kosovo came to an end. Judah argues that the Albanian insurgency in 2001, witnessed through the adventurism of a few Albanians in the Presevo Valley and Macedonia, rather confirmed more stereotypes: "Serbs are good, Albanians bad" (Judah 2001:

15). In June 2020, the War Tribunal publicly accused the leader of the Kosovar Liberation Army [*Ushtria Çlirimtare e Kosovës*] (UÇK) and Kosovar President Thaçi and other Kosovar leaders for crimes against humanity. Of course, Thaçi and others are individuals and none of them represent the Albanian resistance against Milosevic's ethnic cleansing. Although the UÇK fought against Serbian atrocities, Albanians are still persecuted and branded as criminals, while Serbian war criminals are free and involved in Serbian politics. The danger is that this stigma is not only reinforcing the Albanian perception of "humiliation", but it may also have "very negative consequences for European Union political decisions" (Pettifer 2001: 19). Casting the "Muslim" Albanian people as the lowest ethnic group in the Balkans, customises the Balkan's version of Orientalism, and indeed, makes Albanians feel marginalised and excluded. What these stereotypes have shown most clearly is a cohesive Albanian identity that portray Albanians as "Muslims", if not Turks, as "dangerous" people who are situated at the bottom of European civilisation, which can only create more negative stereotypes, whilst the Albanian identity continues to be illusive.

Albanian studies

Since the mid nineteenth century, literature on many aspects of Albania has flourished. Along with rilindja writings, other scholarly literature on Albania has covered much of the process of nation building since the Albanian National Awakening in 1878 (Skendi 1967). Literature has also addressed the creation and consolidation of the Albanian state, the communist era, and the post-Cold War period. A common theme throughout much of this literature has been the constant struggle of the Albanian nation to survive. However, little research has been conducted on the historical relationship between Ottoman Turks and Albanian speaking populations. Exceptions to this are the periods of Skenderbeg (1443-1468), and to some extent, Ali Pasha's upheaval (1790-1822), which focused on Albanian resistance to foreign occupation.

While there has been scholarly engagement on Turkey's new activism during the post-Cold War period in the Balkans and the continuous evolution of Turkish foreign policy, the analyses of bilateral relations between Albania and Turkey after the creation of both nation states at the beginning of the twentieth century has essentially been ignored. Limited research has been undertaken by Tase (2013; 2014), Pajaziti (2011), Limaj (2012) and SÜLKÜ (2010) on bilateral relations between Albania and Turkey after the Cold War.

After the fall of communism in 1990, Albanians struggled to address questions regarding their identity, heritage and belonging in cultural, ethnic, religious, economic and political direction. The aim of this book is to investigate to what extent Turkey's influence over Albania in the twenty-first century will affect the Albanian decision to go West. The relationships between externally constructed representations of Albania and the ways in which Albanians construct their own identities in relation to similarities or differences with Turkish identity will be at the core of this analyses.

Other reasons for undertaking this research

Albanian studies remain largely an internal affair, bounded by a language that few specialists outside Albania have mastered. The current shortage of informed scholarly literature on Albania has prompted the author to undertake this research and offer some contribution in the field. Only small amounts of Albanian literature have been translated into English, while much of the narrative in this book is provided working with original language sources and making relevant sections available to the English reader. The well-known contemporary Albanian writer, Ismail Kadare remains one of the most influential Albanian writers and public intellectuals whose position regarding Albanian national identity in the context of the Ottoman Turks has been significant. It has also provided provocative assertions through his debates with numerous Balkan scholars including the Kosovar Rexhep Qosja. This debate has polarised Albania, its politicians, scholars, media and society, and this book will seek to inform the reader by bringing these authoritative voices to the English reader. Kadare's recent non-fictional works, and much of his fiction, which together comes to twenty volumes in the Albanian complete works edition, have only been translated in small amounts in English. In March 2018, the Albanian media *Mapo* revealed that for the first time, three essays of Kadare were translated directly from Albanian to English by an Albanian native speaker, Ani Kokobobo as *Essays On World Literature: Aeschylus-Dante-Shakespeare* (*Mapo* 2018).

Previously, other scholars have attempted to translate Kadare's works with John Hodgson becoming the leading translator directly from Albanian to English. Others such as Robert Elsie, Peter Constantine and Arshi Pipa have translated various shorter works, and several works were published in communist Albania, including *The Wedding* (trans. Ali Cungu) and *The Castle* (trans. Pavli Qesku) (Morgan 2018). However, most of Robert Elsie's translations of Kadare's works into English, have taken place via French translation by Jusuf Vrioni and Tedi Papavrami. Therefore, much of what has appeared in English has gone through French translations, rather than the Albanian originals, thus bringing to the English reader a doubly mediated version.

David Bellos who has also translated in English from French: *The Pyramid*, *The File on H*, *Spring Flowers*, *Spring Frost*, *The Successor*, *Agamemnon's Daughter*, *The Siege* and *Twilight of the Eastern Gods*, has recognised difficulties of translation in English from French— "a language with extensive, elaborate, and extremely rigid rules about verbal tense and mood"—to the less rigid and "sturdy, verb system of English" (Bellos 2012: 19-20). For Bellos, both

French and English are complex languages as they both have only one tense for the remote past, which is often used in Kadare's writings for example. As a result, there are enormous difficulties when translating from Albanian (which has an alphabet of 36 letters) to French (with 26 letters) due to differences of grammar, tense and structure. Although Bellos does not know Albanian, through translation of Kadare's works, and speaking directly to him, he has realised difficulties of translating from Albanian to English via French.

While Bellos is challenged by these translations, he acknowledges difficulties of working with the Albanian language, which he calls ambiguous or even manipulative. Kadare's mastering of his craft in a such difficult language, and his purportedly creation of universal time in his narratives, makes his powerful imagination and conscious artistry unique, while adding more to difficulties of translation. Although Jusuf Vrioni is considered the best translator of Kadare's works in French (Morgan 2011), according to Bellos, his translations were apparently not perfect (Bellos 2012). Indeed, the title of *Eskili, ky humbes i madh*, contains a mistake when translated in French as *Eschyle ou le grand perdant*. The use of "*ky*" by Kadare is a determinative and clearly does not allow room for speculation—Aeschylus is a great loser. In short, the direct translation from Albanian to English would have been *Aeschylus, this great loser*, or more accurately, *Aeschylus, the great loser*. However, the use of "*ou*" in French, which means "or" in English, may complicate the reader's perception of Aeschylus being a great loser.

Furthermore, lack of scholarly literature on Albania, not only opens the way for the ongoing propagation of stereotypes, but also means that crucial concepts have remained uncomprehended outside their Albanian context. One of these has been the role of religion and its relationship with nationalism in crafting the Albanian nation, which this book will explore.

The approach taken by this study

The methodological approach for this study will be based on political analyses. McNabb discusses the two main methodological research approaches in political science, namely positivist and post-positivist traditions (McNabb 2015). Accordingly, while the positivist approach is based on quantification and statistical analyses, post-positivist research is based on qualitative approaches such as explanatory, critical and post-modern research. This book will make use of quantitative data as evidence for specific lines of investigation. The quantitative research will be based on secondary sources, namely Albanian, European Union and Turkish government archives, their foreign ministry websites and other research institutions such as the Eurostat and the Albanian Institute of Statistics (INSTAT). These sources will not, however, tell us the entire story and must be supported with qualitative and theoretical material, as there are also invisible aspects of Albania's behaviour rooted in the Albanian heritage which exerts a strong influence on Albanian policy makers. In addition, Albania's delay in joining the European Union (EU) due to its limited progress on democratic reforms is a case in point. Thus, a qualitative analysis will help for example to pinpoint whether Albania's corruption has roots in its colonial past, and if so, whether this may further delay Albania's dream to join the European Union.

Qualitative research can give us more understanding about Albania's identity and its self-perception. The qualitative sources include primary interviews published by the Albanian media and secondary sources such as the media, literature from scholars, government reports etc. The research will also bring to light an interview the author had with Ismail Kadare who has been outspoken regarding Albanian-European identity. Thus, the book seeks to cast new light on the issue by drawing on English, through Albanian language sources, and drawing on little known data. Therefore, throughout this study, a large amount of relevant and hitherto inaccessible data primarily from Albanian is translated into English and is used for the re-interpretation of the narrative in this research.

Some limitations of this research

It has to be noted that there are some limitations to this research. Firstly, all government sources, be they Turkish or Albanian, are likely to display a certain level of bias, raising concerns regarding accuracy. Turkey and Albania claim to be liberal democracies, however, the European Union in the review of the two countries' membership applications has raised concerns about their slow path to democratisation. Analysing documents from Turkish government sources needs to be read in light of its poor record on "human rights" within its own country and thus, not only government documents, but also the media can be politically manipulated. Attention is also required when analysing the often-politicised Albanian media and government data, as the government and its opposition parties are still far from being free of bias. However, in this book, media articles from both Albania and Turkey are only used to retrieve concrete facts and not as a source of analyses.

Secondly, there is an issue with accessibility of some secondary sources as these keep disappearing after a certain period of time from some Turkish and Albanian media websites. Some articles seem to vanish from Albanian media sites, whereas since the last attempted Turkish coup d'état in 2016, the Turkish government closed down a number of Turkish newspapers and media sites; removing all material and data from those websites.

Ultimately, the lack of Albanian literature and documentation prior and during the Ottoman period is problematic. An exception is the period of Skenderbeg which is largely covered by many authors such as Frasheri, Barleti, Hodgkinson, Dizdari, Schmitt, Kadare etc., However, Albanian lands missed the European Renaissance, with Albanian literature being under a constant pressure from the Ottoman Turks. The analysis of the interaction between Albanians and the Ottoman Turks are often based on Ottoman documentation archived in Turkey and frequently inaccessible to researchers. Although *rilindja* writings at the end of the nineteenth and the beginning of the twentieth century are valuable secondary sources, the quasi-absence of Albanian literature from the Ottoman period is significant and problematic. Furthermore, the communist regime of Hoxha set Albanian identity on a different path, which raises questions about research outcomes of some Albanian writers during the communist period.

Terminology

To facilitate a better understanding of the theme of this book, it is important to discuss some of the key terms used in this field of research to guide the reader through the study as well as to describe the terminological choices made by the author. Firstly, *Albanian identity* is the overarching concept of this book and one that goes to the heart of this research. Discussing Albanian identity is not only complex but can also be controversial. The first question to be clarified is whether there is an Albanian identity and whether "Albanian identity" encompasses all ethnic Albanians that live in Albania and elsewhere, or whether it relates only to those Albanians in Albania. This book will conceptualise "Albanian identity" as a whole, including the identity of those Albanians who live in Serbia, Montenegro, Macedonia, Kosovo, Albania, but also abroad in countries such as Italy, Greece, US, Australia etc., The author is mindful about similarities and differences of identity between Albanians. An example is the development of a new Kosovar identity. This identity, while according to Mehmeti, still possibly imaginary, may emerge in the future, thus challenging Albanian identity (Mehmeti 2017: 25). Similarities between Albanians in terms of religion, culture, language and identity will be briefly highlighted in order to provide a deeper understanding of what might be considered as Albanian identity.

The East-West dichotomy – on which there is indeed much scholarship – is only provided with a very brief overview in order to elucidate Western Balkan complexities. According to Said, Western European countries are considered "Eurocentric" at the core of the West (usually together with North America); marginalising the periphery of Eastern countries (Said 1985). A more rigorous definition of the East-West dichotomy is problematic, as it is unclear whether it relates to geography, history, culture, politics, identity or religion (Gow 2005: 378-83). In the global era of interconnectedness where the West has more links with the East and vice versa, some believe that the concept of East and West is losing importance. Others use the geographical concept defining Northern European such as Scandinavian countries and Southern European including countries such as Spain, Portugal, Greece and Italy to then finish with South Eastern European countries—a cliché rather than a concept linked to geography. This stereotypical concept can get even more localised to regions, such as the case of Western Balkans, which are considered the "East" by Europe.

The "East" as a concept is a subjective category. For example, "West" Germans consider "Easterners" the same as other ethnic Germans who live further East, Northern Italians consider themselves "more Western" than Southern Italians, Poles are "East" to the East Germans, Greece is considered "East" by Italians, but Greece is considered West compared to Albania that geographically is situated on the West side of Greece. The same concept is also valid within Balkans where a Slovene is more "Occidental" than a Serb who considers a Bosnian an "Easterner", let alone "Albanians, who are perceived as easternmost by the rest of Balkan nations" (Todorova 2009: 58). This is a paradox as geographically Albania is situated in the western part of Western Balkans and much closer to Italy, or what is perceived by Western Balkan countries as the "Occident" or "Europe". Therefore, it is unclear whether this classification is based on geography, culture, democratisation, rule of law, or other criteria. For example, Bulgaria, an EU member, is situated on the Eastern side of Western Balkans, and yet, while it is part of "Europe", it has also been considered a Balkan state with a similar culture. Nevertheless, all Balkan people compete with each other; each of them arguing that they are "more European" than the rest of Western Balkans; leaving Turkey at the end of the regional hierarchy as an absolute "Oriental" country. Turkey is the common "Easterner" for all Balkan states; however, Turkey's self-perception is different, portraying themselves as a Western country compared to "real Easterners," such as Arabs, or a bridge between the East and West (İnalcik 1998). This is a clear imaginary-hierarchical classification of "others" and "superiority" that, in the case of Balkans, leads to historical divisions and a barrier that needs to come to an end.

The definition of the *Western Balkans* region is problematic. The Western Balkans is a region that comprises of Albania and the former Yugoslav republics of Bosnia-Herzegovina, Croatia, North Macedonia, Montenegro, Serbia and Kosovo. Why such a term is used and where is the Eastern Balkans region then? It makes more sense to speak about the Balkans as a region. Maria Todorova's *Imagining the Balkans* (2009) has added to scholarly analyses of the Balkans arguing that the "Balkan concept" has never been seriously considered a central category of identity but is rather a "subspecies of the larger identity problem of small peripheral nations" (2009: 51-57). As a result, Todorova who was "directly inspired" by Said's "orientalism", is convinced that the Western Balkan countries merit a whole genre of work in order to explore stereotypical metaphors (Todorova 2009: 192).

Three decades after the end of the Cold War, Western Balkan countries continue to be "halfway democracies" (Bego 2017) in a region that is challenged by economic poverty, corruption, nationalism, ethnic and religious divisions. Except Croatia—the only EU member state, other Western Balkan countries, Bego argues, are all facing three challenges: the failure of democracy to deliver healthy political competition, Russian interference in the Slavic-majority nations in recent years, which has further complicated the political landscape, and the reluctance of Europe to accept Western Balkan states as EU members. What is missing in the Bego analysis is the influence of Turkey in the Western Balkans – another powerful actor that aims to get closer to Muslims in the region (Türbedar 2011). The main reason to generate these challenges is that Western Balkan countries incarnate the complexity of emerging relations with both West and East. At present, these countries are seeking to re-imagine themselves and bolster their links with the West, while developing concurrent relations with "Eastern" countries such as Russia, Turkey but also economically with China. The reluctance of the EU to include Western Balkans as EU member states create a perfect environment for Eastern countries such as China, Russia and Turkey – a country that portrays itself as "a bridge between East and West" (Heper 2004).

Greater Albania is linked to the concept of Great Powers, and the decline of the Ottoman Empire. While for Albanian nationalists the unification of all those territories into the so called "Greater Albania" would end centuries of humiliation and injustice, Western Balkan nationalists view this as merely an irredentist idea that is trying to destabilise the region. Greater Albania is not the only concept of "greater nation-states" in the Western Balkans. None of the Balkan countries were pleased with the way the Great Powers drew up the Balkan borders in 1913. However, in the twenty-first century, it seems that projects of Greater Serbia (Nacertanie), Greater

Croatia, and Greater Greece (Megali-Idea)—all older than "Greater Albania"—have been put to rest (Bogdani and Loughlin 2007: 233), while, as Tanner mentioned, the ghost of Greater Albania is yet to disappear (Tanner 2015).

In relation to the previous concept of Greater Albania, Kosovo, or Kosova[2] needs further explanation. Following the Ottoman downfall in 1911, Western Kosovo was integrated into the Kingdom of Montenegro and Eastern Kosovo into the Kingdom of Serbia. Various administrative reorganisations of the territory took place during the 1920s and, in 1929, Kosovo was included as part of the new formation of the Kingdom of the Serbs, Croats and Slovenes (Yugoslavia). After WWII, Hoxha subscribed initially to the long-term Moscow policy of merging Albania with Yugoslavia and Bulgaria to create a so-called "Balkan Federation" (Malcolm 1999: 319). Kosovar Albanians were threatened by discriminatory policies in the areas of language and education, and government policies of relocation of Serbs into Kosovo led to further population movements of ethnic Albanians (Morgan 2015).

It was only under Yugoslav leader Josip Broz (Marshal Tito) that Kosovo was recognised as an "autonomous region" and, as a result after 1966, the situation for Albanians improved (Jacques 2009: 43; Malcolm 1999: 316). Stalin became suspicious of Tito's intentions, resulting in the expulsion of Yugoslavia from the Comintern (Communist International) in 1948. Hoxha continued to remain loyal to Stalin and thereby ending the relationship with Tito and Yugoslavia. As a result, Tito developed a distrust of Hoxha and the Kosovar Albanians (Morgan 2015).

The end of the Cold War coincided with the disintegration of the Yugoslav Federation although Kosovo only separated from Serbia

---

2 Albanian official name is *Kosova*, or often called *Dardania*, which was the Illyrian tribe located in the area. For Serbs the official name is *Kosovo-Metohija*. This book will utilise the name Kosovo when referring to it.

in 1999, through NATO military intervention. In 2008, a country with 90 per cent ethnic Albanian population, proclaimed its independence to then become the Republic of Kosovo but this did not stop five European member states: Spain, Greece, Slovakia, Cyprus and Romania, from refusing to recognise its existence. According to Abazi, it would "… impact on relations between regional actors, including the EU, Russia, NATO and Turkey" (Abazi 2008: 2). Citing the Turkish former Prime Minister Bülent Ecevit, Abazi emphasises that Turkey perceives Kosovo, "as a debt it owes to its own history" (2008: 3). While an important issue, an examination of the Kosovar nation-state or state identity is outside the scope of this book. This book will consider the identity of Kosovar-Albanians who live in Kosovo and other parts of Balkans as part of the Albanian national identity.

Albanian identity

Since the collapse of Communism in Europe and the Balkans by the early 1990s, Albanians have wrestled with questions of identity, heritage and belonging in cultural, ethnic, economic and political terms. Communist rule began in 1944 under Enver Hoxha who died in 1985 and which ended in the early 1990; imposing a distinctive brand of nationalism on Albania. Questions from the pre-communist past have re-emerged as the new state struggles to establish a new, post-communist identity. The theme of ethnic Albanians in the adjacent Balkan states of Macedonia, Montenegro and Serbia have reappeared with the break-up of the former Yugoslav Republic, which have further challenged the stability of Western Balkans.

Foreign interests were quick to begin penetrating the once-closed Albanian state soon after the end of the communist government. European and American business interests began to arrive as did Saudi and Kuwaiti money, which was channelled into the country to assist the re-establishment of Albanian Islam (Deliso 2007). Albanians themselves looked to both East and West, as well as to the European Union (EU) and the newly powerful regional state, Turkey, to ascertain their appropriate move towards the old and new partners in the context of post-communist democracy and globalisation.

Turkey has emerged as a powerful player over the past decade in contemporary discussions of Albanian existence and its identity. The reasons for this may be historical as the Ottoman Turks occupied parts of the Albanian Balkans from the late fourteenth century onward, imposing their culture, language, beliefs and more, and drawing the Albanians into the cultural and civil sphere of the Orient, of Islam and Ottoman rule.

The issue of the "Ottoman identity" of Albania has been hotly debated in the wake of the fall of the Berlin Wall. The recent revival of Neo-Ottomanism is but one example of the ongoing debate in the region. The Neo-Ottomans hoped to construct a new Turkey that is based on the Ottoman values, and thus Islam (Yavuz 2020). While Turkish power in the Eastern Mediterranean generally is not to be underestimated, the significance of Turkish engagement in Albania and Kosovo need to be understood.

There have been ubiquitous discussions over the past two decades regarding Albanian national identity; its similarities with "European identity" and the aim to join the 'Euro-Atlantic' family of the West, thereby farewelling its historical legacy of Ottomanism. According to the Albanian government and policy makers, Albania's post-Cold War foreign policy is based on two pillars: the US and the European Union (EU). It is assumed by leaders on both sides of Albanian domestic politics, (Topalli, Nano, Berisha, Moisiu, Meta, Rama and others) that only the "Euro-Atlantic Orientation" will guarantee Albania's survival and prosperity in the international arena.

However, as an old Italian proverb states: *tra il dire e il fare c'è di mezzo il mare* [the difference between words and actions is as big as the ocean]. Albanian politicians may assert that Albania is going West, but what is happening in reality?

Albanians continue to be the most scattered people in the Western Balkans, and the refusal by Greece and Serbia to recognise the independence of Kosovo in 2008, without mentioning the ghost of "Greater Albania" seem to remain painful points for Albanians. The paranoia of a "Greater Albania" evidently has not come to an end. For the First Deputy Prime Minister and Minister of Foreign Affairs Ivica Dačić, the danger of Albanian expansionism seems to be everywhere – in the drone flying over the now infamous Albania-Serbia football match; at Albanian Prime Minister Edi Rama's residence, where a light-display projected the map of Greater Albania for New Year's celebration. In the West's silence, the Greek Defence minister condemned and punished seven Greek soldiers of Albanian origins that formed the Albanian double eagle symbol with their hands. The Greek government has successfully managed to include the issue of minority rights through the European Parliament to condition the Albanian-EU membership, while the issue of deportation of the Albanian-Cham population is historically ignored by Greece. Due to its vulnerability on economic, energy, defence and security, choices for Albania are limited and often forced.

One might also mention the strong historical-cultural bridge that links Albanians in the twenty-first century with five million Turks, who according to Genci Muçaj, the Albanian former Ambassador in Turkey, are conscious of, and proud to mention their Albanian heritage (Mlloja 2015). A more aggressive Turkish foreign policy to get closer to Albania is already using historical-cultural links between Albania and Turkey in their favour, to bring about

Albania's alignment with the East. Turkey may also use Albania's economic, geo-political and security concerns, which remain high for Albanians in the twenty-first century. These are only a few concerns that might affect Albanian's decision to re-align with the East and thus, Turkey. Nevertheless, the question is to whether these cultural links with Turkey are strong enough to force Albanian policy makers to follow Turkey and abandon the West?

The reluctance of both Albanian and Kosovar governments to clearly specify whether Albania will distance its foreign policy from Turkey, while attempting to join the West, creates confusion. Recent arguments between Kadare's thesis and Qosja's opposing position with regards to the Albanian national identity have divided Albanian politicians, scholars and the media. This debate is the best example of Albanian identity contestation, but also shows complexities for Albanian policy makers to decide whether Albania will go West or East. While governments, scholars and media can be instrumental, they cannot stop Albanian people to imagine their identity as belonging to the Western-Christian-European or Eastern-Muslim-Turkish civilisations, but also part of both Eastern and Western civilisations. However, political decisions on foreign policy are made by policy makers and at the moment, all sides of Albanian politics have made Euro-Atlantic orientation the preferred priority for Albania. This book will try to enlighten readers whether Albania will farewell the Ottoman-Turks and thus join the West, or whether EU reluctancy to accept Albania as a member and also Balkans ongoing tensions, pushes Albania to side with Turkey.

Where is Albania?

Albania has a total area of 28,748 square kilometres and shares its borders with Montenegro to its North and North-West, Kosovo to the North and North-East, Northern Republic of Macedonia to the

North-East and East, and with Greece to the South and South-East. To the West, Albania's coastline along the Adriatic and the Ionian Sea is located close to Italy—the distance between Vlorë and the Strait of Otranto in Italy is less than 75 kilometres. Although both Greeks and Albanians live on both sides of the South-Eastern Albanian border, neither are satisfied with borders drawn up by the Great Powers at the beginning of the twentieth century. Nor are Albanians happy with borders that show Albanian speaking people and territories included within Montenegro, Serbia and Macedonia, which according to Pettifer, are a reason for instability in the Western Balkans (Pettifer 2001: 18).

Albania continues to be the poorest country in the Western Balkans, with the majority of the population living on less than 5 US dollars per day. After the end of the Cold War, internal migration to the cities at the expense of rural areas took place. Equally large numbers of Albanians left their country and are now living abroad. In 2005, the number of Albanian migrants living abroad was estimated to be 1,093,000 (see Table 1); which is more than one third of the entire Albanian population of circa 2.86 million estimated by the Albanian Institute of Statistics (INSTAT) in 2018 (Judah 2019). The outward migration of Albanians is an unstoppable phenomenon and seemingly another challenge for Albania in the twenty-first century. Other data from INSTAT shows that from 2006 to 2019, the number of young people in the country has steadily decreased while net emigration is still on the rise (Judah 2019). Even though this data is from government official sources, its veracity is questionable: accurately calculating undocumented migrations is a challenge as my own migration illustrates. The author was one of those migrants who left Albania and moved to Italy for a number of years without informing either the Italian or Albanian authorities!

Table 1 – Estimated number of Albanians living abroad in 2005

Country	Number of Albanians living abroad
Greece	600,000
Italy	250,000
US	150,000
United Kingdom	50,000
Germany	15,000
Canada	11,500
Belgium	5,000
Turkey	5,000
France	2,000
Austria	2,000
Switzerland	1,500
The Netherlands	1,000
TOTAL	1,093,000

Source: Adapted from Government of Albania in Vullnetari (2007: 36)

Who are Albanians?

The meaning of Albanian identity is contested and multifaceted. The complexities start with the ethnic origins of Albanians. Albanian lands have been inhabited since antiquity as stated on the Albanian Council of Ministers webpage: "Traces of life from the period of middle and late Paleolithic (100 000 - 10 000 years ago) are found in Xare, as well as in the Cave of Saint Marina in Saranda" (Albanian Council of Ministers). The Albanian Council of Ministers webpage also claim that Albanians are "direct successors of the Illyrians". This is supported by some scholars who claim that modern Albanians are descendants of Pelazgo-Illyrians. Other scholars posit that Illyrians were the inhabitants of Illyria during the seventh century BC (Vickers [1995] 2001: 1). Based on archaeological analysis, Edwin Jacques states that the origins of Albanians belong to Pellazgo-Illyrians, stating: "... historical sources thereafter demonstrate the unbroken continuity of these Pelasgian and Illyrian forebears down to the additional centuries to the Albanians of our days" (Jacques 2009: 28).

As shown in the figure 1, Illyrians lived within tribal communities of blood relations such as Liburni, Ardaei, Dalmatae, Albani, Dardani, Taulanti, Orestes, Labeati, Amanti, Molossi, Chaones and Thesproti that included Dalmatian coast down to today's Montenegro and Albania (Ceka 2000: 42). They conducted their political and social affairs based on the tribal system. Socioeconomic patterns, such as "clan or tribe living in hilltop towns fortified with walls of huge roughly hewn stones", "burial rites" and ceramic potteries founded in Albania, are three factors that, according to Jacques, "indicate the cultural unity of this entire Illyrian region" (Jacques 2009: 28). Figure 2 shows an example of archaeological discoveries in the South of today's Albania, that belongs to the Illyrian tribes of Amanti.

Although there are complexities in determining the exact "age" of Albania, different archaeological sites in Albania such as Dyrrahium (Durrës), Scodra (Shkodër), Apolonia (near Fier), Lissus (Lezha) and Buthroton (Butrinti near Sarandë) are examples of Albania's ancient past (*Albanian Council of Ministers*). Stocker and Davis argue that Apolonia (an important Illyrian maritime port) was founded in 588 B.C. and not in the seventh century B.C. as

Figure 1: Illyrian tribes from V BC to II AD

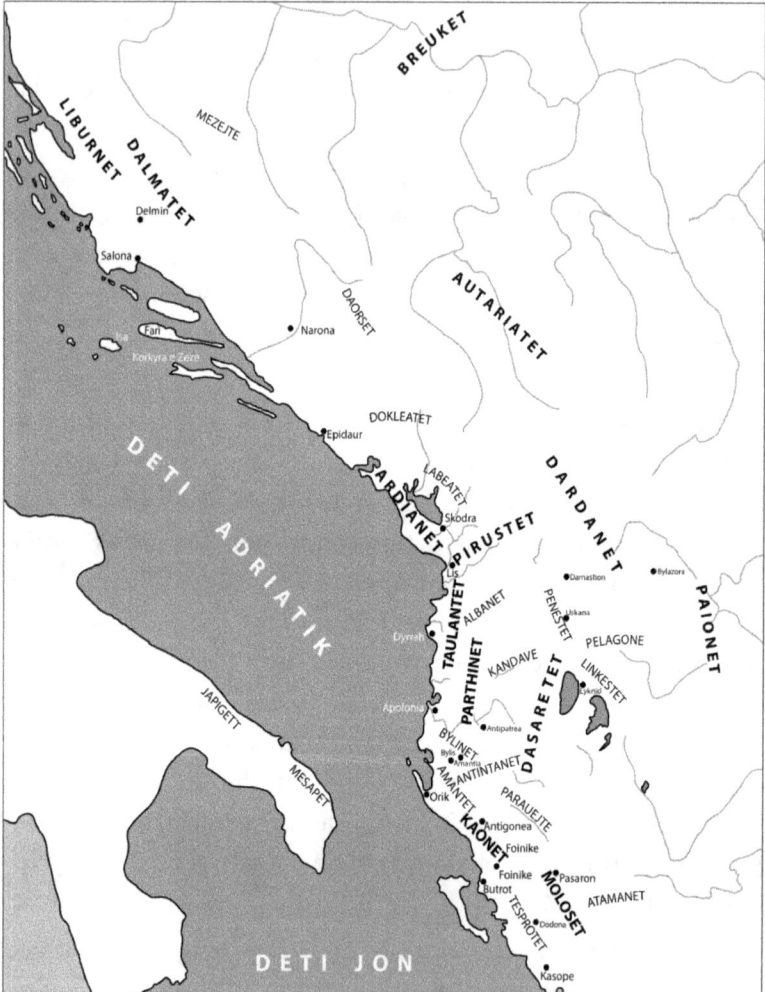

Source: Adapted by Skënder Bushi. Pavilion of Antiquity', *Albanian National Historical Museum*, Tiranë.

This is an adaption of the Illyrian wall map located at the *Albanian National Historical Museum*. It shows the Illyrian tribes situated in the Western Balkans from the fifth century BC to the second century AD. Illyria was situated from today's Croatia in the North to Greece in the South. Traces of Illyrian culture are found also in today's Italian peninsula.

Figure 2: God of Fertility, Amantia, III-II BC

Source: Bushi, Skënder (2018). 'Treasuries from the Pavilion of Antiquity', in *Treasuries Of National Historical Museum*, Tiranë: 20 – 21.
This small stone-relief was found at the Illyrian city of Amantia in South Albania and represents the God of fertility. It dates back to the Hellenistic period and thus, between the III-II BC. The male at the centre of the relief represents the personification of the River Deity. Diety usually appeared in iconography with a floral garland on top of his long, rich and scraggly hair. He is holding a cornucopia (horn of plenty), which has the shape a container overflowed with flowers and fruits. On the other hand, Diety holds a kantharos, which is believed to be an attribute linked with the cult of Priapus. On both sides two companion female figures seem to support Deity with one of them placing her hand on his right shoulder.

claimed by the Albanian archaeologist Neritan Ceka (Stocker and Davis 2006: 85). If anything is clear, it is the fact that the inhabitants of Illyria spoke a different language from ancient Greeks—the Illyrian language, which according to Stocker and Davis, formed part of the old Indo-European family of languages (Woodard 2008: 7-8). Therefore, Albanian language links Albanians with their ancestors, or people who inhabited the region—Illyria. It is also a fact that Albanian language is different from other languages spoken in the Balkan peninsula.

Drawing on the scholarly historiography of Albania, Morgan posits that Illyria was "situated between East and West" and, unlike Greece, it suffered at the hands of the Romans, Byzantines and Ottomans, in "one of the major fault-lines of global civilisation over the following millennia" (Morgan 2010: 5). Greek influence started to be replaced by Latin civilisation after the third century BC. The Illyrian Wars against the Romans started in 229 BC and ended in 168 BC, after the Romans defeated Gentius, the last Illyrian king. As a result, the Illyricum Peninsula "were forced to submit to increased Romanisation" (Fox 1989: xvi). The huge crises of the Roman Empire in the fourth century, and a slow collapse in the fifth century, transformed the Illyrian lands into a battleground, attacked and invaded by Goths, Huns, Visigoths and Ostrogoths (Bushi 2016: 6). The Albanian archaeologist and specialist of the late antiquity, Skender Bushi, has provided a detailed study of amphorae founded in Albanian archaeological sites (as shown in the figure 3) that brings about new scientific evidence that Albanian lands are ancient (Bushi 2016: 324). During the fourth and six centuries, Slavs expanded into the South, and the unsuccessful siege of Thessaloniki in 586 did not stop them conquering and settling next to the Shkumbin River. These invasions weakened the Byzantine Empire until the beginning of the ninth century when the Byzantine Empire expanded again into the present-day Albanian territory and almost the entire Balkan Peninsula. Therefore, the invasion of the Albanian speaking lands did not come to an end as described by Malcom in his essay "Myths of Albanian National Identity" where he cites an earlier Albanian writer, Kostandin Cekrezi, who in 1919 considered the pre-Ottoman invasion of the Albanian-speaking lands by "…the Gauls, the Romans, the Goths, the Slavs, the Normans, the Venetians, and, finally the Turks" as continuous and never ending (Malcolm 2002: 80).

In the fourteenth century, when the Ottomans arrived, the Albanian-speaking people were organised in small groups or clans (in Albanian *fise*), that had blood relationships between members of the same clan. Hodgkinson describes these tribes as formed by "kinship [that] remained in principle", while organised in groups that in "later times, if not earlier", had a strong and capable military, which, as a unit, fought together (Hodgkinson 2004, reprinted

Figure 3: Map of Albanian sites of amphorae of late antiquity (IV-VII AD)

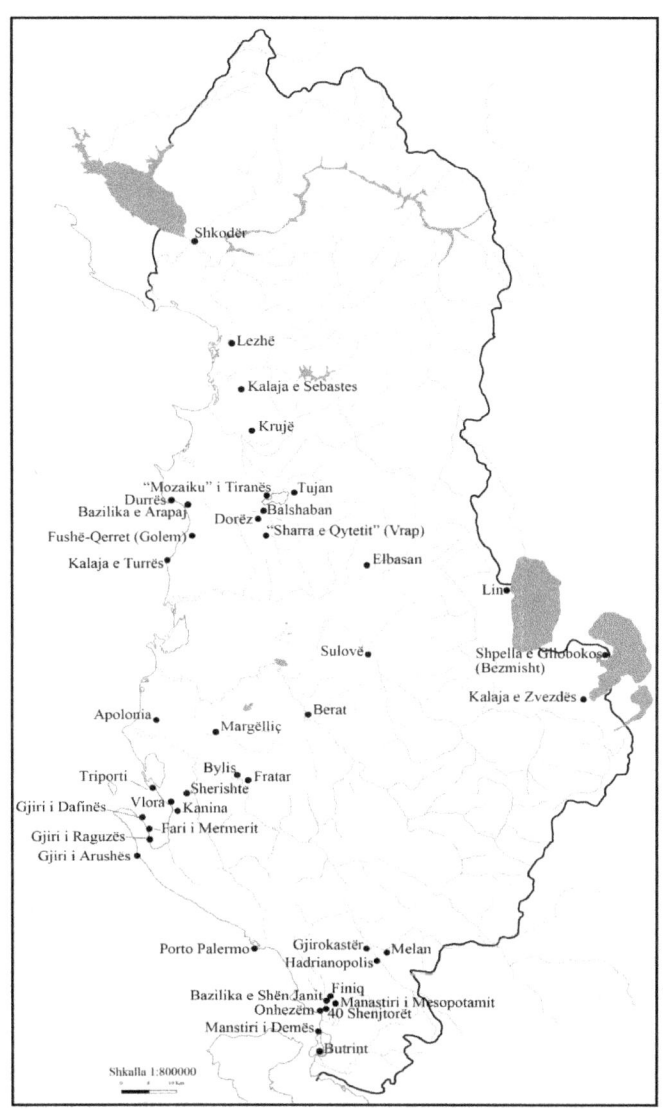

Source: Bushi, Skënder (2016), 'Amforat e Antikitetit të Vonë në Shqipëri (shek. IV – VII m. Kr.)' [Amphorae of late antiquity in Albania (IV – VII AD)], author's translation, unpublished PhD thesis, *Qendra e Studimeve Albanologjike* [Center of Albanological Studies], Tiranë: 323.

2017: 15). The main two ethno-linguistic groups divided by the Shkumbin River—*gegs* (in the North) and *tosks* (in the South) are unique groupings that had Albanian language in common. Despite speaking different Albanian dialects, these two groups also had differentiation on folk and cultural elements that varied across the Albanian speaking lands.

The nature of the Albanian *fise* could not conform to the notion of "civilized society" which according to Crone required a society to be gradually transformed through agrarianism and industrialisation (Crone 2003: 1-10), but rather, as Jenkins discuses, they formed "primitive" organisations of people, grouped together in order to defend themselves from other groups (Jenkins 2008: 16). The question then becomes how to understand those common bonds that at the end of the nineteenth century, forged the concept of the Albanian nation. Answering this question will help examine the Albanian nation and the origins of its existence, a concept which Bismarck, to the detriment of the region, failed to grasp during the Berlin Congress in 1878, where he expressed his scepticism regarding the Albanian Question, which in his view, did not exist.

It is argued that Albanian tribes' rules and legislations, such as the famous *Kanun i vjetër* [Old Kanun], which is known as *Kanuni i Lekë Dukagjinit* [The Kanun of Lekë Dukagjini], dates back to ancient times. According to Fox who translated *Kanuni i Lekë Dukagjinit* [*The Kanun of Lekë Dukagjini*], writen in Albanian by Shtjefën Gjeçov, this jurisdiction was widely used as "customary law" for the Dukagjin region and later, at the beginning of the fifteenth century, expanded to other Albanian principalities (Fox 1989: xvi). Although Roman occupation and its iron rule forced a temporary abandonment of the *kanun*, Fox argues, they could not stop this unwritten law from being transmitted orally to succeeding generations of Albanians. Neither were the Byzantines successful in abolishing it. As Hodgkinson posits:

The old laws of the mountains, though they endured longer than any other system of authority in Europe (and probably still command the loyalty of the older Albanian highlanders) remained essentially the law that great Greek tragedians grappled with and transformed: a law whose sanctions come into operation mechanically, like a natural phenomenon, without regard for the motive of the offender or the gravity or triviality of the offence (Hodgkinson 2004, reprinted 2017: 4).

While in the North, the old *kanun* served as a control mechanism, regulating social and political life as the only code of customary law used in Albania, the centre and South Albania had their own customised legal codes, or different versions of *kanun*. The influence of the Byzantine Empire in the South of the Albanian speaking lands was evident in a number of ways: the manner its legislation was implemented to resolve family disputes; Orthodox religion, music, myths, dress, art, architecture and the influence of the Greek language.

What's in the book?

This book has six chapters. This first chapter introduced the book, its methodology and some key terminology used in this research. Drawing on the existing literature, this chapter provided a short background to the contested arguments that surround Albanian identity. The objective of this chapter was to introduce the origins of the Albanian identity concept and highlight some complexities that have affected it. These debates will then be part of discussion and analyses in later chapters. This chapter also highlighted gaps in the existing scholarly literature, and thus sought to offer this research as a possible contribution to the literature.

Drawing back on Albanian history, since the Ottoman arrival in 1385, chapter two will discuss major implications of the Ottoman influence in Albanian-speaking lands until the declaration of the Albanian Independence in 1912. This chapter aims to discuss how The Porte affected Albanian nationalism and the creation of the Albanian entity. It will explore the Ottomans influence in the Albanian speaking lands, in areas such as social organisation, infrastructure, written language, the system of education and the role of religion. The Ottoman impact on Albanian nation and identity, ethnicity, nationalism and religion will be part of this debate.

The third chapter will focus on survival and recognition of Albania since its Independence in 1912. It will briefly cover periods of the Balkan Wars, World War I (WWI), World War II (WWII) and the Cold War. The chapter will also discuss relations between Turkey and Albania within this period and the political influence of Turkey in fields such as economy, foreign policy, geopolitical alignments and security, which may affect the Albanian "Euro-Atlantic" orientation.

The next three chapters will go to the heart of the book. The fourth chapter will continue exploring identity elements of the modern Turkey. It will discuss whether Turkish intention to escape East and go West is a cliché or reality. Turkey's foreign policy in the twenty-first century will help to explore issues such as "Islamism" and "neo-Ottomanism"—concepts that will further assist to grasp Turkey's seriousness of joining the EU and thus, West. The chapter will then analyse post-Cold War bilateral relations between Albania and Turkey. Analyses will focus on areas such as diplomacy and foreign policy, economy, energy and defence matters; concluding with religion, which is one of the main controversies in the twenty-first century that surrounds Albanian identity in relation to the Ottoman heritage and culture.

Chapter five will attempt to understand whether Albanian identity has in its composition elements of the Ottoman heritage, and thus belongs to Eastern civilisation, or rather reflects elements of the Western civilisation through the thesis of the Albanian prominent writer, Ismail Kadare. This will be through Kadare's own words and direct engagement with some publications of Kadare in the Albanian language. It will also explore Kadare's main opposing voice, Rexhep Qosja, through discussions that while contradicting Kadare's thesis, also shows how debated these arguments are.

Chapter six will aim to explore whether in the twenty-first century, Albania is farewelling the East and thus, Turkey. The chapter will discuss Albanian challenges in areas such as culture resistance and loanwords, Islam and regional security, which are amplified by the political pressure of the Turkish Government over the Albanian domestic affairs. The book will conclude with some remarks to better understand whether, in the twenty-first century, Turkey can halt Albania's Euro-Atlantic path and pull it back to East.

2
THE OTTOMAN RULE (1385-1912)

The Ottoman Empire for over 500 years occupied the Albanian-speaking lands, from their arrival in 1385, until the declaration of the Albanian Independence in 1912. The Ottomans reigned in areas such as social organisation, infrastructure, demography and religion. Drawing on historical narratives of the Ottoman occupation, the aim in what follows is to discuss how The Porte impacted Albanian speaking lands and suppressed the creation of the Albanian entity.

How did the Ottomans enter Albania? According to historic records the feudal lord of Durrës, Karl Topia, invited the Ottoman Turks into what constitutes today's Albania, to assist him in his conflict with the Balsha family (Winnifrith 1992: 77). After five years of attacks from troops led by Karl Topia, in 1367, the Duchess of Durrës, Joanna of Anjou and her first husband, Louis of Navarre, stepped down. Topia, who claimed the title of *Princeps Albaniae*, ruled the regions of Durrës, Elbasan, Peqin, Krujë, Mokra and Gora, as far as the Lake Ohrid, which today represents central Albania, located on both sides of Via Egnatia (Jacques 2009: 169). In 1370, Topia attacked the powerful family of Muzaka in the South and conquered their plain lands situated between the Shkumbin and Seman rivers. This forced Muzaka to ally with another powerful family, Balsha, whose army was led by Balsha II. In 1385, the troops of Muzaka and Balsha II captured the city of Durrës in a surprise attack. Topia called for help from the Ottomans who entered the Albanian speaking lands through Via Egnatia and crushed the Balsha army at the battle of Savra on 18 September 1385. Balsha II was killed and this defeat introduced a new era for the Albanian speaking lands, as the fifteenth century historian and priest Marin Barleti sets out:

> Upon his death, the barbarians set off to tread upon Epirus for the first time and plunder it. From that moment, they [the Ottomans] took over Kastoria, Berat and Kruja… (Barleti 2012: 60).

Other Albanian lords and powerful families soon became *vassals* of the victorious Ottomans, as did local Serbs after the defeat at the Battle of Kosovo (*Polje*) in 1389. Although Balkan forces united in the battle of Kosovo Polje in 1389, the Ottomans crushed the united Balkan army, resulting in the loss of their leader, King Lazar of Serbia. The same night the battle ended; Sultan Murat I was also assassinated. For Albanian and other Balkan principates, Kosovo Polje had a domino effect that resulted in further capitulation to the Sultan Murat II and later to his son, Sultan Mehmed, who was named "the Conqueror".

Although many Albanians fought and died alongside Serbs, including the feudal lord Teodor I Muzaka, Serbian nationalism appropriated Kosovo Polje and mythicised this battle as a spiritual doctrine, using it to describe themselves as defenders of European Christianity against "the other" Asian-barbarian-Turks. According to Payton, Albanians who initially converted to Islam and, later on, all ethnic Albanians regardless of their religion, were viewed by Serbian nationalism as "others" (Payton 2006: 22). Therefore, the Kosovo Polje battle marked a turning point in the relations between Albanians and Serbs, and entered history via Serbian folklore, songs and myths, which were "…enriched with nationalistic tones only in the nineteenth century..." (Kola 2003: 4). One of the central tenets of Serbian and Balkan nationalism, which considered Albanians as Turks, is not only based on a superficial analysis of equating Albanians as Muslims and thus Turks, but is also misleading and unfounded as, under the Ottoman rule, ethnic Albanians experienced the same, if not greater levels of suffering as other Balkan ethnicities.

Charles and Barbara Jelavich emphasise that Albania was identified as one of the "most backward" areas of the Ottoman Empire (Jelavich and Jelavich 1977: 223). Throughout the Ottoman period, the majority of Albanian speaking people—especially peasants, lived within the "limits of what their rural homeland could support" (Anscombe 2006: 93). On the other hand, the national tradition in Balkan historiography tended to equate Albanians with Turks, which for Anscombe is "incomprehensible, incorrigible, intolerable". Although many Muslim Albanian leaders were part of the Ottoman privileged strata, Albanian speaking populations were forced to accept the Ottoman rule.

However, the view that Albanian culture came under siege from the Ottomans is also misleading. It is instructive to explore that the arrival of the Ottoman-Turks, and thus their language, culture and religion in Albanian speaking lands, brought about more confusion for the existing contested Albanian identity. As Fox argues, the Ottomans fostered a new religion along with Turkish customary law that was heavily based on *Sharia* (Islamic law). The ways in which the Islamic doctrine and its way of life slowly blended with that of the Albanians to create a mix of culture and identity that was neither Roman, nor Byzantinian was unique. The arrival of the Ottomans in Albania inevitably introduced terminology and elements of Turkish culture into all spheres of Albanian life such as the military, administration, language and religion. Nor can one ignore the Turkish culinary tradition that was incorporated into the cuisine of Albania, and other Balkan countries, from a simple Turkish coffee to *dollma*, *shishkebap*, *qofte*, or even the turko-Byzantinian *burek*. Many of these culinary elements are still present in Albania and Balkans. Therefore, analysis of this influence, and its positive and negative effects, will help to explore the deep belongings of the Turkish culture in Albania.

Politics of the *millet* society

Prior to the Ottoman arrival, Albanian identity was not homogenous and, in terms of religion, reflected both Christian—Catholic and Orthodox elements. The research conducted by the Albanian scholar and archaeologist, Era Bushi-Xhaferaj, demonstrates that, in Middle Ages, Albanian-Christian monuments were present in the entire Albanian speaking lands (Bushi-Xhaferaj 2016: 110) as shown in the figure 4. The Albanian Catholics of the North, and Orthodox in the South, were dissimilar not only in terms of religion, cultural differences between *gegs* and *tosks* were evident. One of the most eminent scholars on Ottoman civilisation, Speros Vryonis, believes that during the Byzantine rule, Southern Albania was included in a partial Byzantinisation or in a "semi-Byzantinized zone", while the Byzantine effects did not affect Albanian mountain regions (Vryonis 1969-1970: 256). In a sense, this version explains the presence of Albanian Catholics in the North—an area that was ruled by Rome for a considerable period of time. Nevertheless, there were no simple divisions based on religion and culture between *gegs* and *tosks*, as not all Albanian *gegs* were Catholics, and similarly, not all *tosks* were Orthodox-Christians.

Vryonis emphasised that the Ottoman system, in a broad sense, was similar to the centralized bureaucratic theocracy of the Byzantine Empire. However, he argues that on a macro level of analysis,

THE OTTOMAN RULE (1385-1912)

Figure 4: Albanian-Christian monuments in Middle Ages

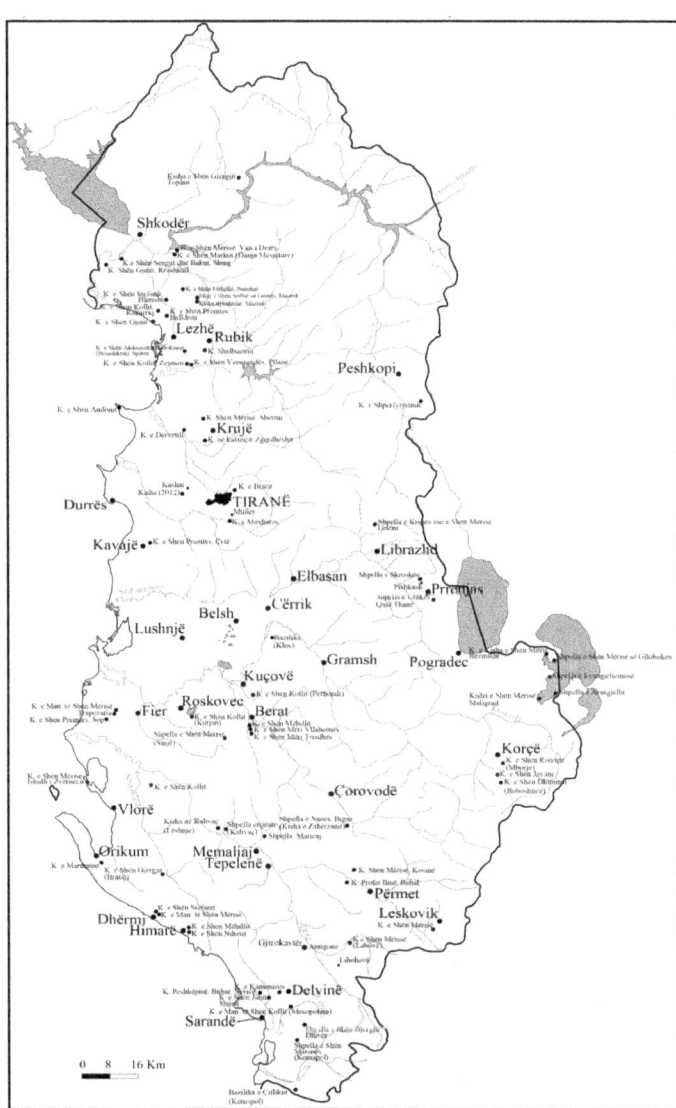

Source: Bushi-Xhaferaj, Era (2016), 'Piktura murale në monumentet e kultit të krishterë në Shqipëri (shek. XII-XIV)' [Mural pictures of Christian cult monuments in Albania (XII – XIV AD)], author's translation, unpublished PhD thesis, *Qendra e Studimeve Albanologjike* [Center of Albanological Studies], Tiranë: 186.

the upper levels of society, the Seljuks and Ottomans were "Islamic rather than Byzantine", whereas with regard to folk cultures, the Ottoman structure isolated the Balkan peoples from developing contacts with the West (Vryonis 1969-1970: 267-308). Historically, Romans, Byzantines and then the Ottoman Empire, transformed Albanian speaking lands into "badlands" but in reality, the impact of the Ottoman Empire was greater (Morgan 2010: 5).

Following an old system used in the Middle East, The Porte organised its society based on the *millet* system. *Millet* derives from the Arabic (*millah*), which means people of a religion other than Islam. This system served to regulate all inhabitants of the Empire who did not believe in Islam and thus, could not use Islamic law to participate in the social structures of the Empire in terms of legal, and administrative jurisdictions. Licursi believes the decision to organise the social structure in *millets* "laid the groundwork for the institutionalized incorporation" of non-Muslim population, which according to Barkey, "would evolve, eventually, into a fluid system of *millets*" (Barkey 2008 in Licursi 2011: 26). All *millets* were considered to be socially at a lower level than Muslims (Duijzings 2000: 28). However, despite the systemic imbalances of *millets,* the system guaranteed a certain language and religious autonomy, provided that *millets* accepted their inferior status compared to Muslims.

As the *millet* system was based on religious affiliation, the concept of the Albanian ethnicity and social groupings were completely ignored. In Albania, deep divisions between powerful families, and the differences between *gegs* and *tosks*, were further jeopardised by the *millet* system. They now had to re-group into Muslims, and Christian-Orthodox that belonged to the Rum *millet*. Albanian Muslims were considered as "first class citizens", equal to Islamic Turks. They were subject to lower taxes and regulated their social interaction through Islamic courts. After the fall of Constantinople in 1453, the Orthodox Patriarchate set the rules under which the Albanian Christian-Orthodox *millet* lived, while reporting directly to Sultan Mehmet II. The situation of Catholic Albanians was different. While they were not "Turks", they were not considered as a separate *millet* either. Since 168 BC, a time that Romans defeated Gentius, the last Illyrian king, Albanian Catholics were part of "the jurisdiction of Rome until 731 [AD] when Illyricum was placed under the Patriarchate of Constantinople" (Doja December 2000: 427). Both Romans and Venetians continued their influence and protection of North Albania, as did Austro-Hungary and France later (Licursi 2011: 28). However, during the long reign of the Byzantine Empire, Albanian Christians "entered further into the orbit of Eastern Christianity" (Doja 2000: 427)—a situation that was further complicated after the Ottoman occupation as Christian Albanians found themselves in the middle of the existing East-West "fault-line and the Muslim faith of the conquerors" (Morgan 2010: 8).

Despite claims of cultural and religious pluralism within the empire (Gawrych Novembre 1983), the coexistence of various ethnicities, languages and creeds proved difficult. As Misha emphasises, at the end of the nineteenth century,

> the *millet* system had resulted in complex demographic patterns throughout the Ottoman Empire. This may explain the confusing mixture of races, faiths and nationalities, which confronted the 'map makers' of Europe when they turned their minds to the Balkans in the second half of the nineteenth century (Misha 1999: 145).

The Porte abolished the *millet* system at the beginning of the nineteenth century, a time that *tanzimat* reforms replaced *timar*—a system that aimed to collect feudal taxes (*timars*) through the "holy" Islamic soil, which was considered to be the property of Sultan (Kaser 2012: 152).

The Ottoman's social, economic and administrative reforms in Albanian-speaking lands

Along with the *millet* system, the *timar* system lasted for more than four centuries and left an indelible mark on Albanian lands. It reduced the majority of Albanian peasants to living in poverty: "many who worked the land, pushed others off it, and contributed to the problems of feeding the [Albanian] population in troubled times" (Anscombe 2006: 95). This not only affected the land and agriculture, but also demographically re-shaped Albanian lands; creating uncertainty in the already fragile Albanian society. The Albanian Christians lived under the constant pressure of paying higher taxes to their chieftains and The Porte. Christian families who lived in these territories paid 10-20 percent of harvest and several days of free service to the Sultan (Kaser 2012: 153). By the end of the eighteenth century, through the *timar* system chaos and anarchy reigned in the Albanian-speaking lands (Zickel and Iwaskiw 1994: 15). At the beginning of the nineteenth century, the religious composition of Albanian-speaking lands changed permanently in favour of Islam, whereas with exception of Bosnia, other Western Balkan countries through the *millet* policy, maintained their Orthodox-religious composition. To an extent, this is one of answers to why, at the beginning of the nineteenth century, the composition of other Balkan societies had less Muslims proportionally compared to Albanians.

By then, following the change in the administration of the Empire, the relationship between landowners and peasants also changed: The "livelihood"—a grant that was "sufficient to support a cavalryman and his horse"—*dirliks* started to be organised in *çiftliks*, which were given to *sipahis*. Based on the number of *dirliks*, the *dirlik* holder was obliged to returning men, equipment and horses, upon the call of Sultan (Graf 2017: 39-40). Larger villages and territories were grouped under a new system that Kaser calls "çiflik economy". The more çifliks concentrated in big feudal families, the more economic disparity increased (Kaser 2012: 153). The Albanian clan-chieftains who had virtually become independent rulers *(beys)*, often took advantage of their wealth and power and refused to pay taxes, while attacking each other (Zickel and Iwaskiw 1994: 14).

From 1826 until 1877, The Porte made a major effort in reforming its empire, which was in decline since the seventeenth century. While The Porte was under increasing pressure to protect itself from external powers who wished to conquer parts of their lands, difficulties of communication between people within the Empire, other external factors such as "outside interests" and the rise of nationalism on the Balkan Peninsula further weakened the Empire economically (Jelavich 1973: 4-5). Sultan Mahmud II was thus forced to introduce *tanzimat* reforms in 1836, in an attempt to strengthen and modernise the state. During the reign of Abdülmecid I (1839-1861) and Abdülaziz (1861-1876), the *tanzimat* reforms aimed "to strengthen the Ottoman State both to resist outside pressure and to preserve inner unity by the adoption of certain Western institutions and ideas" (Jelavich 1973: 22).

The *tanzimat* reform had three aims: the substitution of Ottomanism as an ideology to suppress nationalism, controlling corrupt provincial administration, and a change of the Ottoman constitution in order to be more flexible and inclusive with regard to the non-Islamic population of the Empire. Weiker argues that all three areas of this reform were unsuccessful and thus, the modernisation that required the "abandonment of the Islamic state and [its] absolute monarchy" failed (Weiker 1968: 470). Most agree that *tanzimat* reforms were unsuccessful. The civil service, for example, was also becoming very cumbersome for the Empire, difficult and expensive, if not impossible for The Porte to administer Albanian-speaking living in mountainous region. Despite efforts to reform and changing the entire Ottoman society, insufficient political commitment led to bureaucratic behaviour inconsistent with modernisation, and thus, the predestined failure of these reforms. The *tanzimat* seemed to be a step forward toward the establishment of the Western type of private property, however, in reality, the *tanzimat* reform "was merely an oriental ruse, and not… a serious attempt to rejuvenate the ailing Empire" (Misha 1999: 83).

By the nineteenth century, the expansion and establishment of the Ottoman Empire had come to an end. Insufficient political commitment to changing the Ottoman structure of society, led to bureaucratic inefficiencies that was inconsistent with modernisation (Weiker 1968: 470). As Sugar argues, the golden times of the Ottoman Empire were gradually replaced with a:

> …need to act evasively, if not dishonestly, [that] became a necessity when the well-organised and governed Ottoman state was transformed into the chaotic and corrupt polity…It was the most corrupt, ruthless, selfish lawbreaker among the bureaucrats who prospered the most… (Sugar 1977: 288).

After losing the war with the Eastern Orthodox Coalition[1] led by Russia in 1878, it was too late for the Ottoman Empire to survive on a number of different fronts. The nationalistic movements of Serbia and Greece, the Albanian revolts of "bandits" such as Ali Pashë Tepelena in the South and Kara Mahmud Pasha in the North, the Great Powers, and more importantly, its autocratic and corrupt system had failed to modernise the Empire (Sugar 1977: 287-90). However, the Ottoman system not only drained resources, it also had long-term effects on Albanian lands, collecting taxes but giving little in return. Along with the *millet* system, in Albanian speaking lands, both *timar* and *tanzimat* systems primarily benefited the Sultan, and their servants—Albanian *beys*. In line with Morgan's

---

1 Eastern Orthodox Coalition included Russia, Bulgaria, Romania, Serbia and Montenegro.

"badlands" analogy, Zickel and Iwaskiw agree that during a period of more than five centuries of Ottoman rule, "the Albanian lands remained one of Europe's most backward areas" (Zickel and Iwaskiw 1994: 14).

The Ottoman demographic, social and environmental impact in Albanian speaking lands

By the end of the fourteenth century, a time when the Ottomans controlled Albania, the deep-rooted destructive behaviour of nomadic *Seljuks* was replaced by a more "sedentary" Ottoman culture (Vryonis 1969-1970: 263). Theoretically, the "destructive tendency" of *Seljuks* was supposed to be restrained by a well-organised and centralised Ottoman State. The Ottomans' political goal was to conquer more land, but when they entered Albania, the landscape shocked them. Two thirds of Albanian-speaking lands were mountainous and not arable, and half of the flat land was prone to flooding from the Adriatic Sea. A large part of today's Albanian *myzeqe* flatland from Vlorë to Durrës had no drainage and thus, was transformed into giant, filthy, permanent lakes that spread wide scale malaria. The Ottomans did not have the time, nor were they interested in recovering the Albanian wetlands, as they wanted simply to conquer arable land with a minimum effort. As a result, the Ottomans imposed an iron rule over the Albanian peasants for whom the "land" was the main source for survival.

After the death of Skenderbeg in 1468, many Christian Albanians in fear of their lives migrated to Italy and neighbouring European countries. This forced migration significantly changed the demographics of the Albanian lands. It caused a considerable brain drain effect as demonstrated by the loss of educated Albanians such as the historian Marin Barleti (1458-1512), scientists and philosophers (Gjon Gazulli (1400-1465), Maksim Arioti (1480-1556) and Leonik Tomeu (1456-1531) who continued to work in Italy and elsewhere, rather than using their knowledge and skills for the development of Albania.

It is a fact that the main aim of The Porte was to collect taxes and give little in return failing even to maintain the existing infrastructure, let alone applying development policies. Lack of such policies caused the destruction of the most economically developed Albanian cities of Shkodër, Lezhë, Krujë, Durrës and Vlorë at the beginning of the sixteenth century. Others, such as Deja, Drishti and Sarda, disappeared altogether. Local Albanians who found themselves rivals sold part of their cultural heritage such as sculptures, paintings and other religious objects in return for a few ounces of gold. After ten years of feudal anarchy, rape, warfare and devastation, in 1780, the most developed Albanian town of Voskopojë, with circa 40,000 inhabitants completely disappeared.

The Ottoman rulers never had total control of the Albanian speaking lands, nor were they interested in protecting the Albanian cities and their inhabitants, unless the Albanian "bandits" threatened the Sublime Porte (Anscombe 2006: 103). The Porte turned a blind eye at the beginning of the nineteenth century, a time that rivalry between *ayans* (deputy governors) (Agoston and Masters 2009: 65) brought about more tension and unfair commerce in Albanian speaking lands resulting in a disastrous situation of *reaya* who not only suffered due to malaria and other infection diseases, but also from a shortage of food due to uneven arable land distribution. When a *sancak's* (a district, which derives from the Arabic word, flagg or banner) governor felt threatened by another feudal family and asked The Porte for help, the Ottomans showed little "interest in investigating matters of justice" and thus, the *sancak* was often given to a stronger feudal family. For the state, the main priority was the collection of taxes and therefore, the control of a *sancak* often reverted to another governor (Anscombe 2006: 93-103). By the beginning of the nineteenth century, it was clear that The

Porte was unable to provide economic and social order in Albanian speaking lands.

The Ottoman infrastructure reforms in Albanian lands

Another area that has received scarce attention from The Porte was Albanian lands infrastructure. For the State, the term "infrastructure" was limited to the construction of bridges to connect fortifications, city castles, fortress-walls, which were all used for military purpose and religious buildings. Other scholars such as Charles and Jelavich agree with the concept of "badlands". By 1912, "Albania had remained one of the most backward areas of the empire ... there were only about 200 kilometres of paved roads" (Jelavich and Jelavich 1977: 223). A significant proportion of these was Via Egnatia—a road built by the Roman Empire, which at one time was considered as "the biggest nexus between East and West" (Bulut and Idriz 2012: 9), which the Ottomans took advantage of, but they did not maintain it, nor did they construct alternative roads. A few longer stone-arch bridges built between 1770 and 1780 were used for military purposes, while they also facilitated the transport of people and their goods. However, due to lack of road construction, remote Albanian areas continued to be connected via historical routes maintained by locals. Transport, travel and commercial exchange remained sparse due to the challenge of almost non-existent civilian infrastructure.

Select powerful Albanian pashas enjoyed the privileges of the *tanzimat* reforms and the support of the Sublime Porte. They were able to use the support of The Porte to resolve their rivalries and gain wealth and power. The conflict of Ahmet Kurt Pasha (Ali Pasha's grandfather) and Mehmet Pasha Bushati at the end of the eighteenth century can serve as an example. Ahmet Kurt Pasha managed to gain the support of the Sultan to create the *pashalik* of Berat in 1774. To strengthen his reputation and gain more power,

Ahmet Pasha built the Gorica Bridge over the Osum River between 1777-1780 and Rüfai *teqe* that was then used by the *bektashi* order. The third Head Vezir of Albania and the pasha of Shkodra, Kara Mahmud Pasha, could not afford to stay behind his *tosk* rivals and, in 1780, built the longest Albanian Bridge of Mesi (around 108 meters near Shkodër), connecting his *pashalik* with Prishtina. However, with the exception of religious and military infrastructure, the Ottomans played no more than a passive role in planning and developing Albanian speaking lands. The Porte fail to stimulate planning and the development of Albanian cities and improving living conditions.

The Porte benefited from all of the existing infrastructure in Albania, but what was clear was that the Ottomans invested mostly in religious and military policies. Upon their arrival in the Albanian speaking lands, the Ottomans introduced their faith, Islam. The religious orientation of Albania and the influence of *Sunni* and *Bektashi* Islam "exported" to Albania by the Ottomans will be discussed later in this chapter. For The Porte, Albanian infrastructure came second to religious and military advancement. Ancient Albanian Christian buildings followed the fate of Hagia Sofia after the fall of Constantinople in 1453. They were gradually converted to mosques such as the case of Fatih Mosque that replaced the Durrës amphitheatre chapel (Bushi-Xhaferaj 2016: 42). When the Albanian-Christian buildings were all transformed in mosques, the Ottomans started to invest in erecting new mosques and *madrasas*. One after the other big mosques such as the mosque of Gjin Aleks (1450) Delvinë, Mirahorit (1496) Korçë, Plumbit (1553-1554) Berat, Muradijes (1570) Vlorë, Nazireshtes (1600) Elbasan, Daut Pasha (1605) Prizren and the Ethem Beu (1794) Tiranë appeared. The Mosque complex (1820) in Peqin integrated religious services with more inclusive facilities for people such as local bazars (in Albanian called *pazars*) and small artisan shops.

THE OTTOMAN RULE (1385-1912)

The Albanian occupation by the Ottomans commenced while the Byzantine Empire was falling apart and was fully conquered by the House of Osman on 29 May 1453, after the fall of Constantinople. Some months later, Sultan Mehmet II—"the Conqueror", decided to expand the Ottoman Empire further into Europe (Payton 2006: 12). During the second half of the fifteenth century the attack on Europe through Albania never happened, and Albanian resistance under Skenderbeg was the main reason for this. However, things changed at the beginning of the sixteenth century after the death of Skenderbeg and the rise of Sultan Süleyman I. In 1529, the Ottomans failed to conquer Vienna due to difficulties of logistically consolidating a large force as Vienna was far from the major centres of Ottoman power. As a result of this failure, the Sultan began showing more attention to Albania, from where the Ottomans launched a direct attack on Southern Italy in 1537, expecting a promised French military response in the North, with the objective of a combined conquest of Italy. But according to some, France withheld the diversion, fearing a hostile European reaction to its alliance (Yapp and Shaw 2018).

While it might appear that France was unsure about its support from the Ottomans, scholars agree that the political aim of the Sultan was to expand the Ottoman Empire to the West (Yapp and Shaw 2018). The objective of The Porte was to build a permanent military structure in Albanian lands. Barleti is convinced that "the key of conquering Rome" was to firstly take Epirus, as the only way for the Sultan to achieve his goal (Barleti 2012: 56). The geographic proximity of Albania and Italy explains the Sultan's decision of building permanent military structures in Albanian lands. Some examples were the sophisticated castle of Vlorë that was built by Sultan Süleyman in 1531; the castles of Ishmi (Durrës), which was built in 1574; the castles of Tepelenë, Gjirokastër, Butrint and later, fortification walls in the castles of Janinë, Prevezë, Sul, Artë and Porto-Palermo. Military fortifications were followed by small bridges such as the Prizren, Miraka (Librazhd), Tanners and the Kollorcës (near Gjirokastër), which were constructed to connect military fortifications.

Albanian unity under the Ottoman Empire

Albania is often portrayed in the region as the country which supported the Ottoman-Turks. While there is a degree of truth in this, it can be argued that Albanians implemented strategies of resistance against the sometimes-perceived invincible enemy. This is shown in the ways Albanians resisted the Ottomans during different periods of the occupation. Although the concept of the Albanian nation itself is post-colonial, the League of Lezhë, or Alessio (known in Albanian as *Besëlidhja e Lezhës*), met on 2 March 1444 at the castle of Lezhë, which according to Hodgkinson, was in effect "the first national effort of military and political union" of Albanian speaking people against the Ottomans. Gjergj Kastrioti, known as Skenderbeg, or Lord Alexander, was a genius in waging guerrilla cavalry operations, and under his leadership he kept the Ottomans (described as "the mightiest army of the world") at bay for a quarter of a century (Hodgkinson 1999: 74).

Under the leadership of Skenderbeg, chieftans of the main families of Albanian speaking lands such as Musachi, Balsha, Arianiti, Thopia, the Montenegrin Crnojevic, Dukagjini, Zaharia, Spani and Dushmani united their political and military efforts against the Porte. The secessionist movement under Skenderbeg provoked mistrust from The Porte, as did Ali Pasha's uprising and the Albanian national movement in the nineteenth century. Similar to the post Skenderbeg period, following the assassination of Ali Pasha in 1822, the mistrust of the Sultan increased with punishment for those Albanians who continued to resist The Porte. Perhaps the culmination of this distrust was shown in August 1830, a time that the

Sultan sent the Ottoman General Reshid Pasha to Bitola who invited 1,000 Albanian beys (landowners) to a military celebration-parade against Greek resistance. Reshid Pasha killed 500 of these Albanian leaders (Zickel and Iwaskiw 1994: 15-16), indicating a tightening of the control of The Porte. In the short term, this strategy succeeded in forcing further conversions to Islam and in a sense delaying an Albanian resistance against The Porte. However, according to Vickers, in the longer term, it paved the way for the beginning of the Albanian national movement. While other ethnicities in the Balkans have reinvented myths around contested facts, it is interesting to see how, in the twenty-first century, Albanians do not play much attention to these uncontested facts.

The Ottomans occupied Albania for more than five centuries and their influence was undeniably profound. There are conflicting views in relation to Ottoman occupation of the Albanian-speaking territories. The majority of Turks believe that the Ottoman occupation was welcomed and thus, beneficial to Albanians, whereas others think that Albanians have been oppressed and held back during the time of this occupation (Sulstarova 2010). The particular nuances of the relationship changed with the different stages of the Ottoman Empire. Through these stages, The Porte changed policies based on the will of the Sultan, internal and external developments, the influence of the Great Powers, a number of wars and the dynamics of Balkan nationalism. Analysing the Ottoman policy shifts is not the objective of this book, rather the way in which the Ottoman Turks affected people's lives in the Albanian speaking lands during various stages of the Empire and, may still have existing effects over the Albanian direction of today.

The main contribution to the Albanian literacy regarding the Ottoman period has been that of *rilindja* writers. One of the main *rilindja* figures, Sami Frashëri, identifies three major periods in which the co-existence of Albanians in the Ottoman

Empire significantly differed. In his book titled *Shqipëria – Ç'ka qënë, çështë e ç'do të bëhetë?* (*Albania – What it was, what it is and what it will become*), first published in 1899, Frashëri considers the permanent return of Skenderbeg to Albania in 1443, until his death in 1468, as the first period of resistance. Frashëri views this period as a time when Albanians "protected Europe" from the advance of the Ottomans: "All European governments of that time had hope in Skanderbeg and expected to be rescued by the Albanians" (Frashëri 1999: 34). The second period, according to Frashëri, lasted from Skenderbeg's death until the middle of the nineteenth century. During this lengthy period Albanians became more integrated into the Ottoman Empire—progressing into the high ranks of the Ottoman government, which included some 25 Albanians who served as Grand Viziers (prime ministers of the Sultan). The third period of the Albanian speaking people under the Ottoman Empire is known as the Albanian Awakening (or *Rilindja*). It began in the second half of the nineteenth century and lasted up until the declaration of Albanian Independence in 1912. For Frashëri, this period was characterized by a deep crisis in the entire Ottoman Empire and where Albanians paid the biggest price. He states:

> the Albanians long were comrades of the Turks and not their slaves, but now they are suffering under great oppression and are being beaten and trampled underfoot more than the rest. If this be the case, why are the other nations endeavouring to throw off the heavy burden, while the Albanians are struggling to maintain it? Do they not see that they are leaning against a wall which is collapsing, and which will crush and bury them? (Frashëri 1999: 70-1).

The Ottoman-Islamic polity: Conversions to Islam

Since the eleventh century, sedentary Turks started to replace nomadic Seljuks—a trend that continued until the nineteenth century

(Vryonis 1969-1970: 261). Therefore, tribal chieftains, the highest level of a formal Turkish society, were slowly converting to "rulers of non-nomadic states" (Vryonis 1969-1970: 259). The Ottoman-Islamic polity was built on the Turkish-nomadic-pastoralism culture to that of "jihad against Christians", in an attempt to establish elements of Islamic culture in every aspect of life such as agriculture, education, arts, crafts, religion, commerce, which in short, would contribute to the entertainment, peace and security for the House of Osman (Vryonis 1969-1970: 263). The Islamic religion element became a strong pillar for the Ottoman Empire.

The Ottomans believed in Prophet Muhammad and preached a monotheist religion that included elements of Jewish, Christian, traditional Arabic and some additional Turkish customs (Sugar 1977: 4). The Ottoman society, according to Misha, was divided in two classes: *reaya* and *askeri* and those monotheists who acknowledged Islam as fundamental and were happy to live in a Muslim state under the Ottoman rule were considered as *zimmi* (protected people). For Ottomans, the Islamic element played an important role in the Balkans, as Muslims, regardless of their ethnic background, enjoyed the same privileges within the Empire. In the case of Albania where the Albanian language was prohibited by The Porte, Albanians were forced to become Turks, or be assimilated by the Greeks.

It is often argued that Albanians began converting to Islam, as it was easier for them to live as Muslims rather than Christians within the Ottoman Empire. There was certainly great economic, political and psychological pressure, to convert. Under Ottoman legislation, life was hard for Christian Albanians, as they did not enjoy the same rights as their Muslim compatriots. In short, Doja argues, due to "a cultural situation severely affected by the brutal and harrowing intrusion of ideological, political and foreign domination" (Doja 2000: 435), Albanians did not have much choice.

The State imposed policies of Sunni Islam that were based on the *sharia* law, which privileged Muslims and, disadvantaged Christians. For example, as Misha discusses, if a Muslim physically injured a Christian, it was enough for the former to pay a "blood tax" to *kadi* in order to avoid a Court hearing (Misha 1999: 75). Not only this was not possible for Christians, they could not serve in the high ranks of military, or in civil service and diplomacy (which were highly paid jobs), nor were they rewarded by the Sultan with more *çifliks*, rather they were forced to pay a big *haraç* to the Sultan. Christians were also required periodically to provide one healthy male child to be converted to Islam and trained either for the Ottoman administration or the elite military corps of Janissaries, a policy known as *devşirme*. Under this policy, the Sultan selected children from its *vasal* provinces and brought them to Istanbul through this unique Ottoman invention system—*devşirme* that was a tribute of children levied (Sugar 1977: 31). Many young boys from Albanian Christian families (including Skenderbeg) became great fighters of the Sultan's elite guard—the Janissary (*jeniçeri*) corps. Others served as civil servants in the high ranks of Porte. This system not only caused emotional but also economic hardship for Albanian families; losing healthy young males who might have grown to contribute to their families and community. As Sugar emphasises:

> the disadvantages in human, ethnological, and economic terms were overwhelming and, in balance, far more important than beneficial aspects of the *devşirme* system…It is also the most prevalent example of forced conversion in the years predating the seventeenth century (Sugar 1977: 58-59).

The *devşirme* system was invented by the Sultan to serve his own ends, and it generated hate and resentment in Christian Albanians, especially in the North. Skenderbeg who reconverted to Christianity upon his return to Albania, was mythicised and functioned as a unifying legend for Albanians detesting the Turkish State. Ultimately, Albanian non-Muslims were subject to heavier taxes, *devşirme*, lack of educational opportunities and socio-economic status. It is difficult to misjudge the pressure on them to convert to Islam.

It has also been argued that mass conversion of Albanians increased in the seventeenth century, a time when the Russo-Ottoman wars began to generate more economic difficulties for The Porte. In the mid eighteenth century, the State started to collect more money from all non-Muslim subjects; increasing levy taxes, "while those converted to Islam had their taxes lowered and were given grants of land" (Vickers and Pettifer 1997: 97). The Christian Albanians lacked these opportunities, and were expected to work-menial jobs, while the Albanian Muslims were offered senior administrative positions, where they were considered allies of The Porte that "protected them from the Slavonic and the Greek encroachment" (Vickers and Pettifer 1997: 97). For this reason, Kosovars accepted Islam faster perhaps to resist the pressure of their close proximity, the Serbs, who in 1830, achieved their own autonomous state. Moreover, Anscombe discuses, at the beginning of the nineteenth century in Southeast Albania, the assimilationist threat of the "Hellenisation" idea increased, after the success of Greek independence, and the brutal suppression of the Albanian revolts of Ali Pashë Tepelena in the South and Kara Mahmud Pasha in North. Therefore, it seems that Albanian-speaking populations did not have much choice, but rather were forced to side with the lesser of two evils— protecting their lands from a total annexation by their neighbours. Religion was second to their land. On the other hand, the Ottomans were happy to achieve their long-term goal of planting Islam in Albanian lands.

The conversion could have happened at any time, but Sugar believes that the conversion of Albanians is "...a seventeenth century phenomenon" (Sugar 1977: 52); hence, he thinks, earlier conversions might have been voluntary. It is also known that Islam could not penetrate parts of the Albanian mountains such as the case of Mirditë and other small towns in the North where the mountainous terrain made access for the state difficult. Inhabitants of these remote parts of Albania continued to live as Christians and were less affected by conversions.

The "soft" policy of conversion—Albania's Bektashism

The issue of religious conversion of Albanians is highly debated and scholars have listed forced and voluntary as two ways of conversions (Sugar 1977; Vryonis 1969-1970). Sugar agrees with Vryonis on the four major reasons for massive conversion of Albanians, namely "economic and legal advantages, the influence of medreses and other Muslim institutions, fear, and the adaptability of folk religion" (Sugar 1977: 52). While the first three can be considered as forced conversion, Sugar believes the last reason as more important than others. In fact, the new Bektashism can be considered as a "soft" system of conversion carried out by the Bektashi dervish brotherhood order and supported by medreses and tekkes. Along with Sunni, Bektashi served as a complementary religious system to achieve the aim of the Sultan—diffusion of Islam, and thus, the assimilation of Albanians into Turkish culture and society.

Sunni Islam was very rigid compared to Bektashism—a more tolerant "kind" of Islam that, Hall believes, was introduced into Albania by *jeniçeri* in the fifteenth century (Hall 1994: 43). It is widely agreed that Bektashism originated in Iran and that its theoretical foundations are a mix of doctrines and practices such as "Shiism and Sufism but also preserving pre-Islamic and non-Islamic beliefs and customs originating in Christianity and antique religions as well as ancient Turkic elements" (Doja 2006: 85). Therefore, this moderate Bektashism drew on a long tradition of Sufism including elements of Christianity (Sugar 1977: 53). Although both Bektashism and Sunni were based in Islam, the tolerant Bektashism was more attractive and thus, was more accepted by Christian Albanians.

Since the fifteenth century, the State supported the mission of the Bektashi dervish order, which was supposed to be faster than Sunni in converting Christian Albanians to Islam. Dervishes travelled to remote Albanian villages, where they dealt with daily domestic issues and engaged in a "door to door" conversation. At the end of the sixteenth century, the Bektashi dervish brotherhood expanded into central and southern Albania, where large numbers of *tekkes* and *tyrbes* (in Turkish *türbe*) were established. Inside tekkes, the highest leaders—the dervishi babas were propagating a kind of more inclusive Islamic folk religion that was based on their code—the terikat. For Albanians it was easier to adapt to this folk religion compared to the strict rules of the Sunni Islam and Christianity. Bektashism was not only more tolerant than Sunni Islam, but also had similarities with Christian Orthodox and Catholic rituals. For example, it was believed that a *mekam* (the tomb of a babba whom was the founder and buried in tekke) had miraculous powers at a point that people were praying and seeking help upon the name of the buried baba. This was similar to pilgrimage sacred places for both Christians and Muslims such as Lourdes and Mekka. As a result, this kind of inclusive religion was simpler and more attractive to Albanians, considering that prior to the Ottoman invasion Albanians practiced both Catholic and Orthodox religions.

However, the State changed its position towards the Bektashi brotherhood at the beginning of the nineteenth century, when the *jeniçeri* openly challenged the power of Sultan Mahmud II, who decided in return to reform the elite troops following a Western-French style. For Kressing, the Sultan's decision to suppress Janissaries in 1826 initiated a profound retaliation against Bektashi and forced them to move to the margins of the Empire (Kressing 2002: 66-7). From this moment onwards, the new cast of Sunni-Ottomans persecuted both Janissaries and Bektashi. This was a time when Albanians, especially in the South, had largely embraced Bektashism, and as a result could not escape the Sultan's retaliation campaign that started after the defeat of the controversial Albanian Ali Pasha in 1822. After his successful campaign against the Russians, the Sultan rewarded Ali Pasha with the *vilayet* of Janina, which comprised the Epirus area. Ali Pasha converted to Bektashism and used his power to facilitate the unobstructed growth of the Bektashi order, which in South-Albania, became influential under his rule (Bieber 2000: 18). The revenge campaign of the Sublime Porte continued to blame the Albanian Bektashi for engineering the Albanian uprising that, by the middle of the nineteenth century, according to Norris, a specialist on Albanian Sufism, had become well-known and was identified with an emerging Albanian identity (Norris 1993: 240-41). Along with rising nationalism, Bektashi was becoming very popular in Albania. After the Prizren League (1878-81), it was considered a symbol of resistance against oppressors. Norris describes the effects of the Albanian Bektashi in the late Ottoman Empire as follows:

> the Sufism of Albania, equally popular amongst the masses and in its intellectual appeal to the poets…was compelling and was grafted into local nationalistic aspirations, as in the case in the poetry of the poet, Naim Frasheri, and in the compositions of many poets in Kosovo (Norris 2006: 7).

Naim Frashëri (1846-1900), one of the main figures of the Albanian Bektashism, played a crucial role in the process of Awakening-*rilindja*. Hence, Albanian Bektashism needs to be understood in the context of rising nationalism. The romanticism of Naim Frashëri's writing also had nationalistic undertones. In his book *Histori e Skenderbeut* [*History of Skenderbeg*], Frashëri mythicised Skenderbeg as an Albanian hero, downplaying his triple religious life. Skenderbeg was also portrayed as an innocent Christian child, who was forced by Turks to learn and practice the Muslim religion. He described the Ottoman Empire as "a big beast" that came from Asia and with "cruelty in their eyes" and "a satanic heart", "killed, severed and impoverished" in a way that "grass wouldn't grow" wherever the beast stepped in the "flourishing" Albanian soil (Frashëri 1967: 99-100). On the other hand, in line with his nationalistic ideas, Frashëri propagated the Bektashi religion. In 1896, he published the *Fletore e Bektashinjet* [*Bektashi notebook*], a theological novel that identified "practical principles of Bektashism and the organisational rules governing its functioning" (Abazi and Doja 2013: 860). In this attempt, he promoted the Bektashi religion, which he considered a better vehicle than other religions to unite Albanians. Therefore, Bektashism and nationalism were both embodied in Frashëri's writings. However, it was not his priority to replace the Albanian religious spectrum with Bektashism, but rather to "propagate religious tolerance" (Duijzings 2002: 68), or better, craft a unique Albanian religion that was based on elements of Islam and Christianity. This is the way his brother Sami Frashëri is appealing to Albanians in his book:

> Do not turn to religions and beliefs. Muslims, Catholics and Orthodox – they are all Albanians wherever they are, and they are all brothers. They must all unite under the sacred flag of Albania (Frashëri 1999 in Licursi 2011: 86).

Religious controversies

One of the main arguments that still concerns Albanian identity is why so many Albanians converted to Islam compared to their neighbours? Unlike their Greek and Serbian neighbours, the Albanians did not have real attachment to their Christian religion going back to the Middle Ages. They embraced religion according to the advancements of Roman or Byzantine Empires. The process of shifting religion in Albania happened to both *gegs* and *tosks*. Vickers and Pettifer paraphrased Skendi who mentioned the case of Prince Gjon Kastrioti (Skenderbeg's father) changing his religion several times from "Catholic as an ally of Venice and turned Orthodox as an ally of Stefan Lazarevic of Serbia" (Vickers and Pettifer 1997: 96). It is well known that the Albanian national hero, Skenderbeg, was born into an Orthodox family, educated as a Muslim, and died as a Catholic. Therefore, since the late Middle Ages, the Albanian feudal lords—often followed by their populations—embraced Catholicism when the West was in the ascendant and hugged Orthodoxy at times when Byzantium prevailed. Thus, the process of alignment with the religion of whoever was in power at the time often occurred.

The process of Islamisation in Albania is highly debated and controversial. It was obvious that voluntary and forced conversions often happened simultaneously (Doja 2000: 435). As Sugar discusses, the phenomenon of religious change occurred before, during and after the Ottoman occupation (Sugar 1977: 52). Along with shifting their religion to Islam, Albanians also shifted from Muslims to Christian-Orthodoxy. Karalis argues that "the project of historical Christianity" in Greece, which began in 1453 with the fall of Constantinople, created new opportunities for the Eastern Christendom, culminating with the Greek national uprising in 1821. However, according to Karalis, following this uprising, the Greek "national identity did not really mean religious affiliation" as both Christian and Muslim Albanians, along with other ethnicities fought the Ottomans side by side with Greeks (Karalis 2010: 166). Misha found that during the uprising of Greeks in 1821-1830 many Albanians underwent a process of Hellenisation, a process that was accelerated by their participation in the War for Independence of Greece. Their participation, Misha argues, played an important role as they led a substantial faction of the resistance to The Porte during this war (Misha 1999: 25). While some Albanians converted back to

Christian Orthodoxy, more converted to Islam. In order to further explore this issue, it is instructive to analyse the role of religion during the Albanian Awakening (rilindja) period, which crafted foundations of the Albanian national identity.

The Albanian *rilindja* leaders knew that religion would have been problematic as a source of unification of Albanians in their struggle to create their nation. As a result, little importance of religion prompted the Albanian rilindja leaders to place religion second to "Albanianism". The famous poem of Pashko Vasa "the Albanian's faith is Albanianism" (Vasa 2005: 82-8) was a call to all Albanians to protect their forefathers' motherland, regardless of their religion. However, it is inaccurate to claim that the *rilindja* movement was anti-religious. One example is the position of the influential *rilindja* leader and writer, Naim Frashëri, who commanded all Albanians to have one belief in God; claiming that God cannot be that of unattached religions, but that of "pantheism, included and unified as it is into the nature and universe" (Abazi and Doja 2013: 870).

Albanian language within the Ottoman Empire

The enforced language of the Empire—"Osmanlica", was used for administrative purposes and was incomprehensible to the majority of Turks, and even more to the Albanians who were required to learn and use this foreign language, very different from their own. Trained teachers and religious clerics taught the Turkish language in state schools and *metjepes* in order to offer an education that was based on Islam. The aim of the State was to impose Islam as a holistic theory and practice through the Turkish language. Indeed, the Turkish language introduced knowledge, skills, Turkish culture and religion into Albania.

While the official language for all Ottoman conquered lands was Turkish, the Greeks and Serbs were permitted to use their own written and spoken language. This was not the case for Albanians. As

Albanians were considered neither Turks nor Orthodox *millet*, the official language in all spheres of the Albanian speaking lands was Turkish and Greek. This rule extended to all schools and religious rituals. The Ottomans "did not allow native Albanian schools, nor reading and writing of Albanian" (Byron 1976: 39) until 1880, a time when Albanian nationalism, and with it the demand for the use of the Albanian language, started to increase. Until the mid-nineteenth century, The Porte did not have a policy with regards to education in Albania, and policies of the Ottoman Empire prevented Albanian speakers from developing their independent language structure. Nevertheless, the Albanian spoken language, used in Albanian folklore, songs and epics survived and it was transmitted across generations to provide the basis for the creation of a nation.

In 1879, the Society of the Printing of Albanian Writings was founded in Constantinople. The main goal of this society "was to establish a [an Albanian] standard language which would lead to the publication of books, journals, and newspapers..." (Jelavich and Jelavich 1977: 225). In November 1908, under the presidency of the son of Abdyl Frashëri, Mit'hat Bey Frashëri, the Congress of Monastir (Bitola) not only worked on a standardisation of the Albanian language, its alphabet and orthography, but also appointed the committee of a national union that aimed for "an autonomous Albania within the Turkish empire, which was to include the four *vilayets* of Shkodër, Kosovë, Monastir and Janina" (Pearson 2004: 3). Despite some Albanian Muslim leaders of the North who, inspired by the Young Turks, preferred the scripts of the Koran, the Bitola Congress decided to use the Latin alphabet to transliterate the Albanian language.

The role of language in nation building processes is well known. Wright discusses language as a vehicle of unification analysing the case of France. At the beginning of the fifteenth century, French people adopted a Vulgar Latin and Roman Gaul type of oral language. The expansion of the Kingdom also introduced German, Dutch, Catalan and Italian languages, however, the decision to introduce French as the official language in 1539, created a linguistic homogeneity, and also reinforced French national identity (Wright 2000: 35-36). As Wright puts it, "when a culture production is language-bound it serves to reinforce the homogeneity of the group and mark difference" (Wright 2000: 25).

Until the mid-nineteenth century, Albanian speaking people were unable to unite on any ethnic, religious or any other type of platform. The Albanian language— "very distinct from the languages of its direct (Slav and Greek) neighbours—was the only element that could bridge the differences between religious and regional identities" (Duijzings 2002: 61). Therefore, despite differences in syntax, lexicon, phonology and morphology between *geg* and *tosk* dialects (Byron 1976: 43), the Albanian language was the main pillar of the "bridge" that united Albanians. The translation of the bible by Kostandin Kristoforidhi (1827-1895), in a hybrid of Albanian language that represented both *geg* and *tosk* dialects was an indication of the possibility for Albanians to unite using a collective language. As Misha discusses, the Albanians "were united only by the disaster threatened by the slow collapse of the Ottoman Empire and by their language – Albanian" (Misha 1999: 151). Thus, the Albanian language became an essential vehicle to unite Albanians.

In line with this claim, the Albanian speaking community was united by a "language bond" that was unique and different from the Ottoman language, a fact The Porte feared. As a result of this, on 23 July 1909, the Young Turks organised the congress of Dibër with two objectives. Firstly, to convince Albanians not to separate from The Porte, and secondly, to force the Albanian speaking population to adopt the Albanian language using the Arabic alphabet. Despite their inferior position compared to The Porte, Albanians "gained complete control of the proceedings"; reversing both requests in their favour. The Dibër congress agreed, "...the Albanian language should be taught freely" (Pearson 2004: 7) in a Latin alphabet. The Porte did not give up and, on 19 February 1910, Young Turks organised another congress in Monastir. The aim was to pressure Albanian *hoxhas* to reverse the decision to use the Latin alphabet and replace it with the Arabic alphabet, in line with "the religious law and the interests of Islam" (Pearson 2004: 9). The support of *mullahs*, who were trained in law and theology using Arabic characters, caused resentment in schools around Albania as could be imagined and not all Albanian *hoxhas* supported the Arabic alphabet. An example was the Moslem *hoxha*, Hafiz Ali, who on the same day that the *mullahs* opposed the Latin alphabet, recited a prayer and blessed a crowd of 15,000 people at Korçë agreeing with protesters that the Albanian letters in Latin must be retained due to the fact that there is no connection between the alphabet and religion.

The second congress of Monastir (21-23 March 1910) established that the Latin alphabet was easier to use, as all Catholic schools were teaching in Latin. After a letter from the Supreme Moslem authority of Albania on 22 March 1910, demanding the use of the Arabic alphabet, the Turkish Ministry of Education tried to prevent the implementation of the Latin alphabet (Pearson 2004: 10). At the time, the Latin alphabet represented the West, also considered as "opponents" of the Sultan. The Grand Vezir in March 1910 proclaimed: "The government must do everything, and will do everything, to prevent the adoption of the Latin alphabet [in Albania]" (Skendi in Jelavich and Jelavich 1977: 226). This was a clear sign of the importance the Ottomans placed on the suppression of the Albanian language which would be the strongest element of Albanian unity – irrespective of religious differences. It was also an indication of the Albanian speaking lands to dissociate their language from Eastern Turkish with an Arabic alphabet.

Politics of the Albanian language

The Albanian language was trapped by the political objectives of The Porte and Patriarchate. While the Ottoman schools through the Turkish language taught Islam, the Orthodox schools in Albania used the Greek language as the vehicle "of Helenisation" (Jelavich and Jelavich 1977: 226). The establishment of secular Albanian schools were opposed by both the Ottoman government and the Patriarchate (Jelavich and Jelavich 1977: 226). The Ottomans feared the autonomy of the Albanian people, whereas the Patriarchate, in response to the issue with the Bulgarian Exarchate, feared the same separation within the Albanian Orthodox Church. The creation of Bulgarian Exarchate in the mid-nineteenth century was a result of the Bulgarian Orthodox Church struggling with the influence of the Orthodox Greek hierarchy in the Patriarchate of Constantinople. Therefore, the Rum Orthodox *millet* was divided at the end of the nineteenth century, to now include a Bulgarian *millet*.

These attacks on the use of the Albanian language confirm how central the language was for the unification of Albanians. At the end of the nineteenth century, the sharp rise of Albanian nationalism enabled the establishment of Albanian schools in the *pashalik* of *Janina* and thus, an opportunity for perpetuation of the Albanian language arose. Due to this pressure, the first Albanian school for boys—Mësonjëtoria opened after long negotiations with the State on 7 March 1887 at Korçë, followed by a school for girls four years later. However, Albanian schools were immediately attacked by both the State and the Patriarchate. The Greek Orthodox Church "excommunicated" students who attended the new schools. The Ottoman government went one step further in trying to eliminate Albanian education by deciding in 1902, to ban all books written in Albanian, and disallowing any form of communication in the Albanian language (Jelavich and Jelavich 1977: 227). Any attempt to learn the Albanian language was completely suppressed by the State.

The more the Ottomans applied pressure to suppress the Albanian language, the more Albanians defied the State and learned their language secretly in *bektashi teqes* in the Centre and the South, or churches in the North. As part of the campaign against the Albanian language, both Ottomans and Greek persecuted Albanian teachers. Albanian Awakening—*rilindja* leaders such as Papa Kristo Negovani—a priest who taught Albanian in his church – and Pandeli Sotiri, who although he graduated in Greece, contributed to the propagation of the Albanian language, were both killed by the Orthodox Church as they defied both The Porte and the Greek Patriarchate. Other Albanian language teachers suffered the same fate: Petro Nini Luarasi, Gjerasim Qiriazi, Baba Duda Karbunara, Hamdi Ohri, Siad Hoxha, Balil Tahiri and Sotir Ollani were killed or sent into exile by the State and the *Rum* church (Blumi 2002: 55).

The situation in North Albania was quite different as state schools in the North were almost non-existent and Catholic Albanians were studying in Austrian and Italian schools which, at the time, were more popular than state schools. In contrast to the Muslim and Orthodox schools, the curriculum in Catholic schools was delivered in the Albanian language. The Italian schools appeared to be more professional and better equipped supported by both the Italian government and the Vatican. However, the Austrians soon started to compete with the Italian schools, which were spreading from the North to the Centre of Albania. As became apparent over time, both Habsburg and Italian schools had political and religious aims, which were similar to those of the Ottomans and Greeks. According to Blumi, the two Catholic nations, Italy and Austria, used education as a tool to strengthen their influence in Albania, and thus, advance their main aim of counteracting Slavic influences in the region (Jelavich and Jelavich 1977: 227).

The State recognised the importance of the Albanian language and attempted to destroy it. By 1909, the Young Turks became alarmed at the nationalistic spirit of the Albanians and began systematic persecution. They suspended the constitutional guarantees, shut down Albanian schools and clubs, and suppressed newspapers and magazines. Many Albanian leaders fled the country or were imprisoned. On 2 September 1909, despite attempts by the Young Turks to prevent it, the Albanian leaders organised the Elbasan Congress to discuss the education system. The Congress adopted Monastir's findings that embraced writings of the Albanian language in Latin characters and teaching it in all Albanian schools and, as a result, identifying an immediate need to train Albanian teachers. Based on the last recommendation, on 1 December 1909, a training college—the Elbasan College—opened. Luigj Gurakuqi was appointed Principal and the teachers and children were either Muslims or Christians (Pearson 2004: 8). However, preparation of Albanian teachers started prior to the establishment of Elbasan College, when Kostandin Kristoforidhi secretly trained future teachers at Elbasan and Voskopojë. While the Albanian language survived the assimilation attempt of the Ottoman rulers, the Ottoman religion, Islam, was already widespread in Albania.

Albanian nationalism on the rise

The second half of the nineteenth century saw Albanian nationalism on the rise. During this period, failed attempts at modernising and re-organising the Ottoman Empire coincided with a further weakening of The Porte due in part to their defeat in the war against Russia in 1877-1878. The victorious Russians forced the Ottomans to sign the Treaty of San Stefano in March 1878, which required that the Ottomans cede part of their Balkan territory to Bulgaria, Serbia, Montenegro and Greece. This proposed fragmentation of Albania fuelled the rise of Albanian nationalism, as there were fears that the lands they inhabited would be partitioned amongst their neighbours. Therefore, Albanians were forced to act against their neighbours and not the Ottoman government (Jelavich and Jelavich 1977: 224). Once again, Albania suffered at the hands of more powerful nations. The Treaty of San Stefano "created a large independent Bulgarian state and enlarged Serbia and Montenegro" (Hall 2000: 2) at the expense of the Ottomans. Hall argues that none of emerging Balkan states were happy with the new borders created by this Treaty. Less happy were Albanian speaking people who suffered from both, The Porte and their neighbors.

The Albanians were struggling to be recognized as a different nationality not only from Great Powers but also from their neighbors. The Porte did everything to halt Albanian's secession from the Ottoman territories, which at the end of the nineteenth century seemed to be more difficult than before. On 1 July 1878, Albanian chieftains representing four *vilayets* of Kosovo, Janina, Shkodër and Manastir convened the "League for the Defense of Rights of the Albanian Nation" (Jelavich and Jelavich 1977: 224), known as the Prizren League. The Prizren League was able to secure support from the Ottomans, as it aimed to unite all Albanian territories under the sovereignty of the ruling Sultan and thus, asked for a Turkish governor general to rule Albanian speaking territories.

Originally, all requests of the League leaders were in line with The Porte. However, leaders of the Prizren League had differing opinions regarding whether they should continue to accept the rule of the Sultan in the Albanian-speaking lands. The conservative faction under the leadership of Abdyl Frashëri (1839-1892) desired autonomy from The Porte. Despite the lack of unity between Albanians, the Prizren League carried out Albanian military actions against Serbia and Montenegro for the next three years. In the end, the Sultan refused to grant the League's requests, and brutally crushed it in 1881, but not until after realising its aim of secession from The Porte (Jelavich and Jelavich 1977: 224). The League became the symbol of

THE OTTOMAN RULE (1385-1912)

Albanian's resistance against the Ottomans. *Rilindja* writer's songs, and poems are included in Albanian schoolbook texts, while they became part of the Albanian folklore (Rredhi: 133-38). This also was a wake-up call for Albanian speaking people; marking the consolidation of Albanian nationalism that started to raise the question of an Albanian nation-state. As Morgan correctly noticed, "the seeds of Albanian political nationalism had been sown" (Morgan 2010: 11).

The Great Powers at the time realized the eminent danger that was emerging in the Balkan Peninsula and agreed to hold the Berlin Congress. The Congress started on 13 June and was later enshrined in a Treaty on 13 July 1878. The Prussian Chancellor Otto von Bismarck offered to chair the Treaty as an "honest broker". Although the aim of the Treaty was to resolve territorial disputes in the Balkans, it further fractured already tense relationships and alliances in the region. One example was the fact that the Treaty of Berlin failed to recognise ethnic Albanians and reversed the recognition of Macedonia within the larger Bulgaria, returning its territory to the Ottoman Empire. This infuriated Albanian nationalists. Bulgaria, Greece, Montenegro, and Serbia "perceived in the Treaty of Berlin a barrier to their national aspirations", therefore, after 1878, "all the Balkan states strove to overcome the Berlin settlement and realise national unity" (Hall 2000: 3).

Furthermore, Bismarck's famous proclamation in 1878 that an Albanian question does not exist, terrified Albanians. It was becoming clear to Albanians that Russia had plans on how to end the Ottoman rule and "aggrandize" territories of Macedonia, Epirus, Thrace and Albania (Psilos 2006: 41). At best, there was a real danger that Russia was going to encourage Albania's neighbors, Serbia and Greece to partition all Albanian-speaking territories, considered Ottoman areas at the time.

Young Turks and the Albanian nationalist movement

On 4 July 1908, the Committee of Union and Progress (CUP), one of the main factions of the Young Turk forces, openly challenged the Sultan and demanded the restitution of the 1876 constitution; the establishment of a parliamentary system which was to be generated as a result of free elections, and the change of the state structure in order to guarantee more ethnic unity "irrespective of nationality or religion" (Psilos 2006: 29). On 24 July 1908 the Sultan, Abdul Hamid capitulated and announced the restoration of a new constitution. Albanian leaders who represented Albanian speaking lands during the Parliamentary session in December 1908 sided against the Sultan and supported the Young Turks, who promised democratic parliamentary reforms which would deliver "religious freedom, free education, freedom of the press, freedom of speech and assembly" (Pearson 2004: 2). However, except for the freedom of the press, other requests were not fulfilled by the Young Turks.

According to Psilos, disappointed by the Young Turks and conscious of the risk their neighbors professed, Albanians started to unify their anti-Turkish movement, which in 1909, surged on different fronts. The Albanian resistance during 1909-1910 was not only militarily oriented, in November 1908, the Manastir congress demanded the recognition of the Albanian language. The Tepelena convention that was held on 4 February 1909, demanded protection from the Hellenic expansionist program of Epirus, and for Albanian autonomy; the Dibër congress on 23 July 1909, requested an Albanian Latin alphabet, an education policy and a fair appointment of civil administrators that had a minimum knowledge of the Albanian culture, *doke e zakone*; the Elbasan congress on 2 September 1909, reinforced the demand for an Albanian language and cultural affiliation that underpinned a direct recognition of an Albanian entity (Psilos 2006: 31-37).

The reaction of The Porte was immediate. In April 1910 General

Turgut Pasha led a new military campaign against the Albanians, aiming to restore order, collect overdue taxes, and disarm the Albanian tribes in order to stop them from generating more disturbances. The Ottoman anti-Albanian campaign reached its peak in the summer of 1910 when martial law was proclaimed throughout Albania, with political leaders such as Feim Bey Zavalani and Bekir Suleiman Effendi killed, and many others forced into exile. The Ottoman campaign that aimed to "denationalise the south" and "destroy northern Albania" came to an end in October 1910, leaving Albania in total "devastation and anarchy" (Psilos 2006: 37). This was enough for the entire Albanian population of the North to be organised during the winter and start an armed resistance against The Porte in Spring 1911. The Ottomans called upon Albanian chieftains to agree to a cease-fire.

In June 1911, from the assembly of Greçë in Montenegro, the leaders of the Albanian uprising wrote to the Turkish Cabinet; demanding "territorial and administrative autonomy for all areas inhabited by Albanians, before they would consider a cease-fire". Demands such as the recognition of an Albanian nationality, Albanian language rights, administrative and political self-governance, police agents and gendarmes within Albanian territories should be exclusively for Albanians, taxes collected should be used for Albanian needs, "economic and cultural advancement of the Albanian people"; a general amnesty should be granted for all Albanians, and "Moslems and Christians, who have been sentenced for political reasons" be released (Pearson 2004: 18). Although the Sultan signed an amnesty on 3 July 1911, the Albanian insurgents refused to return home. Expecting to have to assert themselves, the Albanian *Malissori* chieftains, Bajram Curri, Hasan Prishtina, Riza Gjakova, Idriz Seferi and Isa Boletini united approximately 30,000 Albanian forces. On 9 August 1912, the insurgents of Northern Albania sent a memorandum to the Sultan with fourteen demands, similar to that of Greçë (Pearson 2004: 26). Other Albanian leaders increased pressure from the South and captured the towns of Durrës, Krujë and Peshkopi in the vilayet of Shkodër, and Fier and Përmet in the *vilayet* of Janina. This increasing pressure forced the Sultan to cede to some of the Albanian demands, although Albanian autonomy was still off the agenda.

Albanian nationalism, which was transformed into armed resistance, was now becoming a serious challenge for The Porte. This state of play was well understood by Balkan nationalism, whom according to Pearson, attempted to hijack the Albanian resistance. An example was the Albanian uprising of North Albania and Kosovo, which in autumn of 1912, was instigated by "a Serbian terrorist organisation"—the Black Hand Society. Its leader, Dragutin Dimitrijevic, promised help and encouraged Kosovar Albanians in their revolt against the Turks (Pearson 2004: 27). Albanian Kosovars were deceived by Serbs who tricked them. The aim of Serbs was to separate Turks from Albanians, while using the latter to drive the Turks from Kosovo. Some Albanians realised the danger of separation from the Turks, but by then it was too late:

> Far from fulfilling their promises to help the Albanians to liberty, the Serbian and Montenegrin armies fell upon them. The Albanians were trapped and unable to obtain ammunition from either side; the Serbs and Montenegrins massacred them wholesale. (Pearson 2004: 28).

This massacre led to a perception among Albanians that the Ottomans had failed to protect the interest of Albanians (Morgan 2010: 11). It also furthered the anxiety created by the Balkan League agreement. Under the auspices of Russia, in the spring of 1912, Bulgaria, Serbia and Greece signed an agreement to create "The Balkan League", aiming to fight the Ottoman oppressors and drive Macedonian lands out of Turkish dominion. Albanian leaders interpreted the Balkan League to be not only anti Turkish, but also anti-Albanian. As Pearson points out:

...none of the other Balkan States wished to see an independent Albania, but rather envisaged the partition of Albania between them. Thus, they hastened to precipitate war with Turkey, the purpose of which was the annexation of Albanian-inhabited territories that were under Turkish rule" (Pearson 2004: 27).

Albanian independence and the Balkan Wars

By autumn of 1912, the Ottoman Empire was struggling to keep up with pressure coming from different fronts in the Balkans. Italian nationalism started to increase, and Italy took advantage of the Moroccan crisis in 1911 advancing its ambition to establish a colony in North Africa. Italy sent an ultimatum to the Ottomans on 28 September 1911, and the next day declared war against them. Italian troops advanced quickly taking Tripoli, Darnah (Derna), and Banghāzī (Benghazi). Turkey, threatened by the Balkan states, sought peace with Italy. According to The Treaty of Lausanne (18 October 1912), Turkey gave up its rights over Tripoli and Cyrenaica to Italy to now focus on the Balkans.

The first Balkan War broke out on 8 October 1912, and danger for the Albanian controlled lands was imminent. The following month, on 28 November 1912, Ismail Qemali declared Albanian independence, which formally ended the Ottoman occupation of Albanian territories. This meant that "469 years to the day after the return of Skenderbeg into his capital at Krujë, and for the first time since 1468, their [Albanian] country was free from Turkish rule" (Pearson 2004: 34). Following Albanian independence, the only hope for Albanian nationalism was the recognition of an Albanian state. The tasks for the Albanian leaders were enormous: create a united Albanian army; revitalise the Albanian disastrous economy, but most importantly, recognition of the Albanian state by Great Powers.

The cease-fire between the Ottomans and the Balkan League

in December 1912 created a further opportunity for the Balkan League armies of Serbia, Montenegro, Bulgaria and Greece to attack Albanian lands. While exhausted, Turkish troops gradually started to withdraw from Albanian vilayets to mark the end of the Ottoman era in Albania, anxiety among Albanian leaders increased, as Albania's neighbours were already making moves to fill the vacuum left by the Ottomans. As Jelavich points out:

> Certainly, Bulgaria, Greece, Montenegro and Serbia showed not the slightest hesitation or moral qualm in planning the partition of Albanian lands (Jelavich and Jelavich 1977: 320).

The Serbian First Army established another important victory against Djavid Pasha's troops at Manastir in November 1912 – three weeks after the previous win in October at Kumanovo. After controlling the South West of Macedonia, the Serbian Army did not advance through the Vardar valley to Thessaloniki, as their allies at the time, Bulgarians and Greeks were just about to start their own military action over the control of Thessaloniki. Serbia's main focus now became the Albanian Adriatic exit, which at the time was safeguarded by Austrians. Therefore, Serbian troops advanced through via Egnatia and managed to establish control over the north bank of Shkumbin River—a position that they aimed to hold onto in this conflict (Hall 2000: 85). They had no intention of abandoning the north of the Shkumbin River, which would have included both existing ports of Durrës and Shëngjin, thus, ultimately realising Serbia's dream to have an exit to the Adriatic Sea.

The first Balkan War was brief but was not contained solely in Albania. In the Center and North East of Albania, the Ottoman troops of Djavid Pasha supported by Albanian irregulars were fighting Serbs, whereas Esat Toptani's troops and unorganized Albanian guerrillas in the South East fought against Greek armies. Fighting neighbors under Sultan's army suited Esat Toptani, an Albanian chieftain who was a high-ranking member of The Porte.

Greek forces surrounded Ottoman troops of Esat Pasha on 14 December 1912 in what is known as the siege of Janina. A volunteer legion led by the son of the Italian national hero Giuseppe Garibaldi—Ricciotti Garibaldi soon reached Janina to unite with the Greeks. The siege lasted months and ended on 6 March 1913, with the defeat of Esat Pasha troops. The Greek troops quickly advanced North to penetrate Albanian lands and West to secure the Ionian coast and Corfu; demonstrating an effective and agile military capable of functioning in challenging conditions.

During their withdrawal from Janina, Esat Pasha's forces marched towards North Albania to then join troops of Hasan Riza Pasha who were involved in the Siege of Shkodër, which began in October 1912 and lasted until April 1913. Hasan Riza Pasha's troops had no intention of surrendering, and the defeat is also linked to Esat Pasha's order to ambush and kill Hasan Riza Pasha not far from the location where the two had previously dined together. Esat Pasha signed the capitulation and handed over the city to the Kingdom of the Montenegrin Army, which promised to support Esat Pasha's ambition to become the king of what remained of Albania as compensation.

Djavid Pasha's VI Corps on the other hand continued to fight in other parts of Albania, which also included south of the Shkumbin River, coming down to Berat and Lushnje. Serbs concluded the First Balkan War on March 1913 at the battle of Ballagat, a small village near Lushnje. The Ottomans sustained a clear defeat, allowing Serbs to enter Lushnje and then Berat in April. By the end of April, pressure from the Great Powers escalated due to the siege of Scutari; forcing the Serbs to renounce their holdings in Central Albania and, by the first week of May, most of the Serbian forces had withdrawn from Northern Albania. The Austro-Hungarian Army had already entered Bosnian lands and threatened King Nikola of Montenegro that he could not retain Scutari in the face of military action from the Great Powers, forcing him to surrender. After two weeks of occupation from Montenegrin troops, a detachment representing the Great Powers marched into Scutari and assumed control, ultimately ending the First Balkan War.

With the signing of the Peace Treaty in May 1913, the first Balkan War came to an end. However, this Treaty decided that Macedonian lands would be divided between Serbia and Greece, intensifying Bulgarian nationalism. Bulgaria turned its attention to Adrianople, and with the support of Austro-Hungary, in June 1913, they attacked Serbia and Greece, sparking the second Balkan War. While competing with Serbia over Macedonia, Greece signed a "military convention" to attack Bulgaria. It was not a difficult task for the armies of Serbia, Greece, Romania and Turkey to defeat Bulgaria in what is known as the Second Balkan War. The Treaty of Bucharest, which was agreed in August 1913, was negotiated without the presence of the Great Powers and marked the end of the second Balkan War. This Treaty established that Bulgaria would lose control of the Macedonian lands that were now to be divided between Serbia and Greece—both Balkan states that were still banking on dividing Albanian territory.

Russia's strong support for Serbian victories infuriated Austro-Hungary and Germany; countries that were not only planning to teach Serbia and Russia a lesson, but also to oppose Russia's alliance with France and Britain. The Great Powers found themselves in less agreement and as 1914 was approaching, signs emerged that tensions could easily spill over into conflict – something which eventually happened with the outbreak of the First World War in 1914.

3
RECOGNITION, SURVIVAL AND COLLAPSE OF ALBANIA (1913-1990)

The London Conference – and the fate of "little" Albania

Prior to the ceasefire between the Ottoman-Turks and the Balkan League in 1913, the Great powers of the time (Austro-Hungary, Germany, Russia, France, Italy and Great Britain) sensed the potential danger that was approaching from the Balkans. They subsequently met to ascertain if a diplomatic solution to the tensions could be found, including the partitioning of the "Ottoman lands" in the Balkans. The London Conference (also known as the Ambassadors' meetings), chaired by the British foreign minister Edward Grey, was officially opened on 17 December 1912, and continued to meet during both Balkan wars. Although the conference was originally meant to take place in Paris, Austria argued for it to take place in a neutral location such as London. While this London Conference aimed to resolve territorial disputes between the Turks and the Balkan League members, the status of Albania and its territorial boundaries became the main topic of the conference.

In May 1913, at the end of the First Balkan war, the Conference made the important decision to recognise the Albanian state as an individual political entity autonomously from the Ottomans. Although autonomy was not what the Albanians had hoped for, it was officially recognised at the fifty-fourth meeting of the Conference of London in July 1913 (Elsie, 2016). Alongside these decisions, the

Conference also decided that the "boundaries of Albania were to be fixed by the great powers" (The Treaty of London 2011). The political aim of the Conference was to bring peace to Europe. In order to achieve this aim, The Ambassadors Conference assumed the task of re-drawing the ex-Ottoman territories in the Balkans, which meant rewarding Balkan winners with territory from the Ottoman four vilayets of Janina, Manastir, Kosovo and Shkodra. It was agreed that the key criterion to re-draw the Balkans map should be ethnography[1]. However, the Conference struggled to provide solutions after prolonged debates on ethnographic elements, which for people with close similarities such as the Balkans, was indeed challenging. Reaching a peace agreement was the main goal of the Conference, as Gray states that "we could not destroy achievements of the London Conference for some Albanian towns such as Gjakova…" (Grey, 1927). Grey signposted the town of Gjakova as an "Albanian town". Nevertheless, The Treaty left Gjakova and the entire Kosovo-Albanian-speaking lands out of the Albanian borders. While this explains the lack of awareness about the Albanian-speaking territories, it also shows poor decisions creating precedents; foreshadowing future dangers to come.

The London Conference was characterised by disputes between Austro-Hungary and Italy on one side and Russia and France on the other. Grey, who was supposed to represent the neutral position of the UK, showed that in reality, he was protecting British interests, especially when dealing with Greece. Austro-Hungary was known as a strong supporter of the Albanian case, and Russia known for its historical support of Slavs in the Balkans, especially Serbs. The Great Powers presented to Grey two proposals: One from Austro-Hungary and Italy, and the other from Russia and France. The Russian proposal lobbied for Serbian, Montenegrin, Bulgarian and

---

1 Ethnography is the scientific description of peoples and cultures based on their customs, habits, and mutual differences.

Greek interests at the expense of Albanian-speaking territories. It included cities with a majority of Albanian-speaking populations such as Ulqini, Plava and Guzija as part of Montenegro. Russian energy was primarily focused on the Serbian need for securing Adriatic Sea access. Their proposal included within the Serbian territories the plains of Kosova and North Albania. The Russian strategy was clear: at the very least the port of Shëngjin needed to be secured for Serbia. The Russian proposal also excluded the Albanian-speaking territories of today's North Macedonia from Albania but did not oppose the Greek claim to parts of today's Albania such as cities of Korçë, Tepelenë, Përmet, Gjirokastër, Sarandë and both sides of the Vjosa River down to Vlorë.

Unlike the Russian proposal, the Austro-Hungarian proposal strongly lobbied for Shkodër to remain part of Albania. With their decision to deny Serbian access to the Adriatic Sea, Austro-Hungary's aim was twofold: inhibiting Serbian economic expansion and confining the Russian expansion in the Balkans. Austro-Hungary and Italy spent the majority of their energy to secure Shkodër for Albania and to block Serbian access to the Adriatic but compromised on leaving out some territories of today's Kosovo, such as Prishtina. They, however, included Prizren, Gjakova and Pec. They also excluded most of the Albanian speaking territories of Manastir, and other towns that are located within today's Northern Macedonia. However, the Austro-Hungarian plan strongly opposed Greece's claims on South Albania.

All representatives of the recognised Balkan states were invited to the London Conference to participate and present their claims. To its detriment, Albania did not have a recognised government at the time. Upon advice by Austria, the Albanian head of the first provisional government formed on 28 November 1912, Ismail Qemali, did not want to leave Vlorë, fearing a possible uprising or coup. Pro-Ottoman elements, unhappy with the Independence proclamation and the first Albanian government, were still very active. However, Qemali managed to send an Albanian delegation composed of a Muslim, Mehmet Konica, a Catholic, Filip Noga, and Rasim Dino, who represented the Chameria (Çamëria) region. Grey allocated only 13 minutes to hear the Albanian claims. The Albanian chair of delegates, Konica, claimed that Albanian territory should include all parts of Albania shown in the Austro-Hungarian proposal, but also the entire Kosovo region, Ulqini, Plava and Guzije in Montenegro, and the Chameria region, including the coastal North part of Epirus, down to Preveza (Hoxha 2000:16). In order to claim Albanian speaking territories, Konica argued on an ethno-linguistic approach as shown in the figure 5. Konica claimed that the majority of the Albanian population in all four vilayets were comprised of people who speak a unique Albanian language, which had no similarity to Serbian, Montenegrin or Greek languages.

The Great Powers did not agree to any of these proposals. Never losing sight of their own imperial interests, the Great Powers had no clear criteria for designing the borders and used the Albanian speaking territories to satisfy the demands of Albania's neighbours (Danaj, 2012). As a result, none of these proposals submitted to the London Conference were fully implemented. According to the maps proposed, it is clear that the decision made by the Great Powers was to "compromise" between the two proposals satisfying neither of the contending parties and, most of all, angering Albania. Hence, the Chameria region was given to Greece, but not Korçë, Sarandë, Gjirokastër, Tepelenë, Përmet and Vlorë. Kosovo with a population that was 90 percent Albanian was attached to Serbia; Plava, Guzia and Ulqini were handed to Montenegro, and the Eastern part of Lake Ohrid (today's Western part of North Macedonia) was attached to the new Serbian dominated territory, which in the aftermath of the "Great War" became part of the Kingdom of Yugoslavia. Thus, the Conference was responsible for redrawing the Bal-

Figure 5: Albanian border proposals, London Conference (1912)

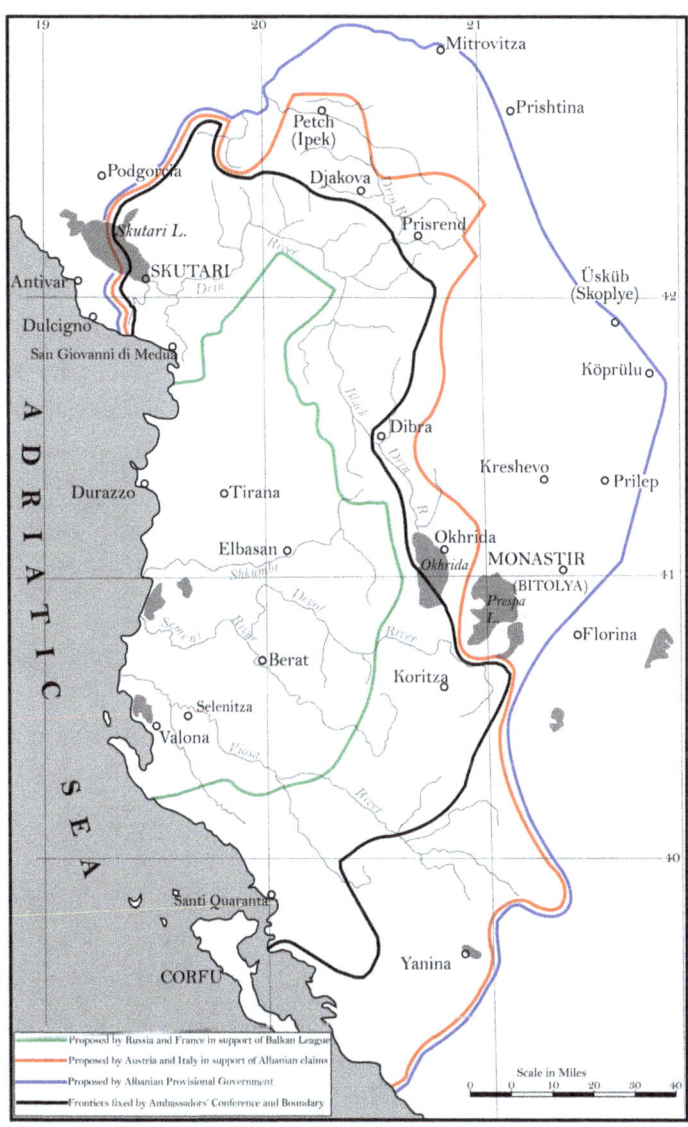

Source: Adapted proposed boundaries at the London Conference. Balkan Map 13, US Commission, DOS, RD 256; Similar version can be found at H.C. Woods (1918), 'Albania and the Albanians', *The Geographic Review*, 5: 259, in Guy 202: 403.

kan map, a map which, for Albanians, remained largely unchanged, and still not conceding full nation statehood and territorial integrity.

By July 1913, The Ambassadors Conference agreed that Albania should be recognised as a nation but mandated its final borders to be decided by the North and South boundary commissions. What was clear was that the Great Powers had little familiarity with the Balkans, its people, its territories and its distinctions. They interviewed people based on ethnographic questions and the border between Albania and Greece proved to be very problematic. The British representative, Lieutenant-Colonel Charles Doughty-Wylie, reported to London that children were waving the Greek flag, speaking Greek and singing Hellenic patriotic songs in towns wherever the border commission was visiting. Entry doors were painted with the Greek national emblem, but they were closed; raising suspicion that Albanian-speaking people may have been inside because they could not speak Greek (Guy 2008: 103-4).

Each time the border commission arrived in a new town or village church bells rang to express the presence of the Greek-Orthodox population. The British representative had no doubt, these welcome parties were orchestrated by Greeks, and this was a Greek strategy to convince the border commission of the Greek heritage of these towns. The Commission proved this in a town where a group of children seemed to have been speaking Greek, however, when the Austrian representative, Bilinski, "threw down a handful of coins, they all started squabbling in Albanian" (Guy 2008: 104). Doughty-Wylie sent a telegram to London requesting not only the "language" to be the main criterion, but he also proposed more investigation on nationality, geographic features, economic and strategic considerations. Austria and Italy sent an ultimatum to the Greek government that if the commission meets any further Greek interference in any town, the town will be considered to be

Albanian. The Greek Prime Minister Venizelos complained directly to Grey who appreciated the internal public pressure Venizelos was handling on issues over borders of Aegean and Northern Epirus. By mid-December 1913, findings of these two commissions were sent to the Geographical Institute of Florence for examination. Greece had to accept the decisions about the border with Albania and on 18 June 1914, Greece issued a Royal Decree, which returned the Sazan island to Albania.

Albania—an autonomous state under foreign protectorate

The Great Powers realized the enormous political challenges for the newly recognized Albania; a quasi-non-existent state. Pro-Ottoman elements were still active[2], and the appetite of its neighbors, Greece and Serbia showed no signs of relenting. Austro-Hungarians lobbied the German Prince Wilhelm of Wied (*Wilhelm Friedrich Heinrich* 1876-1945), to rule over the Principality of Albania which he accepted. From March to his exile in September 1914, Wied was officially recognised as king of Albania.

Upon acceptance of the throne, Wied travelled to the provisional capital, Durrës, and began organising an Albanian government. He appointed Turhan Pasha Përmeti as the head of government which was mostly composed of aristocrats and Albanian notables such as Esat Pasha Toptani and other chieftains. Difficulties for this new Albanian government were enormous. Alongside a disastrous economic situation, the government was under pressure to protect Albania from both Serbia and Greece. While in the South East, the Greek Army penetrated Albanian lands, encouraging a separatist movement of North-Epirus, both the Montenegrin and Serbian Army continued to attack from the North. On 19 December 1913, the Council of Florence reconfirmed and reminded all parties of

---

2 The short-lived peasant revolt led by Haxhi Qamili in May 1914 requested that Albanian lands return under Sultan's suzerainty.

the London Conference's findings on Albanian borders. By February 1914, the Greek government decided to comply with decisions made by the Council of Florence to stop military attacks on Albania. Despite this, fighting continued between Albanian irregulars and Greeks during the spring of 1914.

The same happened to North Albania where in absence of a strong Albanian Army, Albanians were forced to fight with irregular forces. Wied failed to appreciate Albania's complex situation with its borders and its weak military resources. In competition with Austro-Hungaria, Italy also had territorial ambitions in Albania, and financed Esat Pasha's plot to overthrow Wied in May 1914. The Italian plot was exposed and Esat Pasha was arrested, though later released and forced to go into exile. In reality Wied's authority never extended much beyond Durrës. With the outbreak of the First World War, Austro-Hungary requested Wied send Albanian troops to fight the Serbs alongside their allies. Wied's refusal marked the end of his support by Austro-Hungary, which also ended his reign of Albania. On 3 September 1914, Wied fled Albania never to return. Esat Pasha attempted to return to Albania and never stopped dreaming about the Albanian throne until his assassination by Avni Rustemi in Paris in June 1920.

The Albanian government in the inter-war years

In an attempt to bring the Kingdom of Italy on its side, Great Britain, France and Russia (The Triple Entente) signed a secret treaty with Italy on 25 April 1915 in London (Bianchi 2018: 91). According to this agreement, Italy which had not entered the war thus far, was supposed to declare war on the Triple Alliance (Germany, Austria and Hungary), and thus, weaken their alliance while making it more feasible for The Triple Entente and Italy to win the war. The article six of this Treaty, promised Italy a number of spoils for its efforts at the end of the Great War, such as sovereignty over the Albanian island of Sazan, port of Vlorë and its surrounding territories. The following article specified that Italy should not oppose division of the Northern and Southern Albania – territories to be divided between Serbia, Montenegro and Greece.

A month later, Italy declared war on Austria and Hungary, but not against Germany for another year. Despite the agreement on the secret treaty, it remained non implemented largely due to the fact that by the end of the Great War relations between Italy with France and Britain had deteriorated significantly. Another reason which saw the Treaty remain a dead letter was its public release by the Bolsheviks after taking power in November 1917 (Duka 2007: 90). In the same month, Austro-Hungary published their agreement and distributed it in an attempt to mobilise the Albanian population of the North against Serbs who had moved quickly to occupy Albania's North. By July 1917, Greeks, Italians, Austrians, French, Serbian and Montenegrin troops were all present in different parts of the country and once again Albania struggled against foreign ambitions seeking to divide Albanian lands.

In January 1918, the US President, Woodrow Wilson, addressed the US Congress on the new international order created by WWI. In his speech Wilson presented fourteen points, which were crucial for the survival and existence of the Albanian nation. These points emphasised self-determination, free trade and democracy in the new post war world order. Point eleven of this presentation discussed the occupied territories in the Balkans that should be restored to the new nations and point twelve discussed the necessity to secure sovereignty of states that emerged on the Ottoman Empire lands. Wilson's speech also showed increasing American interest in Europe and his fourteen points were instrumental in what would become the Treaty of Versailles.

Being on the victorious side of the Great War in 1918, Italy's expansionist appetite increased. After the London Agreement, Italy never stopped in its efforts to seek gains from the Ottoman territory, especially Albania. However, Italy understood that its expansionist plans to occupy Albania without an agreement with Greece and especially Serbia would be futile (Bianchi 2018: 99-102). As a result, another post-war secret agreement between representatives of Greece, the Prime Minister Eleftherios Venizelos and the Italian Minister of Foreign Affairs, Tommaso Tittoni was signed (Bianchi 2018: 142). It stated that Greece promised to accept Italian claims over Vlorë and the Italian protectorate over Albania. On the other hand, Italy promised to support Greece's territorial claims over North Epirus, and Serbia to annex the Northern part of Albania (Stavrianos [1965] 2000: 710-2). Yet again Albania found itself in the middle of competing powers. For Skendi, Austro-Hungary and Italy were competing for more influence in the North West and the Adriatic (Skendi 1967: 238-56). In 1919, Edith Durham mentions that the strongest support of Albania, Austria, was close to join Russia in opposing an Albanian nation-state and thus realise its interests in the Balkans (Durham 1919: 41).

The Treaty of Versailles officially ended WWI in June 1919. A few months later, the Paris Peace Treaty held by victorious allies decided on the peace terms for the defeated central powers. The Albanian Provisional Government formulated again its claims on ethnographical lines (as shown in the figure 6), arguing[3] with decisions made by the Berlin Congress in 1878 and London Conference in 1913.

Albanian leaders had neither the strength nor the support to oppose these treaties. At the end of WWI, Albania was partitioned and occupied by Serbian, Greek, French, British and Italian armies. The dysfunctional government of Durrës was operating under Italian protection and could not extend its authority over the Northern tribal chieftains and Southern landowners. Nevertheless, Albanians

---
3 See the entire speech of the Albanian delegation in the Appendix.

Figure 6: Albanian Provisional Government claims (1919)

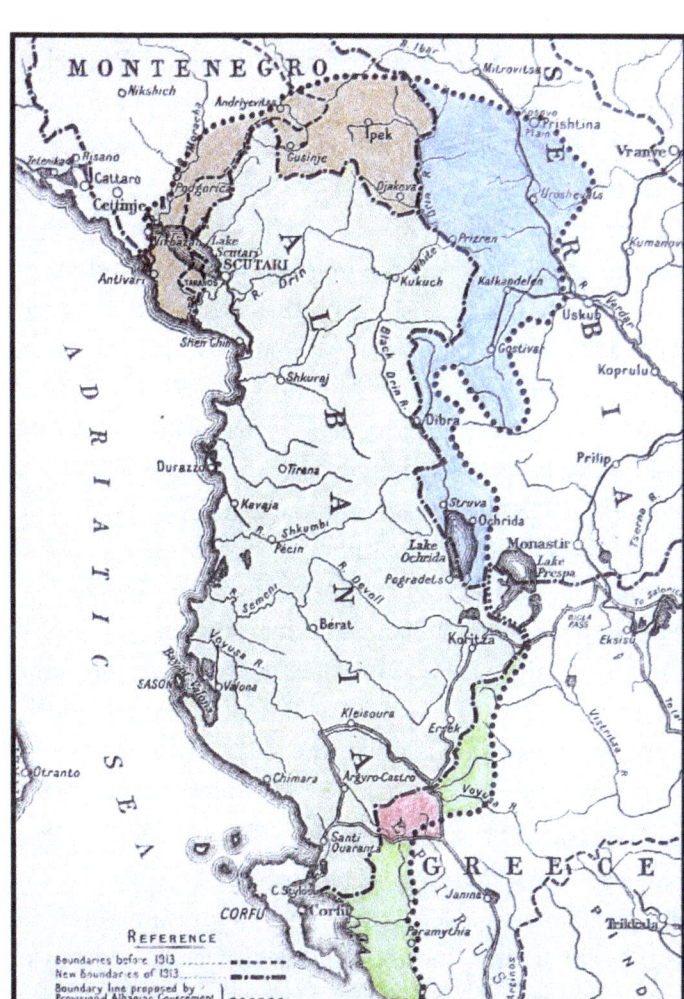

Source: Adapted, Temperley, *History of the Peace Conference*, IV, p. 338, [Kindly reproduced with permission of Royal Institute of International Affairs], in Guy 202: 416. This indicative map shows territories of the Albanian speaking majority populations that were left out of today's Albanian borders.

sensed the danger of partition once more, and decided to react. In their very last attempt, Albanian representatives from all parts of Albania convened the Congress of Lushnje from 21 January until 9 February 1920. The Congress of Lushnje aimed to protect Albanian lands against the possible invasion from foreign armies.

Although it did not have any state authority, the Congress of Lushnje operated on the *besa*[4] approach (Crampton 1997), which according to the *Kanun* was the most powerful institution for Albanians. The Congress of Lushnje produced the first constitutional document and elected a four-man supreme council composed of a Catholic, an Orthodox a Sunny Muslim and a Bektashi. The Congress sent a letter to the Conference of Paris asking that Albanian territorial unity be protected, and decisions made by the London Conference in 1913 to draw up boundaries of Albania be reversed. The Congress also decided unanimously not to recognise the Durrës government, which was supported by Italy, and to lead the armed resistance against Italian and other occupations. To assist its cause Albania finally became a member of the League of Nations on 17 December 1920 (Steed 1927: 172-3). On 9 November 1921, the Conference of Ambassadors under the authority of the Great Powers assigned to Italy the right to act in Albania (Fischer 1984: 85-6).

From 1920 to 1939, Albania was characterised by a political rivalry between Fan Stilian Noli, a Harvard-educated scholar who believed in parliamentary democracy and the muslim Ahmet Zogu, an authoritarian figure educated at Lycée de Galatasaray in Costantinople and leader of the important Mati tribe. Noli and Zogu represented two sides of the same coin with Noli embracing Western ideology and Zogu mirroring the authoritarian rule of Constantinople. This is the period when the Albanian state started to con-

---

4 In Albanian culture precept *besa* is considered as a pledge of honour. Since ancient times, *besa* has acted for Albanian people as an 'oath', which means 'to keep the promise' and the 'word of honour' regardless of its consequences.

solidate as an actor. Zogu initially got the upper hand and came to power in 1922, establishing an authoritarian regime that filled the political vacuum left in Albania after WWI. Despite the support of some tribe leaders, his popularity was never high, and he began to lose legitimacy, fleeing to Yugoslavia after the so-called "June revolution" in 1924. Reformist and liberal Noli was appointed Prime Minister in June 1924. In December 1924, Noli's government fell to Zogu, who was backed by Albanian tribal supporters and the Yugoslav military (Vickers 1998: 157-8). Noli fled to Italy and then to the United States. As a gesture of recognition to his Yugoslav supporters, in June 1925, Zogu ceded a small part of Albanian territory called "Saint Naum Monastery" to Yugoslavia (Pearson 2005: 248). He declared himself the King of Albania in 1928 and remained attached to his "declared" throne until 7 April 1939; when Italy occupied Albania forcing Zogu to flee.

Post-Ottoman bilateral relations between Albania and the Republic of Turkey

The collapse of the Ottoman Empire by the end of WWI necessitated a new struggle for Albania to protect its territorial integrity. Cultural similarities, commonalities in dealing with oppressors, but above all, a desire to survive, brought about new ties between Turkey and Albania at the end of WWI. This was a time when Turkey was dealing with its own internal and external struggles to maintain its territorial integrity and trying to replace the Ottoman Caliphate with a modern Republican state. The name that has become synonymous with the end of the Ottoman Empire and the creation of the Republic of Turkey—Kemal Atatürk— has been described "for all intents and purposes, the moral and intellectual epitome of the Young Turk[s] movement" (Gingeras 2016: 5). Atatürk and other Turkish Republican leaders rejected the Ottoman past as a backward and "non-Western" society. This shift suited Albanian needs, and a new chapter in the relations between Turkey and Albania began (Xhaferi 2017b: 45).

Despite Turkey's domestic and international challenges, Atatürk assumed a friendly posture towards Albania. He believed in a republican and modern Turkey, and he hoped for Albania to become a free and prosperous country (Limaj 2012: 33). For example, in 1920, Atatürk sent several scholars of Albanian origin back to Albania to help the establishment of the Albanian state. One of them, colonel Selaudin Shkoza, a man with Albanian heritage, was appointed as the defence minister in the Albanian government in 1920. Shkoza's appointment laid the foundations for new diplomatic relations between Turkey and Albania. In March 1921, addressing the National Assembly of Turkey, Atatürk explained "sanctuary" links between Turks and "brother" Albanians stating that "we [Turks] are going to help as much as we can" and provide whatever this brother nation-state needs (Limaj 2012: 29). Therefore, in December 1923, nearly a month after the Declaration of the Republic of Turkey in October 1923, a "Memorandum of Friendship Agreement" between the two states paved the way for another five years of increased diplomatic relations. This was now a post-colonial agreement between the Republic of Turkey and the Albanian government, led by the Muslim leader of the Mati tribe, Ahmet Zogu.

The Republic of Turkey was internationally recognised by the Treaty of Lausanne in July 1923. From this Treaty, Bulgaria was obligated to withdraw from the Western Thrace, and have this territory join Greece. Greece, on the other hand, returned territories of Eastern Thrace and Smyrna (Izmir) back to Turkey; territories acquired through the Treaty of Sevres in 1920. The return of these lands to Turkey became problematic for Greece, as Christian Greeks also lived in these territories, while Muslim Turks were living in Western Thrace, Thessaly, Macedonia and Epirus—all territories that were now part of Greece. The Venizelos proposal for an agreement of population exchange with Turkey had the approval of Atatürk. As such, Turkey and Greece reached an agreement to facilitate the exchange of circa one million Christian Greeks, and 400,000 Muslim Turks. The agreement that formed part of the Treaty of Lausanne in 1923, provided legal rights to Turkey and Greece to exchange population, while both governments agreed to protect rights of all minorities living within their territory. In order to classify other minorities, both Greece and Turkey decided to follow the lines of the millet system, which further complicated the position of Muslim Albanians who were living in big numbers in Epirus. According to the Ottoman *millet* system, Muslim Albanians were classified and detailed in the Ottoman documents as Turks. When the Treaty started to be implemented, many Muslim Albanians who were living in Greece decided to stay in their homes and protect their properties, rather than leaving what they considered to be their lands.

The only way for the Greek state to comply with the Treaty of Lausanne was to protect the rights of the Albanian minorities. However, hiding the presence of the Albanians could also make the Greek state comply with the Treaty. The Greek state chose the second option, and registered the Orthodox-Albanians as Greeks, and Albanian-Muslims as Greek-Muslims. Therefore, the Greek state aimed to justify the non-existence of the Albanian Chams, after much concern in covering the issue of Arvanitas-Albanians (Baltsiotis 2011: 19), who fought the Ottomans alongside Greeks and inevitably, they were part of the Greek Revolution in 1821 (Karalis 2010: 166). As a result, Chams were under the constant and systematic pressure by the Greek government and the Orthodox Church to either leave the country or assimilate using the Greek language and religion. In 1923, the Greek state and the Orthodox Greek Church reached an agreement that affected Albanians: they both agreed to follow a structured plan; crafting a historical experience of "the state sponsored Church...", which, according to Karalis, is still present in the twenty-first century and needs to be changed (Karalis 2010: 174-84). The undesirable Muslim Albanians continued to live under the pressure of the Greek state and its spiritual leadership—the Greek Orthodox Church.

Why was the Greek state disturbed by Albanian Chams situating in the West coastal part of Epirus? On superficial analysis, one may think the Greek state did not want Muslim Albanians to be part of Christian Greece, but the issue was deeper. It is linked to *The Megali Idea*[5], which played a significant role in Greek politics since the War for Independence in 1821. Since then, Greece expanded its territory several times as shown in the figure 7. Since the Greek constitution in 1844, until the end of WWII, all Greek governments promoted the *Megali Idea*, which basically means Greece's claim to extend its territory following that of the latest Byzantine Empire. As part of these claims, "North Epirus" and its territory would belong to Greece. An old map crafted by Giacomo Cantelli in 1683 (figure 8) shows the South of Illyrian tribes called Epirus. The Epirus is known through successful campaigns against Romans led by the famous Illyrian, Pyrrhus (Myrdal and Kessle 1976: 52) who reigned Epirus lands from 297–272 BC. As shown in the above map, Epirus inhabitants lived South of the Illyrian lands and it is believed that Pyrrhus built the theatre of Butrothon (Gilkes 2013: 97) (figure 9), which is now located in Albania. It became clearer when Skenderbeg fought the Ottomans from today's Albania, while he declared himself to be the King of Epirus. Unlike Albanian nationalism that is firm on its national hero, Skenderbeg, Greek nationalism and historiography has attempted to appropriate both Pyrrhus and Skenderbeg as Greek; calling Skenderbeg with a Greek-sound name, George Castriotis.

---

5 According to *The Megali Idea*, Greece should have had its capital (Constantinople), and extended its territory on "Two Continents (Europe and Asia) and Five Seas", namely: Ionian, Aegean, Marmara, Black and Libyan Seas.

Figure 7: Stages of Greece's expansion of territory

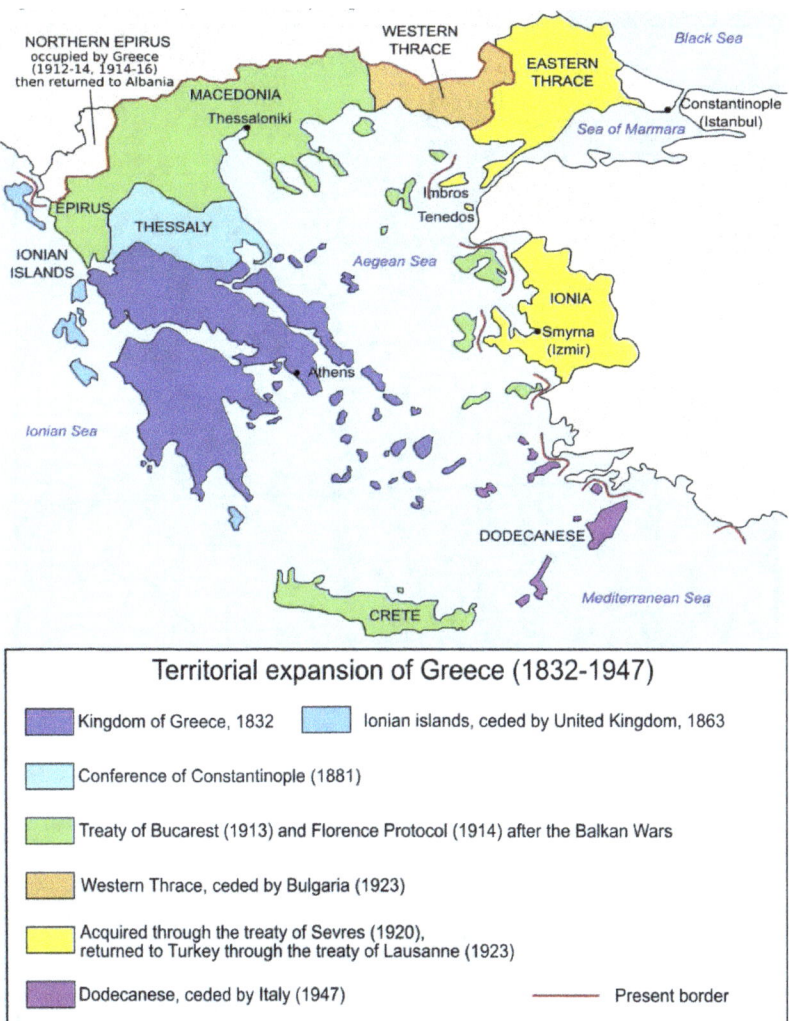

Source: Wikipedia,
https://en.wikipedia.org/wiki/Megali_Idea#/media/File:Map_Greece_expansion_1832-1947-en.svg
The map shows different stages of Greece's territory expansion following the *Megali Idea* (Great Idea). Through the concept of *Megali Idea* Greece aimed to extend its borders; constructing claims of historical and ethnic Greek territories that existed within the borders of the Byzantine Empire, which is considered by the Greeks to be their medieval national state.

Figure 8: Albania and Epirus with names of the Illyrian tribes

Source: Adapted and extracted from *The antique compared to the modern Greece,* a map crafted in Italian language by Giacomo Cantelli in 1683 and published by the *Albanian National Library.* The map shows that Albania and Epirus were inhabitated by Illyrian tribes.

Figure 9: The theatre of Butrothon (modern Butrinti)

Source: Photo taken by Skënder Bushi. The *Butrint* theatre is believed to have been built in the third century BC, under King Pyrrhus of Epirus (306-272BC) (Gilkes 2013 97-99). The theatre was enlarged by Romans after they conquered Illyrian lands. Only part of the *Butrint* complex is excavated and most of these ancient treasures, especially in the south part, remain still unknown.

However, a famous writer who was born in Epirus, Kostas Krystallis, in his valuable work reveals symbolically similarities of Greeks and Albanians—people with different religion, but one leader—Skenderbeg, the King of Epirus (Potts 2010: 237).

In 1923, the Albanian government of Zogu was rather weak and not able to protect the Albanian Muslim minority living in Greece. After overthrowing Noli in 1924 and taking back the control of the state, Zogu sought to re-establish good relations with Turkey. However, Zogu's decision, in 1928, to turn Albania into a monarchy annoyed the Republican Atatürk who, despite his sympathy for Albania, had little time for a monarchy and terminated diplomatic relations by recalling the Turkish ambassador Tahir Lütfi from Tirana as he considered the shift to an Albanian monarchy as a backward step. In response, Zogu closed the Albanian embassy in Ankara, leaving the fate of many Albanians living in Turkey in the hands of the Italian Consulate in Ankara. In reality, the conflict was deeper, as Kadare noted that the Albanian-Muslim King Zogu, attempted to create a new "European Muslim" through legislation, which regulated Albania's three religions and the state (Kadare 2006: 35-36). Although Zogu was a Muslim himself, the legislation contained policies such as prohibiting men from wearing the white Turkish fez and women from wearing the veil. Other laws regulated the physical posture for prayer: standing, rather than kneeling – as this would clash with the old Albanian *kanun*, which protected the pride of Albanian males. The conflict lasted three years, until the second Conference of the Balkans in 1931. Later, in May 1933, the new Albanian ambassador, Xhevat Leskoviku, met with Atatürk, who subsequently sent Ruşen Eşref as Turkish ambassador to Tirana in April 1934 (Limaj 2012: 34). Upon his arrival in Albania, Eşref met King Zog, who then echoed Atatürk's previous words in describing Turkey as the "big brother" of Albania. Despite Atatürk and Zogu having different beliefs—one a convinced republican and the other in favour of a monarchy—it seems what united them was more important. While Zogu's Albania needed to secure Turkish support, Atatürk's Turkey could not find a better friend than Muslim Albanians to help Turkey come back into the Western Balkans.

As Zogu's returned to power in 1924 was backed by Serbia and Montenegro, he had no intention to oppose agreements between Serbia and Turkey. In 1938, Serbia and Turkey implemented a secret plan to "empty Kosovo". This project was initiated in 1937 by a Serbian academic, Vasa Cubrillovic [Čubrilović], known as "Iseljavanje Arnauta" [The expulsion of the Albanians] (Cohen 2013: 44), which, according to Kadare, "shows its explicit aim in its very title" (Kadare 2011: 33). In 1938, Turkey agreed with Serbia to "empty Kosovo" accepting 40,000 Albanian families to be transferred to Turkey (Rexha 2015: 89). The excellent diplomatic relations between Albania and Turkey were again disrupted in April 1939, when fascist Italy occupied Albania. Although the Turkish Embassy in Tirana was closed, during WWII, the Turkish Consulate of Vlorë operated until Hoxha's provisional government closed it down in 1944.

In June 1940, Mussolini declared war on his ex-allies France and Great Britain. He then sent an ultimatum to Greece in October of the same year; requesting Greece hand over parts of its territory. The Greek Prime Minister Ioannis Metaxas rejected the Italian request and once the ultimatum expired, Italian troops based in Albania, occupied Northern Greece. Although Italian troops penetrated Greek territory, they were halted by the resistance of the Greek Army on the Albanian-Greek border and, in little more than a month, Greek resistance managed to stop Italian advances inside Greek territory. By the end of winter and the beginning of spring, the Greek Army started to push the Italian forces back, forcing the Italians to reorganise their forces for another attack from Albania. Greek troops were now attacking Albania from Korcë to Gjirokastër, arriving close to Vlorë. Britain was quick to send aid to the

Greek Army, but this could not support large numbers of Greek soldiers and reserve forces for the entire summer. Hitler, aware of the danger posed by Britain in Greece, invaded Northern Greece in April 1941. Greek troops then surrendered to Germans on 20 April. After the collapse of fascist Italy in July 1943, with only two divisions and minimum effort, Nazi-Germany occupied Albania until winter 1944.

The rise of the Albanian Communist Party

The effects of the October Revolution in 1917 and the rise of communist ideas, spread to Europe, the Balkans and Albania soon after. The first Albanian communist cell was created in Korçë in 1927, followed by others in Shkodër and Tirana. From 1927 until 1930, its future leader, Enver Hoxha, studied at the French High School of Korçë (Le Lycée de Korça). He secured a scholarship from the Albanian government to study at the University of Montpellier in France but, due to his poor academic performance, lost the scholarship in 1934 and returned to Albania in 1936. During his time in France, he embraced communist ideas. In France, he met Isuf Luzaj who commenced his studies at the University of Sorbonne in 1933. Luzaj abandoned their studies due to economic difficulties in 1936 and returned to Albania, however, he continued with his studies. He started to work as a teacher at the French High School of Korcë for two years, and so did Hoxha who joined the school a year later. Luzaj, who had embraced liberal ideas in France was a social justice activist. In 1937, Luzaj graduated from the University of Sorbonne with a Doctor of Philosophy and managed to publish his first book, *Rrefimet*, where he criticised Zogu's regime while hunger was widespread in Albania. After Korçë's hunger march in 1938, he was transferred to the Vlorë Institute, whereas Hoxha continued at the French School from where he started to express communist ideas and influence his students. Hoxha became an active member of the Communist Group of Korcë, supporting Albanian uprisings against the Zog monarchy. Although divided, communist groups started to collaborate and share information that was received by other communist members across Albanian borders. However, the communist movement in Albania suffered a setback in 1939, after Zog's troops arrested and imprisoned nearly all communist members of the Shkodër Group.

In April 1939, fascist Italy attacked Albania and, due to the weak and unorganised resistance of Albanians, the occupation succeeded with little resistance. Luzaj was amongst those Albanians who resisted the occupation with arms. He was arrested at the end of April 1939 and sent to jail in Gjirokastër until March 1940, and then sent to the Italian prison camp of Ventotene, from where he was released in August 1942. While out of jail, Luzaj met some Albanian nationalist elements led by Mit'hat Frashëri in Italy who were not in support of the communist programme and formed their own political grouping, Balli Kombëtar. Luzaj then returned to Vlorë in Autumn 1942, but soon was forced to escape to the mountains after fascists discovered his intention to mobilise his ex-students against the fascist regime. From the labëria mountains, he then led the armed resistance of the Balli Kombëtar in South Albania.

After the French School of Korçë was closed by Mussolini in 1939, Hoxha's activities attracted the attention of the Italian regime. In order to escape the arrest, the Communist Group of Korçë sent Hoxha to support revolutionary activities alongside the Tirana Group. The task of unification against fascist-Italians became imminent. Therefore, despite factions and divisions, communist Albanians managed to form the Albanian Communist Party, *Partia Komuniste Shqiptare* (PKSH), in 1941, with the participation and support of two Yugoslav Communist Party delegates, Mugosha and Popovic (Skendi 1957: 77).

Another Albanian prominent figure who played an important

role in this period, Musine Kokalari, was a close-relative of Hoxha, and known as the first Albanian female writer to have published in the linguistic field. Kokalari graduated in modern literature from the Rome La Sapienza University (Italy) in 1942. She embraced the anti-fascist ideas in Italy, and upon her return to Albania in 1942, Kokalari attempted to join the high ranks of the PKSH. However, the rivalry with Hoxha's future wife, Nexhmie Troplini, was problematic (Wagner 2016: 10). Kokalari, whose ideas about social justice were very close to those of Luzaj and Skënder Muco, decided to form another political entity in 1943, the Albanian Social-Democratic Party; attempting to unite *LANÇ* and *Balli Kombëtar* in a united political organisation in order to fight Nazi-Fascist troops (Wagner 2016: 10). Kokalari's strong social justice beliefs were embedded in the Social-Democratic Party programme, which promised speech and religious freedom to all Albanians.

Zogu's supporters were still active and they also formed part of the Albanian resistance during the occupation by Italy and Germany. They were, however, struggling to be accepted by the Albanian Anti-Fascist and National Liberation Movement (*Lëvizja Antifashiste Nacional-Çlirimtare*) known as *LANÇ*. Both PKSH and *Balli Kombëtar* fought against foreign occupation, but they had differing opinions. In August 1943, PKSH and *Balli Kombëtar* tried to resolve their differences in the Conference of Mukje, where Luzaj was present. While both, the PKSH and *Balli Kombëtar* aimed to fight for the liberation of Albania from all foreign powers, *Balli* also proposed the National unification of all Albanians.

At this point, the Kosovo question came to the fore. Yugoslavia aimed at keeping Kosovo within their federation, and *Balli's* "national unity" request did not suit them. Hoxha followed his Yugoslav comrades and dashed away from the Mukje proceedings (Vickers and Petiffer 1997: 292). This was the deal breaker between Balli and PKSH. After this episode, due to strong support from the Yugoslav communists, the PKSH became the leader of *LANÇ*. After the Mukje conference, members of *Balli Kombëtar* were not welcomed in talks with the PKSH anymore, as they were identified as anti-communists. By November 1943, Hoxha became the leader of *LANÇ* and declared war on *Balli Kombëtar*, as well as on the Legality Movement led by a Royal officer—Abaz Kupi, who declared loyalty to Zogu. The f*LANÇ* was now fighting the Germans, *Balli Kombëtar* and the *Legaliteti* (Legality) resistance—a situation that suited Germans who supported forces opposed to the communists. In December 1943, the Albanian government used its army to support the Germans – a move welcomed by the Reich. The Albanian troops were mainly recruited from Kosovo and led by a German commander (Seton-Watson 2019).

Hoxha became the Head of the Albanian provisional government at the Congress of Përmet in May 1944. The PKSH took an active role in the Albanian resistance that lasted until winter 1944 when German troops left Albania. From November 1943 until June 1944, the German-supported Albanian government was led by a nationalist leader *Balli Kombëtar*, Rexhep Mitrovica. After his resignation, Germans appointed another Prime Minister from *Balli Kombëtar* who had links with *Legaliteti*, Fiqiri Dine, who also resigned on 29 August 1944 to allow another pro-German, and the third member of *Balli*, Ibrahim Bicaku, to become the Albanian PM under the German occupation. By Autumn 1944, the German Army started to withdraw their troops from Albania, followed by allied bombardments and partisan attacks from Greece, Albania and Yugoslavia. It was not difficult for the PKSH to take the lead after the support *Balli Kombëtar* and *Legaliteti* received from the Nazi-Germany.

In November 1944, the Albanian Communist Party, which had led the Albanian resistance against Italian and German occupation, became the leading force in the country. This signalled a new era for the Albanian state and its foreign relations. Most leaders of *Balli Kombëtar* and Legality, including Abaz Kupi and Luzaj realised the danger of the communists coming to power and fled Albania. It was now easy for PKSH to fill the political vacuum and take control. They began a systematic campaign of persecuting their opponents, who at the time were well known intellectual, political and religious figures. Kokalari well understood the danger that would come after November 1944, a time that communists arrested and killed without trial her two brothers and a dozen people from her family. Kokalari, or what Luzaj calls in one of his poems "the icon of the Albanian history" (2020) was imprisoned to 30 years by the Hoxha regime and died in misery in 1983. She is remembered for her courage during and after the trial where she never apologised for having preferred to serve the country as a non-communist. The other Albanian prominent philosopher and writer, Luzaj fled to Italy, to then migrate to Argentina and later to the US. He left his wife and five children in Albania, and only reunited with them in 1990. Literature of both Kokalari and Luzaj is not widely known in Albania. Nevertheless, they were both two great Albanian scholars who were purged by Hoxha's regime.

Post-WWII Albanian Foreign Policy: From Sino-Soviet Cooperation to Isolation

The rise of the Albanian Communist Party to power generated some immediate reaction by both Western and Eastern countries. The US, British and Soviet governments refused to recognise the communist Albanian Provisional Government until November 1945 (Pearson 2005: 477-8). The Allied forces requested democratic elections in Albania. Between 1944 and 1945, opposition political forces were weak to non-existent in Albania. The request sent to the Allied forces by Kokalari to extend elections until the formation of communist opposition was ignored by the British representative who thought that communists deserved merit for fighting Nazi-Fascists. In one of his interviews, Luzaj admitted that communists were advantaged due to their better structure and the fact that some feudal *Balli* leaders from the North Albania were not interested in fighting the oppressors, but rather competing for leadership, while they collaborated with Nazi-Germans on "at least" one occasion (Luzaj 2020). Therefore, there was little to no resistance to the Albanian Communist Party in winning the 1945 elections which saw them take power officially. Since the declaration of Independence in 1912, Albania had finally created the strongest state to oppose endless attempts of its neighbours to split the small and fragile Albania. However, Hoxha's rise to power also came with costs for the political pluralism and Albanian people.

In their program the Albanian Communist Party declared war on all forces that occupied Albania. This decision appears to have also affected the bilateral relationship between Albania and Turkey. In July 1945, the Turkish Ambassador, Muzaffer Kamil Bayur, departed Albania after holding this position since the Albanian occupation by the fascist Italy in 1939. Thus, political relations between the two countries remained static for a decade, until Albanian leaders requested to move diplomatic relations forward.

At the end of WWII, Albania was at war with Greece, which technically started when fascist Italy invaded Greece from Albanian territories in October 1940. Similar to Albania, Greece's main resistance in WWII were guerrilla-communists of the National Liberation Front–National Popular Liberation Army (*Ethnikón Apeleftherotikón Métopon–Ethnikós Laïkós Apeleftherotikós Strátos*), known as EAM-ELAS and the Greek Democratic National Army (*Ellínikos Dímokratikos Ethnikós Strátos*) well known as EDES. While Germans started to withdraw from Greece, the mass expulsion of Albanians living in the Chameria region in 1944 was completed. What is worth noting was that after the German withdrawal, massacres and expulsion of Albanian-Muslim-Chams were completed not by the communists of ELAS, but from the right wing—EDES forces led by Napoleon Zervas. The fact that the expulsion of Chams was then accepted and claimed by the Greek government shows that the real reason was not the collaboration of Chams with Germans, but rather to cover up the existence of the Albanian minority in Greece—an old policy that Greece could not implement after the Treaty of Lausanne in 1923 (Baltsiotis 2011: 19-20).

While the Greek Army was again penetrating the Albanian South-East in 1946, Yugoslavia was Albania's main ally immediately following WWII. However, this changed in December 1947 with the introduction of the Yugoslav plan for the annexation of Albania as the "Seventh Republic of Yugoslavia" (Pearson 2006: 242-3). The deputy Prime Minister and the Minister of Interior, Koçi Xoxe, who was supported by other pro-Yugoslav elements, agreed for the Albanian economy and military to unite with that of Yugoslavia. This fraction of the Party seriously challenged the power of Hoxha who secured the Soviet support. Tito, on the other hand, decided to send two army divisions in Albania to fight the Greek Army. This was reported by Hoxha to Stalin who expressed his disagreement. Moreover, the deterioration of relations between Belgrade and Moscow in June 1948 after the expulsion of Yugoslavia from the Communist Information Bureau (Cominform) also signified the end of the relations between Tirana and Belgrade. Xoxe was arrested and executed in 1949 (Morgan 2011: 26). The following decade marked significant attempts of the Albanian Communist Party to eradicate pro-Yugoslav elements.

Albania was also in conflict with the British government due to the mining incident in the Corfu Channel in October 1946 that resulted in damage to a British Navy vessel and the death of British military personnel. The US followed with the suspension of the diplomatic relations with Albania at the beginning of November

1946. Hoxha then considered both Britain and the US as a threat to Albania (Hoxha 1982), after their failed attempts to challenge Hoxha's regime between 1949 and 1952. The Albanian government was largely helped by Soviet support to manage these developments (Bethel 1984).

The Cold War polarisation of political systems was emerging in which each system had actors with different capabilities and different rules. Across this polarisation, however, the basic tenet remained, that the rules within these systems were imposed by the most powerful states. Interestingly, Albania was aligned neither with the West, nor the East bloc until 1949 and yet, managed to survive on the international stage. The hostile attitudes of neighbouring countries, as well as Albanian economic situation led Albania to look to the Soviet Union as the best option to fill the vacuum created by the termination of its alliance with Yugoslavia. Hoxha's Marxist-Leninist ideology was in line with that of Josef Stalin and by the beginning of 1949, Albania was allied with the Soviet Union and Soviet economic aid would play an important role for Albania.

Some years later, Albania was pleased to join the Warsaw Treaty Organisation (known as the Warsaw Pact) in 1955, hoping that Albania could indeed be protected by the pact that was signed by the communist-bloc countries under the leadership of USSR. However, as Hoxha notes though, the Albanian government did the right thing to sign the Warsaw Pact and the USSR government fulfilled its military commitments, Albanian participation was merely ceremonial, as they felt excluded from discussions (Hoxha 1983: 21).

Following Stalin's death in March 1953 and the introduction of a new Soviet policy of "peaceful co-existence" few years later, Hoxha mentions that the ideological and political differences between the new USSR leader Nikita Khrushchev and Hoxha became more evident. Khrushchev's speech in February 1956 about the cult of Stalin was seen by Hoxha as betraying the USSR and Stalin. Hoxha interpreted Khrushchev's position as a deviation from orthodox Marxism-Leninism, which he called "revisionism" (Hoxha 1983: 25). As such, Soviet economic aid to Albania started to decline, and by 1960, the possibility for Albania to secure long-term loans from the USSR ended. Khrushchev's shift also affected Albanian domestic politics. In 1960, Hoxha's government survived the plot organised by the Soviet trained-Albanian Admiral Teme Sejko. Sejko was arrested and then sentenced to death; followed by purges of high pro-Soviet members of the Party such as Liri Belishova and Koco Tashko. The split between China and the Soviet Union in 1961 farewelled diplomatic relationships between Tirana and Moscow with Albania now shifting its attention to China.

On 14 December 1955, Turkey's vote helped Albania to become a full member of the United Nations (UN) (Albanian Ministry of Foreign Affairs 2015: 4). As a result, Albanian-Turkish diplomatic relations resumed, culminating in the official re-establishment of diplomatic relations in June 1958 (Elsie 2010: 455) and the re-opening of the Turkish embassy in Tirana in June 1959. Following the Turkish military coup in 1960, diplomatic relations remained formally in place, but without significant interaction. Although, Turkey became a NATO member in 1952, during the Cold War era, Albania and Turkey had "few noticeable direct political contacts" (Elsie 2010: 455).

Hoxha and Chinese leader Mao Zedong met only once in 1956 in China, however, the relationship between the two countries was considered to have "steel-like unity" (Tretiak 1962). Albania's communist government was happy to secure Chinese aid and enjoy their special relationship. In Mao's speech, on 3 November 1966, Albania was claimed as the only Marxist-Leninist state in Europe stating:

... an attack on Albania will have to reckon with great

People's [Republic of] China. If the U.S. imperialists, the modern Soviet revisionists or any of their lackeys dare to touch Albania in the slightest, nothing lies ahead for them but a complete, shameful and memorable defeat (Hamm 1963: 43).

As China at the time was both consumed by its own internal dilemmas and conflicts and lacked the power and political importance it has today, Hoxha's decision to side with China attracted some attention in high places. For something small and weak like the Albanian state should have remained allied with the Soviet Union, in order to ensure protection, but this was not the case. During the communist period there were no open hostilities between Albania and Turkey. On the contrary, the Turkish support for Albania in 1955 and the Albanian vote on the Cyprus issue in 1965 revealed that both Albania and Turkey agreed on crucial issues in the international arena. Despite the fact that their vote was unsuccessful, and Cyprus was granted recognition (with the General Assembly resolution 2077 being approved), this vote not only boosted relations between the two countries, but also showed that, while continuing to march alongside China, Hoxha had no intention of abandoning its Turkish alliance. During his visit to Albania in 1968, the chairman of the Turkish National Assembly, Ferruh Bozbeyli, discussed ways to improve "Ankara's ties with the communist leadership of Tirana" (Tase 2014), at a time when, politically and economically, China was becoming important to Albania. After 1968, for another decade, the entire Albanian economy, its health system, the industry, defence and foreign policy relied on the support of Mao's China, and as a result, ties with the rest of the world were severed.

However, the "steel-like unity" started to deteriorate in July 1971, after the Chinese premier Zhou Enlai agreed to meet with US President Richard Nixon during his visit to China. In 1973, Hoxha wrote in his diary (published in *Reflections on China*) that:

> Albania is no longer the "faithful, special friend" [of China] ... They are maintaining the economic agreements though with delays, but it is quite obvious that their [China's] "initial ardor" has died (Hoxha 1979: 41).

To create even more uncertainty, Tito's visit to Beijing in August-September 1977 convinced Hoxha that his hopes regarding the Chinese leadership were entirely dashed as he stated in his diary. "To hell with them! We shall fight against all this trash, because we are Albanian Marxist-Leninists and on our correct course we shall always triumph!" (Hoxha 1979: 107). At this point Albania lost both Western and Eastern support, following Hoxha's unwise decision of complete isolation of his country from the world, which proved disastrous for Albania's economy. By the time of the formal break with China in 1978, Albania had become isolated, with an economy on the verge of collapse. Once more, in difficult circumstances for Albania, trade with Turkey resumed. In December 1980, a Turkish delegation visited Tirana, and the visit was returned by an Albanian delegation almost a year later led by Nedin Hoxha, a minister and cousin of Enver Hoxha (Elsie 2010: 455).

Following the death of Hoxha in 1985, Ramiz Alia (who survived Hoxha's political purges), came to power as the First Secretary of Albania's Socialist Party [the new name of Labour Party of Albania (PLA)]. In August 1987, Albania resumed diplomatic relations with Greece, which was an indication of more openness in Albania's foreign policy.

In 1988, after a historic meeting of the Albanian foreign minister Reis Malile with the foreign ministers of Yugoslavia, Bulgaria, Greece, Turkey and Romania in Belgrade (Binder 1988), Hoxha's successor—the Albanian Chairman of the Presidium of the People's Assembly, Ramiz Alia—welcomed the Turkish foreign minister Mesut Yilmaz to Tirana (Tase 2014). The visit was returned in 1990 by an Albanian delegation. Despite the political position of Hoxha, Turkey helped Albania during the Cold War every time a request was made for help. The end of Hoxha's regime in Albania ushered a new era of continuous and uninterrupted relations between Turkey and Albania. At the end of the Cold War, Albania's economic needs were enormous, and Turkish authorities did not wait to help their "little sister", Albania. The way to East was again open for Albania.

Life in Albania during the Cold War

Due to Albania's regime faith in "Stalin orthodoxy", King and Vullnetari compares Albanian collectivisation policy to that of the Soviet rural areas, or what was known as *kolkhoz* and *sovkhoz* (King and Vullnetari 2016: 2). According to these authors, the regime kept urbanisation to a bare minimum, while fostering growth of rural areas. Rural Albanians were initially offered to join agricultural "cooperatives", a system that could offer them a higher possibility of automation, in order to maximise their yields. Voluntary actions were followed by forced collectivisation, until all private property was in the hands of the state. Albanians in rural and industrial areas were merely paid by the government that became slowly the owner of all goods, from land to services, infrastructure, buildings, education and so on. The Party decided government apartments Albanians should live in cities or towns but also, the place and type of work they should be employed in (Albanian State and Society 1944-1990). The permission to have a TV at home was given by the Party, while Albania's only TV channel was strictly monitored by the secret police. The regime considered obsolete the Ministry of Justice, which was eliminated in 1966; abolishing the profession of lawyer a year later; followed by forced termination of all religious activities and sites. By then, Albania was declared the first atheist country in the world!

Before the arrival of communist regime in Albania, Albanians were relatively-free to trade and travel to other countries. Hoxha's regime made restrictions for individual citizens to enter and exit Albania. While the average Albanian citizen faced restrictions on movement, with tight controls on exit and entry into the country, only a few organised groups were supported by the Albanian regime. However, all members of these groups were strictly scrutinised and controlled by the regime, as were any figures who enjoyed external contacts or travel, such as writers and cultural figures. Although Albanian writers had better pay and conditions, they were kept under closer scrutiny by the communist regime. As Morgan argues, even the work of the well-known Albanian writer, Ismail Kadare, was censured by Hoxha's regime (Morgan 2010: 23).

Voluntary activity was promoted and strongly supported by communist propaganda. Albanians worked six days per week and Sundays were considered as societal "voluntary" days. The regime-built railways, roads and infrastructure with organised "volunteers". Volunteers were young Albanians who worked in large building enterprises for months. The large participation of young Albanians and especially woman inclusion in these activities merits special attention. The Albanian social revolution was profound, and the propaganda machine was considered extremely serious. The propaganda about the new proletarian class included all levels of social strata such as children, youth, woman, farmers, blue and white-collar people who achieved free education. At a certain period of the year, Albanian intellectuals, students and workers had to wear military uniform, or what was called in Albanian *"zbor"*. These compulsory activities were designed by the Party to support the Albanian Army and the country from attacks from both "imperialism and revisionism" (Albanian State and Society 1944-1990). This unique social organisation could not prevent Albanians from living in one of the poorest countries in Europe—a country with a poor economy that was challenged by peoples' needs. An example was the voucher regime, which for the state propaganda was fair, but the Albanian reality was different. By 1989, education was free and compulsory for up until year eight, however, most of further studies required a scholarship from the Albanian regime. As Vickers mentions:

> Although the country benefited from improved agriculture, industry, and in particular health and education, such initiatives were overshadowed by a horrific legacy of brutal repression... The Albanian people had been cowed into a fearful state of submission, which led them, like their country, to withdraw into themselves with their thoughts kept secret, paranoid and suspicious of all around them (Vickers 1995: 209).

Hoxha enacted a dictatorship under his personal control and the Albanian sigurimi (secret police) kept society in check. Albanian totalitarianism was considered to be one of the most extreme in the ex-Communist countries (O'Donnell 1995: 18-22).

4

MODERN TURKISH AND ALBANIAN IDENTITIES IN THE POST-COLD WAR PERIOD

Turkish national identity is no less contested than Albanian identity and, since the creation of the Republic of Turkey in 1923, has become even more contested (Yavuz 1998: 19). Turkey is geographically located at the crossroads of Europe and Asia and debates about Turkish cultural belonging has engaged scholars on the dilemma as to whether Turkey is an Islamic or a Secular society? Is it Western, Eastern, or a bridge between Western European and Middle Eastern civilisations (İnalcik 1998), or simply is it a bridge between East and West? Mango suggests that Turks are "experiencing a crisis of identity, torn between East and West" (Mango 2004: 4).

The concept of Turkey as a "torn" country was previously addressed by Samuel Huntington. In explaining his concept of "the clash of civilisations", Huntington mentions that countries with "a fair degree of cultural homogeneity", which on the other hand, have a divided society that "belongs to one civilisation or another", are "torn countries" (Huntington 1993: 42). He posited:

> The most obvious and prototypical torn country is Turkey. The late twentieth-century leaders of Turkey have followed in the Attaturk tradition and defined Turkey as a modern, secular, Western nation state... however, elements in

Turkish society have supported an Islamic revival and have argued that Turkey is basically a Middle Eastern Muslim society (Huntington 1993: 42).

Nevertheless, Huntington believes that the "central focus of conflict for the immediate future will be between the West and several Islamic-Confucian states" (Huntington 1993: 48). The Turkish elite sees Turkish national identity as being part of Western culture but, according to Huntington, the "West refuses to accept Turkey as such" because, he notes, Turkey is culturally a Middle Eastern Muslim society that has the opportunity to become the leader in the region (Huntington 1993: 42).

While Turkey's Ottoman past has placed Turks as Easterners, a new Republican era began to embrace the famous sentence of the late Ottoman intellectual, Abdullah Cevdet, who stated: "Civilisation means European civilisation" (Rustow 1987: 14). The post-Ottoman Turkish elite praised European civilisation, which, following Cevdet's thought, "must be imported [to Turkey] with both its roses and thorns" (Rustow 1987: 14).

The "father" of modern Turkey and the President of the first Republic of Turkey—Mustafa Kemal Atatürk—initiated stringent reforms that aimed to secularise Turkish polity and society. Atatürk's pragmatic reforms aimed to separate the state from religion in a similar way to what occurred in some Western polities. Heper argues that the abolition of the Caliphate, replacement of religious courts with secular counterparts, introduction of a Western-style education system, substitution of the traditional Arabic-Islamic scripts with the Latin alphabet, and adoption of the European theatre, music and law codes from different European countries aimed at "*reformation* rather than the *renaissance* of Islam" (Heper 2004: 5). Atatürk attempted to bring Western culture closer to Turkey, but his legacy was challenged and questioned soon after his death in

1938. In the post-Ottoman era, religion has divided Turkish society into two political groups: those who subscribe to a secular, republican view, known as "Kemalists" and those who side with "Islamic neo-Ottomanists" views (Taspinar 2008: 28). Hence, according to Taspinar, Ankara will be careful to "balance its neo-Ottoman and Kemalist instincts" (Taspinar 2008: 28). For Yavuz, from 1947 to 1974, Turkey's foreign policy was driven by the new "statist elite" (Yavuz 1998: 27) who tried to split the Ottoman era from the modern-day Republican Turkey; portraying the former as founded on Islamic ideology. However, this scholar argues, the policy of "disengagement" with Islam created a considerable gap between the general populace and the Turkish elite. Perhaps the radical reform of Islam, in such a short period of time, meant changing everyday life, customs and laws, and it was a very ambitious task.

Another characteristic of Turkey's new elite was its aspiration to be part of Europe—a decision that, Mango argues, was reinforced after 1 December 1964 when Turkey became an associate member of the European Economic Community (EEC, later EC, and more recently EU) (Mango 2004: 258). During the Cold War, the Turkish political elite adapted to the international system of two poles (Yavuz 1998: 27); joining NATO in 1952, which ended Turkey's long struggle to be portrayed as anti-European. Analysing Turkish foreign policy, Erickson discusses positive relations with Western Europe and the US, which became temporarily strained in 1974 when Turkey invaded and occupied Northern Cyprus (Erickson 2004: 26) ultimately leading to economic and military sanctions against Turkey. The US ban on the provision of spare parts and logistics support for previous armaments sold to Turkey, and for Erickson, Turkey's first coup in 1960, diminished the capacity of the Turkish military (Erickson 2004: 26). The US embargo ended in 1980, when the US realised the importance of Turkey as an ally against the USSR, while a secular and pro-western Islamic state (Erickson

2004: 27). However, according to Erickson, six years were enough for the Turkish economy to deteriorate, generating much social unrest. A second military coup occurred in 1980; relative normality was re-established in 1985, and since then, the Turkish state has been in the hands of "conservative, moderate, and Islamic parties" (Erickson 2004: 27).

Since 2001, when the current Turkish President Recep Tayyip Erdoğan founded the Justice and Development Party (*Adalet ve Kalkınma Partisi* (AKP), which came to power in 2002, the Turkish political and religious orientation started to shift. AKP was established on the foundations of a moderate Islamic ideology and united a number of existing conservative Parties. It was successful in five consecutive elections, in 2002, 2007, 2011, 2015 and Presidential elections in 2018. While AKP seems to be Turkey's preferred Party in the twenty-first century, attempts to re-introduce Islam as the foundation of Turkish society, remain constant in Turkish political life. On the other hand, Turkish coups of 1960, 1980, military memorandums of 1971, 1993, 1997 and 2007, followed by the last attempt to overthrow Erdoğan's government in 2016, are all indications of the ongoing struggle between secularism and Islamism in Turkey.

Turkish priorities in the twenty-first century: Islamism and neo-Ottomanism

Islam is an important link with the Ottoman past when Turkey enjoyed relative prestige. In the twenty-first century, a new Turkish middle class, close to the Turkish government, is embracing Islam as an ideological tool in order to craft a new Turkish national identity. The concepts of "neo-Ottomanism" and "Islamism" in contemporary Turkish politics are associated with the Islamist AKP. In November 2002, AKP secured control of the Turkish parliament allowing Erdoğan to become prime minister the following March.

Soli Özel considers a paradox the fact that Turkey is being led by the (AKP), a Party that in appearance seems to rush toward reforms in order to join the EU, while, on the other hand, is discovering values of Islam and the days of the Ottoman glory (Özel 2007: 21). Others such as Ömer Taspinar believe that Turkey is not aiming to resurrect the Ottoman Empire, but is rather extrapolating Turkish influence in a way that bolsters Turkey as "a bridge between East and West, a Muslim nation, a secular state, a democratic political system, and a capitalistic economic force" (Taspinar 2008: 3). The declaration of the Turkish Head of Parliament, Ismail Kahraman, in April 2016 stating that Turkey is a "…Muslim country and this is why we need an Islamic constitution" was immediately criticised by Opposition Leader Kemal Kilicdaroğlu who argued that the "father" of modern Turkey, Atatürk, built the modern state based on laicism and religious freedom.

Erdoğan's centre-right wing AKP, is an Islamic Party that is aiming to align Turkey to the Middle East; away from the West. It is questionable whether Turkey has achieved any separation of religion and state. The alliance between the AKP and the far-right Nationalist Action Party (*Milliyetçi Hareket Partisi*, MHP), regarding the 2019 presidential elections, was secured in February 2018 (Kucukgocmen 2018); further supporting Erdoğan's rule in the future. During the parliamentary and presidential elections in June 2018, the AKP lost its controlling majority in the assembly after nearly 16 years; having to rely now on the support of its nationalist MHP allies, who outperformed expectations to win more than 11 percent of the vote (*Reuters* 2018). As an extreme-right party, MHP espouses a mix of nationalism and scepticism towards the West, which is now added to the Islamic ideology of the AKP.

Erdoğan, however, expanded new powers under a powerful executive presidency narrowly approved in the 2017 referendum. The opposition group led by the centre-left wing of secular Kemalists or the Republican People's Party (*Cumhuriyet Halk Partisi*, CHP), allied before 2018 elections with the pro-Europeans—*Iyi Parti* (Iyi Party), and the Sunni far-right-conservative—*Saadet Partisi* (Saadet Party) (*Reuters* 2018). The pro-Kurdish Peoples Democratic Party (HDP) was not part of an alliance and earned 11.7 percent of votes to become the assembly's second largest opposition party after the CHP. However, opposition parties are struggling to challenge Erdoğan. As Aksoy argues, criticism continues to rise regarding Erdoğan's move towards abandoning the West and aligning Turkey with the Middle East by using sectarian politics to help him turn himself into a regional leader, a sort of "new caliph", or the leader of the Islamic world (Aksoy 2015).

Nonetheless, it is not clear whether domestically, Turkish people voted AKP due to its Islamic orientation or whether the majority of Turks support Erdoğan's aims against the Kurds. Erdoğan's decision to position Turkish's foreign policy against the Syrian regime of Bashar Al Assad, the self-declared "Islamic State" (ISIS) and Kurds of Syria that helped to defeat ISIS is contentious. As Brown argues, for Turkey, the Kurds are a big "imbroglio" (Brown 1995: 116), despite the fact that Syrian Kurds demonstrated to be the best coalition ally in fighting ISIS on the ground. Republican Kemalists also see Kurdish ethnicity in Turkey, Iran, Iraq and Syria as a threat to the Republic of Turkey, whereas, according to Taspinar, the "Neo-Ottomanist" approach of the AKP, "seeks to rise above this Kemalist paradigm" (Taspinar 2008: 3); portraying a sort of Muslim "macro-identity among populations that share the Ottoman Islamic heritage" (Yavuz 1998: 40). The reality on the ground is different: Kurdish people who also practice Islam are considered second-class citizens in Turkey. Turkey's aim is to stop every attempt for recognition of the Republic of Kurdistan, to avoid its secession from Turkey. Although the assimilation of ethnic Kurds in Turkey failed (Brown 1995: 129), according to Schoon, persisting economic underdevelopment and "longstanding social inequality" might further exacerbate the ethnic Kurd's relationship with Turks (Schoon 2015: 17). The Kurdish struggle can also raise a question: Why is Turkey trying to protect their Muslims-brothers in the Western Balkans and fight Kurdish Muslims in Turkey?

Turkish politics in the twenty-first century

Modern Turkey remains politically divided between the two broad-based affiliations, the governing and the opposition alliances. The ruling alliance is led by Erdoğan's AKP in alliance with the far-right Nationalist Action Party (MHP). On the other hand, the fragmented opposition group is led by the centre-left wing of secular Kemalists or the Republican People's Party (CHP). Up until the June 2018 elections, CHP officials considered outdated the agreement with the *Iyi Parti*, and *Saadet Partisi*, and the pro-Kurdish Peoples Democratic Party (HDP) was not part of any alliance (*Reuters* 2018). The Turkish political landscape has changed since 2016 when the Turkish military carried out an unsuccessful coup, which according to the Turkish government was organised by Gülen's movement. Fethullah Gülen who spent the first part of his life as an Imam, is influential in Turkish civil society, a reputation that arose in 1980-90's, while he was promoting his Islamic organisation and educating followers in his schools; making them feel a personal debt to the divisive preacher (*Deutsche Welle* 2018). Since 1999, Gülen who was under investigation for seeking to overthrow the Turkish government, is living in self-imposed exile in Pennsylvania, US, from where he is still running his religious popular movement called *Hizmet* (in Turkish Service). In 2000, he was convicted in absentia by the Turkish tribunal, but the common Islamic agenda aligned him with Erdoğan's values, after the AKP won Turkish elections in 2002 (*Deutsche Welle* 2018). Gülen had the tools to serve Erdoğan and up until 2011, they were allies, but soon after they fell out. Since

2013, Erdoğan is blaming Gülen for organising unrest in Turkey and specifically for his involvement in the planning and organisation of the 2016 attempted Turkish coup (Beaumont 2016).

Erdoğan is a master of geopolitical manoeuvring. Turkey's foreign policy is a mixture of requests to ally with Europe and the West, while shifting eastwards to the Middle East and Russia. However, Turkey's increasing military power in the twenty-first century is notable. Erdoğan's decision to purchase armaments from Russia is jeopardising Turkey's relations with NATO, making unpredictability one of the main features of Turkish foreign policy. Despite this, Erdoğan's Turkey is seeking to become a regional power, and thus, revive the past Ottoman "glory" in the Western Balkans, where actors such as Albanians became crucial components. Shifts by the Turkish government from the West to its "comfort zone"—the Middle East are not unknown; rather they show fluctuations in Turkey's foreign policy and its international reputation that according to the former Canadian defence attaché to Turkey, Chris Kilford, is "in free-fall" (Kilford 2016).

Nonetheless, Turkish power, proximity and Eastern Mediterranean influence, impacts on Albanian domestic and international affairs and offers Turkey the potential of returning to the Western Balkans as a major player. Although there is no willingness by Albanian and Kosovar government to distance their respective countries from Turkey, do both the Albanian and Kosovar governments have the political will to escape the Ottoman heritage?

Turkey's foreign policy towards Western Balkans in the twenty-first century

Although it claims to be a "secular" and "democratic" state, Mango describes Turkey as a "non-Western country" that is attempting to organise "its society on Western lines" (Mango 2004: 253). Turkish society is no more homogenous than Albanian society. Taspinar describes Turkish society as "...deeply polarized over its Muslim, secular, and national identities" (Taspinar 2008: 2). However, all sides of Turkish politics support the Turkish foreign policy in the Balkans, especially the relations with Albania. Some believe that Turkey is shifting its foreign policy focus to the Western Balkans as "relations between Turkey and the Western Balkans have never been more intensive since the foundation of the Turkish republic" (Petrović and Reljić 2011: 169). Davutoğlu's speech on 16 October 2009 at the "Ottoman legacy and Balkan Muslim Communities" conference in Sarajevo is described as a shift in Turkish foreign policy in the Balkans. By 2009, Turkish political initiatives in the Western Balkans went far beyond the "bandwagon" approach with the US policies in the Balkans. For Petrović and Reljić, Turkey "has leverage and increasingly capacities in the Western Balkans" which must be accepted and recognized by the EU (Petrović and Reljić 2011: 159). For others such as Erickson, there is no doubt that Turkey is working to become the main power of the region, and it is merely a question of when it will happen (Erickson 2004: 42):

> Turkey uses its influence in the Balkans as an example of its geopolitical importance and Ankara wants to demonstrate that a permanent peace in the Balkans is unattainable without Turkey's help (Türbedar 2011: 154).

Winning the Turkish elections in July 2011, Erdoğan claimed that AKP's victory aimed to serve not only the Turkish people, but maintained further that "The Middle East, the Caucasus, and the Balkans have won as much as Turkey" (Cornell 2012: 13). A year before, Turkey's former foreign minister Davutoğlu revealed the country's twenty-first century foreign policy. Its slogan "zero problems with neighbours" encapsulated the policy, known as the "Davutoğlu doctrine". In this foreign policy Davutoğlu states that:

> Turkey has multiple goals over the next decade: First, it

aims to achieve all EU membership conditions and become an influential EU member state by 2023. Second, it will continue to strive for regional integration, in the form of security and economic cooperation. Third, it will seek to play an influential role in regional conflict resolution. Fourth, it will vigorously participate in all global arenas. Fifth, it will play a determining role in international organizations and become one of the top 10 largest economies in the world (Davutoğlu 2010).

Davutoğlu provides strong evidence of Turkey's desire to step forward onto the global stage. Davutoğlu's tone and the strength of his language shows Turkey's aim to play an influential role in regional conflict resolution. While it is not clear whether Turkey's "influential" role is referring to the Balkans, the second and third goals of Turkish foreign policy are a direct involvement with regards to security, economic cooperation and conflict resolution in the region. However, "Turkey's region" needs to be clearly identified. Is it the geographical territory of the old Ottoman Empire in the Middle East, Asia and Balkans, which comprises modern nation-states that have in their composition people of the Muslim religion?

According to Davutoğlu, "Turkey's actions are motivated by a great sense of responsibility, entrusted to it by its rich historical and geographic heritage, and by a profound consciousness of the importance of global stability and peace" (Davutoğlu 2010). However, historical facts of the Ottoman engagement in the Balkans are different. From their first involvement in the region, the Ottomans who conquered and ruled Albanian speaking lands and the entire Balkan Peninsula for centuries were not interested in investing and developing the region, but rather in benefitting from it as a military imperial conquest. Although the situation in the twenty-first century is different, the re-emergence of Turkey in Albania is again challenging the Western Balkans. It seems that in 2018, Davutoğlu's previous dogmas regarding the revival of the Ottoman glory in the Western Balkans is not just media speculation, but it has been transformed into a neo-Ottoman Platform based on "religious nationalism" (Parllaku 2016). It has been observed that politically, the Albanian and Kosovar governments have quietly bowed to Turkish pressure.

In the last decades, Turkish foreign policy according to Cornell has shown to have a "less predictable force than it used to be and one whose policies will occasionally clash with those of the West" (Cornell 2011: 23). The absence of common values between the West and Turkey makes Turkish foreign policy unpredictable and unique, but it also poses a further challenge for the Albanian and Kosovar governments to align with Turkey.

Turkey and the European Union

While Turkey is aiming to get closer to Europe and thus, the Balkans, Erdoğan and his AKP are also seeking to convince the Turkish people that the EU is not the only alternative. Erdoğan's ambition to become the regional Muslim leader may influence the EU to not embrace Turkey's application for accession. In return, Europe's reluctance to accept Turkey as an EU member, may generate more "'Islamically' shaped neo-Ottoman foreign policies in the future" (Yavuz 1998: 41). This may shift Turkey's foreign policy position towards Asia, the Middle East and perhaps an attempt to drag the Western Balkans back to the East, enabling Turkey to become the regional "hegemon" (Erickson 2004: 44). However, the deadlock between Turkey and the EU has gone through rollercoaster scenarios. The EU is waiting for Turkey to resolve its issues with Cyprus and quickly progress with the EU recommendations on the issue, such as corruption, free media and human rights. Nevertheless, the question to be asked is whether Turkey will wait endlessly for Europe's decision to include it as a member state or whether it will redirect its energy toward the alternative of becoming a regional leader? Membership of the European Union represents not only an aspiration but also a challenge for Turkey (Mango 2004: 4). Since 2015, Turkey's leverage towards the EU has increased due to Europe's difficulty in accommodating large numbers of refugees fleeing ISIS and the Syrian war. Turkey has received so far, the largest number of Syrian refugees in Europe, functioning as a buffer zone for Europe. Turkey is a crucial player for the NATO forces using the proximity of Turkish bases to defeat ISIS and the Syrian regime.

As mentioned, Turkish government has argued that the last attempt of the Turkish coup d'état, in July 2016, was organised by Fethullah Gülen's movement—Hizmet; trying to avoid persecution by the government (Uras 2016). In 2013, Turkish opposition made officially allegations of corruption against two Turkish ministers and other high officials. This sparked the arrest of Turkish Minister of Economy and EU affairs, both accused to have been receiving bribes by an Iranian born, Reza Zarrab, who is believed to have helped Iran evade UN sanctions with its nuclear program (Garbuz 2014: 3). At the beginning of the twenty-first century, politics in Turkey are marked by titanic contradictions. If anything is clear, Erdoğan's authoritarianism goes hand in hand with Islamic ideology and will be challenging not only Turkey, but the entire region.

Bilateral relations between Turkey and Albania in the post-Cold era

Similar to other ex-communist countries in Eastern Europe, the end of the Cold-War was a big event for Albania. Albania restored diplomatic relations with the US in March 1991, and with Great Britain in May 1991, just after the first three round multi-party elections in March and April 1991 (Binder 1991: 3). In June 1991, Albania established diplomatic relations with the European Community (EC) (Pano 1997: 317). However, since 1991, Albania's aim to go further West has been obstructed by the Turkey factor.

In April 1991, Sali Berisha was elected Albanian President, after the Albanian Democratic Party (PD) won the first democratic elections. One of the main challenges for the new fragile Albanian "democracy" was its dire economic situation.

Turkey came to Albania's economic aid when in 1991, through their President Özal, Turkey delivered approximately USD14 million to Albania through *Eksim Bank*—the first country to offer a post-communist donation of this scale to Albania. A number of visits from both Turkish and Albanian leaders in years to come brought about an increase in economic, political and defence support to Albania. Funds donated to the Albanian government were followed by Turkish investments to restore mosques and religious buildings, ambulances and equipment for hospitals, motor vehicles for the Albanian police forces, along with scholarships for Albanian "civilian and military" students to study in Turkey (Vickers and Pettifer 1997: 221). In 1992, the Turkish government granted a further USD 29 million on food and technology to support Albania's economic revival (Tase 2014).

Some consider the help of Özal's Turkey as opportunistic, taking advantage and using Albanian poverty to its favour. According to Tase, Turkey stepped in when Albania's need was at its greatest, taking advantage of Albania's weakness in order to potentially exploit the old imperial subject and subsequent Eastern Mediterranean ally. He states:

> Turkish Foreign Policy in the Balkans was significantly influenced by Turkish President Halil Turgut Özal who took tremendous advantage of Albania's weak economy and its state of extreme poverty (Tase 2014).

Turkish authorities re-commenced their official visits to the now "democratic" Albania in November 1991 with the visit of the Turkish General Doğan Güres. Six months later, in June 1992, the Turkish Prime Minister Süleyman Demirel visited Albania and signed an agreement of bilateral friendship and cooperation (Limaj 2012: 36). Demirel was elected as the Turkish PM in 1965, at the time when Albania voted in favour of Turkey in the UN on the Cyprus issue (Security Council Report 2008: 10). As a figure known for his pro-Albanian sympathies, Demirel reassured Albanian leaders in 1992 that "Turkey was committed to provide USD 50 million in humanitarian and logistical assistance to Albania" (Tase 2014). This humanitarian aid to Albania reinforced the idea that Turkey was its best supporter in the region.

The bilateral relations between Turkey and Albania intensified after the first ministerial meeting held in Ankara in July 1992, which was followed by the visit of the Turkish President Özal to Albania in February 1993. Özal, addressed the Albanian National Assembly, and signed "a fifteen-year economic agreement with Albania that would cover a wide area of cooperation from infrastructure projects to military assistance and growth of the tourism industry" (Tase 2014). Two months later, in April 1993, the Albanian President, Sali Berisha returned the visit, followed by the Albanian PM Aleksander Meksi at the end of the same year. During meetings between the two presidents, Özal sought to convince Berisha to recognise the new independent state of Macedonia (now North Macedonia); arguing that this will make the Balkan region a more peaceful place. On the other hand, Berisha raised concerns regarding tensions with Albania's neighbours, Greece and Serbia, and asked for total economic and defence support from Turkey (Tase 2014). The term "total" used by Berisha is clear: at the end of the Cold War, Albanian authorities, once more, aimed to fully rely on Turkey. On the other hand, Albania's position created perfect conditions for Turkish authorities to advance their influence over Albania. As a result of this Turkish pressure, in December 1992, under the leadership of Berisha, Albanian delegates decided Albania would become a member of the Organisation of the Islamic Cooperation (OIC), without consulting the Albanian parliament (Vickers and Pettifer 1997: 105). This shift triggered a fierce debate between Albanians who then questioned whether Albania's identity was shifting towards Islam and the East (Young 1999: 11). At this time, Albania secured economic assistance in the form of donations from Turkey, Kuwait and Saudi Arabia, to restore old mosques and build new ones and Islamic schools (Bogdani and Loughlin 2007: 82). While for Albania—the poorest country in the Balkans—this aid was critical, instead for Turkey, this was a step towards bolstering its support for Muslim Albania, and thus re-establishing an official presence in the Balkan region.

The collapse of the Albanian government in 1997 (due to failed pyramidal investment schemes) alongside the worsening situation in Kosovo, brought about another opportunity for Turkey to support its "brother" Albanians. Pyramid schemes caused further political crises verging almost to the point of a civil war. Albanian and the international media reported over 2,000 deaths and in 1997, the Albanian government actually lost control of some areas of the country (Jarvis 1999: 31). In the absence of government authority, armed gangs took control of entire areas such as the city of Vlorë, which was taken over by two gangs that were related to the Albanian main political opponents: Gaxhai's gang was supported by Democratic Party and Zani's gang, that served the Socialist Party (*Panorama on line* 2017). The Albanian government lost its legitimacy, creating again another opportunity for the Serbian and Greek territorial grab. During this revolt, according to Limaj, there were, once more, international plans to divide Albania. Albania's historical neighbours, Serbia and Greece advanced again their own agendas, as they had done at the beginning of the twentieth century.

The "ghost" of North-Epirus was resurrected when the Greek flag was flown in protest in Sarandë, Delvinë and Gjirokastër in South Albania while the North and the rest of the country was under a real danger of a Serbian invasion (Limaj 2012: 106-08). Once again, Turkey stepped in to protect the territorial integrity of Albania during this political turmoil in 1997 and following the advice of the Turkish General Karadaj, on 29 March 1997, the Turkish PM Tansu Çiller reassured Albania that Turkey would protect the territorial integrity of Albania and would not stay passive in the face of threatens to divide Albania (Limaj 2012: 108-09).

The Albanian President, Rexhep Meidani welcomed the visit of the Turkish President Demirel in April 1998, which was not a simple meeting between the two presidents, given that Demirel was accompanied by many high ministerial figures, leaders of different Turkish institutions and members of the business community. A sign of its importance within Turkey was the wide Turkish media coverage (Tase 2014). The stated aim of this visit was again to reassure Albania as President Demirel standing before the Albanian parliament claimed that "65 million Turks are close to the Albanian people", anytime they need help (Tase 2014). Demirel's strong words were in line with Atatürk's historic sentiments and reaffirmed again Turkish support for Albanians, calling for an immediate halt to the Serbian atrocities in Kosovo (Tase 2014). After warning the international community that Turkey could not "allow the terrible tragedy of Bosnia [to] happen again", in his speech to the Albanian parliament President Demirel argued that it was necessary to:

> immediately halt the bloodshed in Kosovo; restore the fundamental human rights and grant full freedom to Albanians in Kosovo; start a dialogue between all parties immediately and ensure people who were forcefully chased and driven out of Kosovo return to their respective lands (Tase 2014).

On the other side of the Albanian border, Kosovar Albanians were facing ethnic cleansing as a result of the atrocious activities of Slobodan Milošević and his supporters. Therefore, Demirel's visit was highly significant in re-confirming Turkish support for the Albanian people during the most difficult period since the end of the communist regime. Albanian President Rexhep Meidani applauded the Turkish support and noted that "Turkey particularly in the decade of the 1990s, has extended a hand of hospitality like no other nation to Albania". This was repeated by the Albanian Assembly Speaker, Skender Gjinushi, affirming that the "Albanian Assembly and all political parties, despite their program differences, [...] all want to strengthen bilateral ties with [the] Turkish government" (Tase 2014). Demirel's visit concluded with the signing of a bilateral agreement on social policy and labour reforms, reviews of the migration policy, employment monitoring and analysis, media and research on the impact of social policies in Albanian communities. The Albanian Telegraphic Agency signed a memorandum of cooperation with the Anatolu Ajans (AA) Turkish news agency. In addition, the Albanian national TV channel signed a further agreement with the Turkish TV channel ARD, which included a series of programs, training and logistics that Albania would receive from the ARD. These agreements ensured that by the end of the twentieth century, relations between Turkey and Albania finished on a high.

Political relations in the twenty-first century

Early in the new millennium two major events took place for Albania, further suggesting Turkey's place alongside Albania. The Kosovar parliament declared independence from Serbia in 2008, and Albania became a NATO member in 2009. In both cases, Turkey was in the forefront recognising the Republic of Kosovo from day one and lobbying for Albania's entry into NATO. However, Turkish support for Kosovar-Albanians was not welcomed by Albania's neighbours Serbia and Greece who both considered Kosovo to be part of Serbia. The situation was somewhat different when it came to the security issue. Greece, a NATO member, found itself united with Serbia to again fight the ghost of "Greater Albania". For Albania, Turkey's foreign policy become even more closely aligned with the Albanian foreign policy. Visits from political leaders and higher officials from both governments intensified the tradition of maintaining periodic meetings. The visit of the Albanian President, Alfred Moisiu, in May 2003, was returned a week later by a visit by the Turkish PM Erdoğan who returned again to Albania as President in 2013 and 2015. The next Albanian President, Bamir Topi, and the Albanian PM Sali Berisha visited Turkey in April 2012, followed in October of the same year, by the Albanian foreign minister, Edmond Panariti who held talks with the then Turkish foreign minister Ahmet Davutoğlu.

Since his election as Prime Minister, in June 2013, Edi Rama highlighted the need for "strategic relations with Turkey", which were to be given an immediate and "special priority" (Tase 2014b). This decision moulded a new momentum for bilateral relations and Turkish foreign minister Davutoğlu, visited Albania two months later, in October 2013. During his visit, Davutoğlu aimed to establish high-level strategic cooperation mechanisms, and create sustainable political, economic and trade relations between the two countries. The Albanian Defence Minister, Mimi Kodheli and the foreign minister Ditmir Bushati returned the visit to Turkey in April 2014. While Kodheli signed a secret treaty with her Turkish counterpart, according to which Turkey donated another considerable amount to rebuild the Airport of Kuçovë, military equipment and training (Mesi 2014), Bushati's first visit as the Albanian foreign minister to Turkey aimed to further extend bilateral cooperation, bringing these relations to a new level in the twenty-first century.

According to Davutoğlu, Albania and Turkey are endeavouring to work together to achieve common goals through the "High Level Cooperation Council" that was established (Tase 2014b). This Council was established as a bilateral body of two foreign ministries that would maintain close relationships between the two governments in order to discuss items of mutual benefit (Tase 2014b).

Davutoğlu's statement about "common goals" for Albania and Turkey is an interesting point, which shows the Albanian-Turkish political motivations. According to the Albanian foreign affairs ministry Albania signed 74 bilateral agreements with Turkey between 1992 and 2013, more than with any other country, except Italy and Germany. The majority of bilateral agreements between Albania and Germany and Albania-EU were focused on finance and technical subjects, while in 1992 and 1997, Albania signed only two agreements to collaborate on military and defence matters respectively with Italy and Greece. It is significant to note that 29 of these agreements with Turkey (40 per cent) concern military and defence matters. The majority of these agreements—71—were signed in the twenty-first century, indicating a sharp increase in defence and military agreements, but also an intensification of Turkish diplomatic relations with Albania.

Cultural ties are another reason that has consolidated this relationship. The population of Turkish citizens with Albanian heritage is estimated to be around five million according to the former Albanian Ambassador in Turkey, Genci Muçaj (*Telegrafi* 2015). This is a significant number, comparable to the number of Albanians living in Albania, Kosovo and North Macedonia combined. Although the majority of these are assimilated and no longer provide large source of financial remittances for Albania, the cultural bridge between the two countries is consolidated through further areas of mutual interest described by Muçaj as "bilateral relations, economic and cultural diplomacy" (*Telegrafi* 2015).

Bilateral post-Cold War economic relations

An increase in economic relations with Turkey is further hope for the weak Albanian economy. The Turkish economy started to improve after the mid-1980s economic expansion as a result of the policies of the Prime Minister, then President, Özal. Both agricultural and industrial production between 1980 and 1998 rose by 38 to 41 per cent respectively (Erickson 2004: 28); proving Özal's economic reforms to be successful. According to the Turkish former Prime Minister, Ahmet Davutoğlu, Turkey's economic future was felt to be positive, and his government's plan was to become "one of the top 10 largest economies in the world" by 2023 (Davutoğlu 2010). While the Turkish economy grew in the previous decades, by 2016, it showed signs of decline going "from 17th to 19th place in the rankings of the biggest economies" in the world (Aksoy 2015). In the first months of 2016, Turkish exports to Western partners, Germany, Great Britain, Italy and the US, declined by 14.4 per cent, whereas exports to Saudi Arabia and Egypt rose by 30.5 and 15.1 per cent respectively (*Hürriyet Daily News* 2016). The Turkish government was working to finalise free trade agreements with Iran, and improve its relations with Israel, which would bolster Turkey's ambition to become a regional leader.

Nevertheless, Turkey is a much bigger, richer and more powerful country than Albania and, therefore, an important strategic partner for Albania whichever way one wishes to examine it. Turkey's population of approximately 80 million is 27 times bigger than the number of Albanians who still live in Albania. In 2019, the Turkish Gross Domestic Product (GDP) passed US$ 750 billion, which was circa 50 times greater than the Albanian GDP. More importantly, Albanian trade with Turkey is crucial for the Albanian economy. According to the European Commission, at the end of 2019, Albania's imports from Turkey were in second place with 9.5 percent, whereas export to Turkey had an insignificant value of 0.7 percent of total Albanian exports (EU 2020).

Albania is central to the new Turkish engagement policy in the Balkans. During an interview for the Albanian *Top Channel* on 19 June 2017, Erdoğan proudly announced that Turkey had already invested three billion euros in Albania, stating: "I don't know how many investments have arrived from the EU, but ours will not stop" (*Top Channel* 2017a). The economic connections between the two countries are rapidly strengthening.

Leading Turkish companies have invested and operate in crucial sectors of the Albanian economy (Mlloja 2015). Large Turkish companies such as ENKA, Gintaş, Armada, Metal Yapı, Aldemir, and Servomatik are involved in construction and the building industry in Albania. Others such as Çalık Holding, Türk Telekom, Makro-Tel and Hes Kablo are involved in telecommunications. The only Albanian national telephone company, Albtelecom, along with Eagle Mobile, are owned by BKT, a Turkish company. Similarly, the Turkish Çalık Group owns Albania's second biggest bank—The National-Commercial Bank. Şekerbank-BKT is present in banking and telecommunications. Kürüm has invested in the iron and steel industry, managing a steel factory, the only functional part of the previous backbone of the Albanian mineral industry—the Elbasan metallurgic factory.

Turkish investments are also very present in other sectors of the Albanian economy such as health with Universal Hospital Group; mining with Ber-Oner and Dedeman; manufacturing and consumer goods retail with Yilmaz Cable, Merinos, Everest, Pino and RM Kocak. Education is another sector influenced by Turkish organisations: Turkish Gülistan and Istanbul Foundations have invested heavily in all stages of education from primary schools to tertiary education. Turkish companies manage four medium-sized hydro-power plants, the largest port of Albania—Durrës goods terminal, and important parts of the Albanian infrastructure, such as the construction of the North-South freeway *Rruga e Kombit*, which connects Albania with Kosovo. In the first quarter of 2018, nearly 270 licenced Turkish companies operated in Albania.

To support these companies, the number of Turkish citizens on work permits who reside in Albania is greater than that of Italian and Greek citizens (*Mapo* 2013). In September 2018, Turkish workers residing in Albania reached 32 percent of the total foreign workers—in first place, followed by Chinese workers (*Tema on line* 2018).

While the Albanian media has described Turkish economic involvement as "the second invasion" (Shala 2018) of Albania, Can argues that the Turkish government does not seek to economically dominate the region. According to Can, the increase in import-export with Albania is a result of the Turkish economy growing rapidly in the region (Mapo 2013). Can's diplomatic statement does not negate the increase of Turkish influence over Albania. In reality, the Turkish Ambassador, Bayraktar, was "not satisfied with these [economic] figures, when comparing the excellent level of our [Turkish and Albanian] political relations" (Mlloja 2015). This was also confirmed by the new Turkish Ambassador, Murat Ahmet Yörük, who in February 2018, stated that Turkish investments in Albania although having reached 2.7 billion Euros, needed to increase (*Ora News* 2018). Strengthening bilateral economic ties in the future will help the Albanian economy, as well as bringing Turkey closer to the Western Balkans.

The Turkish government is facilitating economic and cultural ties with Albania through Turkish agencies such as Maarif Foundation, Cooperation and Coordination Agency (TIKA), the Yunus Emre Turkish Cultural Center and Religious Affairs (Diyanet). It needs to be mentioned that Erdoğan is using these agencies as a leverage to also invest in religious institutions (Ben-Meir and Xharra

2018). Following requests from the Albanian government, TIKA is investing to restore "mosques, bazars and historical houses" in Albania (Mlloja 2015). A significant proportion of that contribution has been dedicated to cultural and religious restoration, with the aim of increasing support for Albanian Muslims (*The Economist* 2016). For example, the Great Mosque *Namazgja* (shown on this book's front cover), which is the largest mosque in Albania, cost around 36 million USD and was fully financed by Turkey's Presidency of Religious Affairs (Diyanet) (Ben-Meir and Xharra 2018). When meeting the Albanian diaspora in the US, Bushati denied Turkey's influence on Albania; and claimed that the Great Mosque was built to satisfy needs of Albanian Muslims (Ben-Meir and Xharra 2018). This shows that Turkey is indeed seeking to gain influence in Albania through religion, while the Albanian government, when questioned, is denying Turkish interference in Albania's cultural and religious matters. The Albanian government is hiding from the public of at least another dozen mosques in Albania, which are fully financed and inaugurated by Erdoğan (Ben-Meir and Xharra 2018). This might be considered as not economic help for Albanians, but rather a continuation of the Ottoman policy; investing on Islam as a permanent-long-term-strategy for Albania (Shala 2018).

Turkey as Albania's guarantor?

The defence sector has been seen the strongest cooperation between Turkey and Albania. The post-Cold War era has been a period of reformation in the Turkish armed forces. This has brought about a modern and capable Turkish army, operating within NATO since 1990 in missions in places such as Bosnia, Somalia, Kosovo and Afghanistan (Erickson 2004: 32). Erickson believes that Turkey "has shown the willingness to defy the US" and according to him it is not a question to whether Turkey will become a powerful political and military regional player, but it is rather a question to when it will happen (Erickson 2004: 42).

Under the NATO mandate, Albania had a unit of soldiers operating in Afghanistan, "serving within the Turkish command deployed in Kabul" (Tase 2014b). Although Albania became a NATO member in 2009, since the end of the Cold War, Albania has depended heavily on Turkish "assistance in training and supply of cutting-edge defence technology, as well as the reconstruction of Albania's military bases and their maintenance" (Tase 2014b). A new era of military partnership between the two countries started on 19 November 1992, with the signing of a partnership agreement to instruct and train the Albanian forces. For the former Turkish Defence Minister, Nevzat Ayaz, the "agreement focused on broadening bilateral cooperation in the areas of military education and technology" (Limaj 2012: 38).

As part of this agreement, Turkish military personnel of the infantry, land, naval and Air Force bases have trained Albanian Armed Forces; providing technological equipment and helping to "rebuild its military infrastructure" (Tase 2014b). There has been an increasing number of high-level military visits between Albania and Turkey since then. For example, between 19 January and 20 November 1992, the Albanian Army General Kristaq Karoli, Defence Minister Safet Zhulali and General Ilia Vasho visited Turkey. The Turkish General Doğan Güreş and the Defence minister Nevzat Ayaz returned the visit in the same year stating that it is Turkey's "obligation" to help its little "sister", Albania. The Albanian defence minister, Safet Zhulali, visited Turkish military bases and factories; sharing sensitive information when no other defence minister from a country that was not a NATO member had done before (Tase 2014a).

A month later, after the Albanian delegation returned from Turkey on 28 August 1992, "the Turkish Gearing Class destroyer, TCG Mareşal Fevzi Çakmak," visited the Albanian port of Durrës (Tase 2014a). Both of these episodes demonstrated the high level of trust between the two countries, as well as Albania's need to demonstrate Turkey's power in the Western Balkans. More recent evidence of this military demonstration and strong ties between the two countries includes high Albanian military officials proudly welcoming the visit to Durrës of the Turkish submarine "TCG Sakarya" on 10 November 2014 and "TCG I. INONU 'S 360'" on 30 March 2017. The collaboration between Albania and Turkey in defence matters seems to bolster political relations between the two countries.

Analysing some official statistics, Limaj claims that Turkey has spent more than any other country in training all levels of the Albanian military (Limaj 2012: 39). Turkey equipped the Albanian Guard of the Republic, trained the Albanian special troops, reconstructed the Albanian military base at Pashaliman, the Marine Academy of Vlorë and the Air Force Academy of Kuçovë. It also modernised the munitions factories at Poliçan and Gramsh. Between 1992 and 2000, more than 1000 Albanian students and military officials were educated at the Turkish Universities, and Turkish military officials trained 3491 Albanian troops in Albania (Limaj 2012: 41). In the last two decades, "many Albanian military students [graduated or are] studying in the Turkish War Academies", and "from 1998 onwards, over 100 Albanian students graduated from the National Police Academy" (Mlloja 2015). It is clear that as a result of this involvement, Turkey has an intimate and detailed knowledge of Albanian security matters.

These indicators show Turkey as a trustworthy strategic partner for Albania's security matters in the twenty-first century. Similarly, at the end of the nineteenth and the beginning of the twentieth century, Turkey was considered by some Albanian leaders as the only hope to protect Albania from being partitioned by its neighbours. It seems that Albania's need for Turkish military muscle at the beginning of the twenty-first century is similar to that of the previous century.

Energy security drivers

In the twenty-first century, Albania is hoping to strengthen its geopolitical position in the region with two main projects: The Trans Adriatic Pipeline (TAP) and the Pan-European Corridor VIII—*Via Egnatia*, which has remained a cultural and archaeological site once considered as "the biggest nexus between East and West" (Bulut and Idriz 2012: 9). While the Corridor VIII is still waiting to be classified as a priority by the EU, the TAP project is currently going through its implementation stage.

In February 2013, after ten years of negotiation and assessments, TAP was selected as the best project to bring Caspian natural gas from the Shah Deniz gas field to Italy and from there to Europe. This pipeline will be connected to the Turkish Trans Anatolian Pipeline (TANAP) at the Greek-Turkish border. TANAP will then connect to the South Caucasus Pipeline Expansion (SCPX) that runs across Georgia and Azerbaijan. TAP will be 870 km long and will cross Greece, Albania and the Adriatic Sea to deliver the gas to Santa Foca (Italy).

The aim of TAP is to diversify Europe's energy sources, which at the moment is heavily dependent on Russia. TAP's significance was amplified after Russia annexed Crimea in 2014. After this event, disagreements between a number of EU countries and Russia deepened, and consequently, American and European sanctions were placed on Russia. All countries involved in this project: Azerbaijan, Georgia, Turkey, Greece, Italy, and Albania hoped to advance their relations with the EU, as TAP will place them in a favourable position compared to other regional neighbours. It remains to be seen whether bilateral relations between the not-yet EU members—Turkey and Albania—may bear fruit as a result of energy and security matters.

Nevertheless, TAP offers an economic win-win situation for

all countries the gas pipeline runs through. Through TAP, NATO members such as Turkey, Greece and Albania will generate income for their economies. For Albania, TAP is currently the biggest international investment, placing it along with Turkey and Greece at the centre of energy security policies within the EU. TAP may also improve trilateral relations between Turkey, Greece and Albania after centuries of extremely troubled relations (Demetriou 2013: 2).

However, the latest shifts of Turkey's foreign policy designed to develop a closer relationship with Moscow (*Panorama on line* 2017a), allow Russia to deliver its gas to Turkey through the "Turkish Stream" pipeline situated only 10 km from TAP. This project will challenge TAP. Turkey will be a key player here as both TANAP and Turkish Stream are running through its territory, and Albania can only hope that TAP will be the preferred pipeline for Europe.

Post-Cold War Islam in Albania

Since Albanian independence in 1912, along with Christian Orthodox and Catholic faiths, Albanians followed two forms of Islam: Sunni and Bektashi. All these religious concepts survived and flourished after the restoration of religious freedom by the Albanian parliament in December 1990. Between 1991 and 1996, Young writes that "120 new sects and faiths" were formally registered as entities into a legal register under the Albanian State Secretariat of Religious created in 1991 (Young 1999: 11). Albania's official religions, Sunni Islam, and Orthodox and Catholic Christianity, along with the "traditional community" of Bektashism, re-emerged (Clayer 2012: 203). While there are significant divisions between Catholicism and Orthodoxy, the two religions are united by the cross. Similarly, Sunni and Bektashi Muslims are united by the crescent moon, and thus, Islam. Clayer finds it "striking" that administratively, Bektashi and Sunni-Islamic institutions are separated, while on the other hand, their "Islamicisation" can be interpreted as the "affirmation of a Muslim identity" (Clayer 2012: 202). Therefore, the August 2017 participation of the Albanian President, Ilir Meta, in the annual five days Bektashi rituals at Tomorri mountain, where the tomb of Baba Tomorri is situated, did not come as a surprise. In his speech Meta echoed Bektashi religion and recited Vasa's poem, "The Albanian faith is Albanianism", underlining that "Bektashi faith and Albania are the same body" (Top Channel 2017). Although Meta's aim might not have been that of placing Bektashism above other religions, it is noted that Bektashi is one of "ingredients" of Albanian identity.

As a result of a disastrous economic situation inherited from the Albanian communist regime, in the early years after the end of the Cold War, atheism and religious concepts were superseded by people's needs for basic commodities such as food, shelter, and employment. Due to political instability, in 1992, both Europe and the US were reluctant to invest in Albania. As a result, the slogan: "Toward Europe or Islam" became part of Albanian media and politics (Vickers and Pettifer 1997: 105). On the other hand, Islam became a powerful tool for the Albanian government when Kuwait, Saudi Arabia, Egypt, Libya and Turkey started to funnel money to re-build Islam in Albania (Deliso 2007: 30-31). In contrast to other ex-communist countries in eastern Europe, the post-Cold War era in Albania triggered a bigger challenge with regards to religious orientation not only for the Albanian government, but also for Albanian society. Although the Albanian governments of the post-Cold War period have proved to be more materialistic than secular, it seems that a lack of a clear platform has created issues for Albanian politicians in the last two and a half decades. Vickers and Pettifer observe that:

> the intellectual disorientation being caused by the religions struggle in terms of the traditional national identity is considerable and has been an important factor in the

difficulties the government has faced (Vickers and Pettifer 1997: 117).

After a long-time being a member of the Organisation of Islamic Cooperation (OIC), Albania through the head of Parliament and the current President, Ilir Meta, refused to participate at the OIC's ninth Parliamentary Assembly held on 18-19 February 2014 in Tehran. His predecessor, Josefina Topalli, on the other hand, had been part of the Albanian delegation to the OIC's seventh Parliamentary Assembly in Indonesia (Mejdini 2014). Meta downplayed his absence, blaming his government's budget, but it is commonly accepted that Albania's Euro-Atlantic commitments are the major driver; preventing the participation of the Albanian delegation in further OIC forums (Mejdini 2014). Albanian authorities also blamed the short notice given by the organising country, Turkey, for the country's inability to participate in an urgent OIC meeting in December 2017, which had the objective to counteract the decision of the President Donald Trump, to recognise Jerusalem as the capital of Israel. However, the Albanian pro-Turkish and OIC vote not only shows clear signs of hesitancy and explains that it is hard for the Albanian government to disassociate itself from Turkey and OIC.

Although in the twenty-first century, there is little tension between the Turkish government's way of supporting Islam and the Albanian multi-religious approach, the effect of Islam in Albania is provocative. Religious matters have been instrumental in bringing Albania closer to Turkey after the Cold War. Since 1992 the number of Turkish primary and secondary, religious and secular schools in Albania started to emerge. In 1994, a secondary school for four hundred students was built in South Albania, with a curriculum to be delivered in both Turkish and English (Vickers and Pettifer 1997: 107). As Krauthamer mentions, not only the Turkish government but also a "Turkish-based Islamic movement committed to interfaith dialogue, globalisation, and making money is changing the face of the country's school system" (Krauthamer 2012). Vickers and Pettifer believe that at a cultural level, relations are still close for many Albanians and "a major growth of Islamic influence in Turkey would certainly have effects in Albania" (Vickers and Pettifer 1997: 108). According to these same scholars, these cultural similarities explain the traditional white Albanian fez, which is "a glimpse back to the Ottoman world in the centre of a small European city" (Vickers and Pettifer 1997: 116-17).

The question whether Islam is increasing in Turkey is not the purpose of this book. Nevertheless, the controversial "religious democracy" of bringing back the headscarf for 9-10-year-old girls, as well as the idea of building a mosque for every University in Turkey cannot go unnoticed (Stafa 2014). These are indications of Turkey's religious policy shifts. On this controversial topic, Kemal secularists are concerned with "creeping Islamisation" as a hidden agenda by the AKP aiming "to Islamize Turkish society" (Rabasa and Larrabee 2008: Summary, xii.). Concerns still remain with developments of Turkish Islam that could influence the Albanian position towards religion, at a time when the Albanian government and religious communities are promoting Albanian religious harmony (Squires 2014).

5
Albanian Identity and the Ottoman Culture in the Work of Ismail Kadare

No other writer has written on Albanian political direction more than the Albanian prominent writer, Ismail Kadare. Kadare's extensive work in Albanian language was compiled in 2009 through a twenty-volume set. Kadare has tried with his fiction and non-fiction books to illuminate the historical past and the future of Albania. He has formed his own understanding of Albanian identity, which is in need of examination. This chapter discusses Albanian identity in relation to the Ottoman heritage not only through the work of Ismail Kadare, but also his detractors such as Rexhep Qosja and other Albanian scholars, politicians and the media. Ismail Kadare claims that Albanian identity is European, whereas others say the opposite. While helping the reader to understand Albanian identity, Kadare's thesis is steeped in controversy, and is strongly opposed by some Albanian scholars such as the Kosovar academic, Rexhep Qosja who argues that Albanian identity also reflects elements of Turkish culture, and thus, Eastern civilisation.

Kadare— the Albanian Master of literature
In January 2020, the chief of the Albanian Academy of Science again put forward Kadare's candidature for the Nobel Prize; com-

paring him with two great Albanians: Skenderbeg and the Nobel Prize holder, Mother Teresa. So much of what we know and understand regarding Albanian identity is due to extensive narratives of Ismail Kadare. This is particularly true at the level of the emotional, physical and psychological trauma of the Albanian nation, which often gets lost in larger narratives of the Ottoman period. According to Carey, Kadare, who creates the entire map of Albanian culture, its history, passion, folklore, politics and disasters, "is a universal writer in a tradition of storytelling that goes back to Homer" (Kadare 2011). Morgan, whose work has closely studied Kadare's writings, reminds us that Kadare's aim is to connect the period between the Illyrian and the modern Albanian cultures, in the same way Aeschylus did (Morgan 2010: 292). For Kadare, Aeschylus is the character "who forged the transitional path from the oral legacy of the Homeric Greek to the written forms of modern literature" (Morgan 2010: 285). Similarly, Kadare, or what Morgan describes as the "Albanian-Aeschylus", offers his contribution to defining Albanian identity. He is convinced his duty to his motherland lies in conveying its ancient folklore and epic songs (as Aeschylus did with Greek literature) into a structured literary. No other Albanian writer has written more than Kadare on Albanian identity and its links to the Ottoman heritage and therefore, analyses through his work is paramount.

Kadare's Albanian-European identity

Kadare has been persistent in his effort to uncover the ancestral roots of Albanian identity. In his seminal essays *Aeschylus, the great loser* and *The Palace of Dreams*, Kadare has asked questions about his origins and the authentic core of the Albanian existence, as he did in *The Shadow* going back to the period of Christian Albania in the Middle Ages, before the Ottoman conquest. For Kadare, there are two main reasons for demeaning Albania's European culture:

The Ottoman occupation and the communist regime. Therefore, Kadare's aim is to discard culture remnants of the Ottoman and communist periods and reconnect Albania's pre-Ottoman era with that of the Post-Cold War period.

Inspired by Greek mythology, Kadare argues that Albania's culture belongs to its geographical ancestors—the Illyrians, who, together with the Greeks are the most ancient people to have lived in the Balkan Peninsula, or what he considers "the cradle of civilisation" (Kadare 2006: 59). Based on archaeological facts and historical studies, Kadare envisages the Greco-Illyrian civilisation as the oldest in the Balkan Peninsula. In his essay *Aeschylus,* Kadare advances his "imaginative evocation" of similarities in "the original Greek and Illyrian civilisation of Homeric antiquity" (Morgan 2010: 299). Kadare claims that Illyrian-Albanian culture existed in the Balkans before the Slav migration, as "Albanian Christianity was older than that of Serbia" (Kadare 2006: 44). While Illyrian history is used as a powerful foundation myth to pave the formation of the new Albanian nation, the Ottomans are considered as "hegemonic occupational powers" (Morgan 2015: 3).

For Kadare, as a result of the clash of two civilisations, the Oriental-Ottoman Empire and Occidental-Europe, the Balkan Peninsula was removed from the body of "the mother" Europe (Kadare 2006: 59). However, Kadare is convinced that Albanian identity was not affected by the Ottoman conquerors, as he emphasises, "nations cannot be changed by occupations, or conversions" (Kadare 2006: 51). While in the earlier *Aeschylus* Kadare discusses Albania's European credentials, in his 2006 essay *Identiteti evropian i shqiptarëve* [*The European identity of the Albanians*], he aims to craft the intellectual and spiritual foundations in order to facilitate "a new and more profound reattachment of Albania to its European heritage" (Morgan 2010: 299). In fact, throughout his writings, Kadare maintains his thesis that Albania is part of Europe. In the same essay, he supports this claim arguing that geography, race, the Albanian national hero Skenderbeg, whose name was mythicized by Albanians and Europeans alike, the similarities of the Albanian *kanun* with European epics and the early Albanian literature which was written in Albanian and also in Latin languages, are all indications of the European identity of Albanians. His argument begins with the geography, which according to Kadare, "is hard to argue with" (Kadare 2006: 20-21). He points out that Albania is on the periphery of Europe to the East; however, at least, on the map, three more countries are located further East: "Macedonia, Greece and Bulgaria, not to mention what is called 'European Turkey'" (Kadare 2006: 20-21). Therefore, the line of separation between Occident and Orient, which according to Kadare does not cross Albania, is a validation of Albanian European-ness (Kadare 2006: 21). In order to prove his argument, Kadare argues that three Albanian ancient cities: "Durrës, Shkodër and Berat have nearly the same age of Rome" (Kadare 2006: 21). In short, Kadare is convinced that geographically and physically Albania is part of Europe.

Kadare's second justification is based on race. His argument is that the Albanian population, as the entire European continent, is white and its ancestors are "at best Illyrians, or at worst Thrace-Illyrians" (Kadare 2006: 21). Kadare's genetic differentiation of the human population of Europe proves that he is not interested in issues of race, but rather posits himself "on a mission" to enlighten Europe that the Albanian race was "mistaken" for Turks, and thus, non-European. Kadare's analysis based on race/skin colour is a simplistic approach that excludes Albanian minorities and multiethnic Europeans, and thus, can be counterproductive to shifting Albanian identity closer to that of Europe.

The third argument advanced by Kadare is the fact that the Albanian national hero Skenderbeg, the mention of whose name in Albanian lands was prohibited until the end of the Ottoman occupation, "became firstly a European myth" (Kadare 2006: 22), and then, an Albanian myth. Kadare is convinced that Skenderbeg does not rest in his tomb at the castle of Lezhë as his "dead body was never found from the beginning" (Kadare 2013b: 123-24). While it is speculation that Ottoman officers opened the tomb and stole Skenderbeg's bones, the disappearance of Skenderbeg's dead body is a major theme in Albanian epic songs and occupies a large part of the Albanian narrative—the Albanian myth that protected not only Albanian lands but also Europe from the Ottoman barbarians, to the point that the mystical disappearance of Skenderbeg's body was considered by Kadare as a resurrection: "the same as Jesus" (Kadare 2011: 54).

Kadare believes that another link, and reason for Albanians to be proud of their European "roots" is the fact that the Albanian *kanun* and epic poems share similarities with European epics. The controversial "blood feud" as part of the Albanian *kanun*, which in the twenty-first century, is still present in Northern Albania, creates challenges for local Albanians and for the government (Foster 2016). The reputation of *kanun* as the best issue resolution policy, due to weak state has been paradoxically the historical rule in Northern Albania. However, Kadare is interested in the historical narrative of the Albanian *kanun* and *këngeti e kreshnikëve* [epic songs], which he reveals, are all part of the European epics, from Diogenes, one of the creators of the European culture, to the "Saxo Grammaticus, which in 1200, dedicated around forty pages to the history of the blood feud" of the prince Hamlet (Kadare 2006: 22-23). Therefore, according to Kadare, preservation of the Albanian *kanun* is further proof of the connection with the European tradition.

Kadare's main argument is that Albanian language has similarities with other European languages. Historical linguists have agreed that the Albanian language is different from the Greek and Slavic languages, hence according to Kadare, the closest option is to think it originated from "ancient Illyrian" (Morgan 2010: 29). Kadare has a high regard for the Albanian language—the main constituent that played a crucial role in keeping the imaginary of the Albanian nation alive: he positions the language above the state (Kadare 2011: 69). For him The Porte knew the power of the Albanian language and that was the reason as to why it was targeted:

> there are a thousand Greek schools in Albania, the same as Turkish. There are three hundred Slavic schools, Vlach, Bulgarian, why not Albanian? Why is there no Albanian? (Kadare 2011: 69).

Kadare also thinks language was more important than religion in the formation of Albanian identity. He argues that, for the Ottomans, religion was "less dangerous than language…the language was going to still be one; the same as it was people's identity" (Kadare 2006: 25). Not only does Kadare equate the Albanian language with Albanian identity, he is convinced that correlation of Albanian and European identities is demonstrated by the fact that Albanian writers such as Pjetër Budi, Frank Bardhi, Gjon Gazulli and Pjetër Bogdani published their books mostly in Europe's Latin language.

With regards to religion, Kadare thinks that Albanian Christian religion was "contaminated" by the Ottomans, as "a new faith, added to our ancestors, Muslim faith and its mosques" (Kadare 2006: 25). The Albanian famous sentence "where is sword, lays religion" has a cultural meaning in Albanian language, which relates to the fact that religion is not to be trusted—it rather generates wars through the symbolic use of swords. It is believed this sentence was crafted by the father of Skenderbeg, Gjon Kastrioti, who remained disappointed with his Catholic, Orthodox and Islam religions he embraced throughout his life. Kadare asserts that the *rilindja* period was pivotal in laying the foundation of today's Albanian national identity: during the *rilindja* period, from the scrimmage of three

Albanian faiths, Catholic, Muslim and Orthodox, "the miracle happened" as three faiths showed respect and loyalty to *"Albanianism"* (Kadare 2011: 68). As he emphasises, the harsh medieval formula, "where is sword, lays religion", was replaced with the soft approach: "The Albanian faith is Albanianism'" (Kadare 2006: 33). Thus, following Albanian independence, religious differences did not affect Albanian identity, as *Albanianism* was above religion. Religion could not force an Albanian man to sit on his knees (Kadare 2006: 35). In short, for Kadare, *Albanianism* remained above religion.

Kadare urges Albania to join Europe, this "beautiful creature", that for Kadare represents a star in the sky. Thus, in one of his last novels, *Bisedë për brilantët në pasditen e dhjetorit* [Conversation about brilliants on a December afternoon], Europe is described as "a strange star, very dense, a sort of a colossal diamond…a brilliant" (Kadare 2013a: 111-12) that is more important than anything else. While Kadare deliberately distinguishes Europe as a "diamond", on the other hand, Europe has also been contemplated as "cold and useless such as death" and helpless to protect the Balkans—its "cradle of civilisation" (Kadare 2013a: 112). However, for Kadare, this enormous diamond is illuminating Albania's way to re-join Europe. Although the "mother" Europe has been non-existent and late for many years, the rediscovery of the mother continent makes Albanians not less European than others (Kadare 2013a: 111). On the contrary, it marks them more (Kadare 2006: 59). Thus, the Albanian nation with a "European-Latin" language and cultural similarities to those of Europe needs to re-join the European Union. Kadare is as obsessive in his quest to attach Albania to Europe, as he is anxious to distance Albania from its Ottoman past.

Kadare's "others"

At a time when the Albanian nation-building process is underway, Kadare "remains fuelled by the same fears" that this process can also "capitulate again to internal as well as external forces of destabilisation" (Morgan 2015: 14). In short, Kadare's emotive language is addressed externally to the West, Orient, and Albania's neighbours, but also to the Albanians themselves – "the four others of the Albanian nation" (Jing 2013: 48) that Jing Ke has found scrutinising the work of Kadare. However, Ke's analysis of Kadare's shift from considering the West as "the hostile other" to becoming "the dear Mother" (Jing 2013: 226) of the Albanian nation is simplistic. While Kadare never denies the West's indifference on the Albanian fate, his analyses need to be read in the context of the time and the environment he wrote in. Kadare's three "others" are unchanged: the Oriental Turk, Serbian nationalistic ideology, and those Albanians who since the fourteenth century have been working against Albania's interests, have been his constant adversaries.

However, for Kadare, the main opponent for Albanian identity remain the Ottoman-Turks. He is a master of crafting fiction-narratives without a specific chronological time. In one of his last essays, "Secret relation", Kadare's creative characters speak an emotive language that is directed to different audiences. His invented character, "Tuz *effendi*" (a high Ottoman figure who may be a representation of Sultan Mehmeti II) is coming to visit Albanian *pashaliks* after the death of Skenderbeg. Kadare's Tuz considers the European continent as "threatening, without soul" (Kadare 2013b: 125). While some Albanian people speculate about the purpose of his visit, others claim that Tuz *effendi* is preparing a big attack against Europe. Tuz himself cannot stop thinking about Skenderbeg (Kadare 2013b: 118). Skenderbeg's disappearance deeply troubles him. One local-"other" Albanian, speaking to Tuz *effendi* states:

> Our Osman state soon will swallow Europe. I once saw a python swallowing a gazelle. It was terrible, but beautiful. This is what is going to happen; the swallowing [of Europe] will start just here; the Balkans (Kadare 2013b: 134).

This fiction narrative aims to reach different audiences in the past, present and future. While it articulates the Albanian resistance to halt the destructive effects of the Islamic Turks that arguably might have come to occupy Europe, it also compares the Turks with a snake that swallows a beautiful gazelle. On the other hand, Kadare's message is clear: These "other" Albanians are meeting and supporting Tuz *effendi*. This fiction-element can also be relevant to current and future times; aiming to warn Albanians in the twenty-first century. Bellos has realised difficulties with translating Kadare who manipulates chronological times of his narratives; providing "the backbone and the whole point of his often quite peculiar sentence structures, which simultaneously assert and deny the mono-directional flow of time" (Bellos 2012: 19). Bellos is correct about Kadare's deliberate use of writings. He is a master of historical narratives in Albanian language; knowing how to draw readers into his fiction scenes.

The second "other"—Serbian nationalistic ideology, is no less dangerous for Kadare. Kadare infers in his thesis that "Albanian Christendom was older than the Slav" (Kadare 2006: 44). Thus, Albania's ancestors—the Illyrians inhabited the Balkans before the Serbs. In fact, in contradiction to Serbian claims that consider Kosovo as the "cradle of Serbia", Kadare correctly states that Albanians had settled in Kosovo many centuries before Slavs (Kadare 2006: 44-45). However, for Kadare, the main issue lies with the Ottoman-Turks, who continuously jeopardised conflicts between Albanians and their Serb and Greek neighbours; trying to convince the audience that Turkey did not protect Albanians "from this unfaithful" Orthodox world (Kadare 2011: 71). While the Greeks were against the Albanian Latin alphabet, for Kadare, Serbs attacked Albanian identity in a more aggressive way (Kadare 2006: 36); exploiting Albanian conversions to Islam and using it as a vehicle in order to destroy it (Kadare 2006: 40). After Albania's recognition as an independent entity, Kosovo was left alone to handle the Yugoslav racist policies against Kosovar-Albanians. According to Kadare, the Serbian policy was very clear: to break the link between Kosovo and the Albanian nation. In order to achieve this, the Serbs turned to the "old Turkish policy: Mosques are enough; you do not need schools" (Kadare 2006: 41).

Kadare is concerned with negative effects of The Porte, as during the occupation of Albanian speaking territories, the State not only benefited from Albanian lands and its soldiers, but after the collapse of the Ottoman Empire, a large number of Albanians never returned to their country. Kadare then embarks on uncomfortable discussions that consider these Albanians as being assimilated, to the point that their "women continued to deliver Turks" (Kadare 2011: 35). Serbs on the other hand, he claims, could have enjoyed Kosovo's plain land without the unwanted Albanian population (Kadare 2006: 42-43). The Kadare analysis of policy links between Turkish and Serbian governments shows once more the effects of Turkey with regards to Albanian identity, while Serbian atrocities came to an end after NATO's Euro-Atlantic intervention in 1999.

Ultimately, Kadare's last "other" are all those Albanians who damage the Albanian cause. Kadare is convinced that "new *Albanologists*" who envisaged the Albanian existence as merits of two protectors, that is the Ottoman and the Communist State, also helped the Serbian cause (Kadare 2011: 206). He classifies Albanians in three main categories: those who "did not exchange anything" with the Ottoman Turks, others that "threw the cross" (but they did not forget Albania, nor did they accept Islam) and those who "sold everything for their own interest" (Kadare 2011: 67-68). Kadare's main focus again is to highlight Albania's destruction at the hands of her own:

give up the cross to get prestige. Keep the cross; give up the Albanian language... Keep the gun; give up the cross. And the main thing: to be a Turk...so unfaithful, you will be punished (Kadare 2011: 67).

For Kadare, one of these destroyers was Enver Hoxha who in 1947 wrote his "only historical prose"; mythicising Haxhi Qamili (an Albanian-Ottoman officer) and making it easier for Yugoslav propaganda to damage Albanian identity. Although Hoxha threw away both the cross and the crescent moon, according to Kadare, due to his isolationist policies, he allowed Europe to forget Albania for some decades (Kadare 2006: 38). However, Hoxha was not the only Albanian leader to have changed Albanian identity. For Kadare, the long line of leaders who have shown sympathy to or sided with the Turks begins with the Ottoman occupation and is still alive in the twenty-first century. Examples are continuous efforts of Albanian political leaders to hide the statue of Skenderbeg when meeting with their Turkish counterparts (Kadare 2011: 41). On the other hand, the statue was proudly presented when meeting with other European leaders. Kadare interprets these attempts as nothing less than a demonstration of Albania's ambiguity towards abandoning the Eastern way, or at best, this is a confirmation of the influence of Turkey. Kadare's concern is that these Albanians may impede the Albanian march to join Europe and allow Turkey to pull Albania back into its sphere of influence as the Ottomans did in the past.

Kadare's Albanian identity through Qosja's lens

Kadare's Albanian identity thesis is strongly opposed by the opposing voices who think that the "Islamisation" of Albanian-speaking people enriched the Albanian culture; creating "a new identity" (Shehu 2011: 407) that was more dynamic than the Christian religion was. The leader of this camp is Rexhep Qosja, a long-standing intellectual figure in Kosovo and another "giant" of contemporary

Albanian literature, a historian and critic also very active in politics and social science. The debate between the two was fuelled in 2006, after Kadare's essay *Identiteti Europian i Shqiptarëve* (The European identity of the Albanians), which was then published in a small book by Onufri. The argument became fiery when Qosja responded in the same year with his essays *Idetë raciste të Ismail Kadaresë* (The racist ideas of Ismail Kadare), *Ideologjia e Shpërbërjes* (Disbanding Ideology) and *Realiteti Shpërfillur* (Neglected Reality), all published by Toena in 2006. The two-way argument between Kadare and Qosja is central as it goes to the heart of Albanian identity establishment and the direction of Albania.

Unlike Kadare who is convinced that Albanian identity has remained unchanged and clearly belongs to the European-Christian civilisation, Qosja believes that it is a mixture of two civilisations: Christian and Islamic. However, for Qosja, "Islamic civilisation" in Albania is more widespread than the "Christian civilisation" (Qosja 2006). Qosja centres his claim on Albania's culinary culture; folk dress; songs and dances; death and birth ceremonies and their rules; gender culture; morals and laws; pop art that have Turkish and Arabic similarities; religious, illuminist, pedagogical and moral literature written in Arabic; architecture of Albanian cities; bridges, mosques, *tekkes* and *tyrbes* built during the Ottoman occupation, which, according to him, are all part of the "Islamic civilisation" (Qosja 2006). While for Kadare the Ottomans represented Islam, backwardness, intolerance and barbarism, Qosja disagrees, arguing that the Ottoman Empire was also "tolerant" such as in the case of religion (Gawrych 1983).

The Albanian religious dichotomy creates strong divisions between two schools of thought. In a similar way to Edward Said's argument of the superiority of West versus East, Qosja thinks that Kadare's thesis put forward in the essay, *The European Identity*, reveals "the cultural disagreement between Europe and Muslim-East, while...it shows superiority of European identity towards...Muslim identity!" (Qosja 2006). Qosja argues that equating Albanian identity with that of Christian Europe, which according to him, was not less "barbarian" than the Ottomans, as shown during the period of Christian crusades, is a racist assumption and ignores the fact that the Albanian Muslim community is the majority group in Albania and Kosovo (Qosja 2006). Hence, while for Qosja, Islam is part of the Albanian national identity, Kadare simply posits Islam as incarnated with the Ottoman-Turks, and thus, the main "other" for Albanian identity. Downplaying the religious importance, Kadare thinks that during their protests against Serbian regime in 1981 and 1989-1990, Kosovar students fought for freedom, not for Islam (Kadare 2006: 43-44).

On the other hand, Qosja believes that Kosovar students did not fight for Christianity either, but for a simple request: to see Kosovo becoming a Republic, and unite with "what was then called, the mother state – Albania" (Qosja 2006). Qosja went as far as revealing his position against "mythicising Mother Teresa" in Albania, who for him, is a religious figure and, therefore, the "name, portrait and her statue must be present at religious, humanitarian or health institutions, but not at Tirana airport, political, state institutions and city plazas" (Qosja 2006). Qosja thinks that Albanian politicians (including Kadare who is not a politician) use religious figures "in a multi-religious country" to achieve their political ends. It is not hard to grasp Kadare's alignment for Christian Europe, or Qosja's writings with regards to "the Albanian Muslim heritage". In relation to Islam and Albanian identity, both positions, Kadare's and Qosja's, have been politically instrumental for the Albanian nation-building process of the post-Cold War period (Xhaferi 2017a).

While Qosja tries to paint a realistic picture of Albania's current religion, Kadare is going back in history to discover the "unchanged" Albanian-Christian identity. Qosja argues that Albanians have different religious identities such as "Catholic, Orthodox, Muslim, Protestant, Atheist", however, they are all united in what he calls "the Albanian national identity" (Qosja 2006). Kadare instead, ignoring the overall religious composition of Albania, thinks that it is clear for Christian-Albania to join Europe. This is not the case for Qosja's Albania with its mixed religious identities, or "more" Muslim identity, which, following his logic, is not yet ready to join the Christian Europe (Frashëri 2015).

Kadare argues with Qosja that identity is not something fleeting that can change quickly, whereas for Qosja, national identity can be transformed and changed, absorbing new elements, as it did in Albania's case. Kadare thinks that Albanian identity cannot be "half", which in the Albanian language means "torollak [fool]" but must be entirely Occidental—the same as European identity (Kadare 2006: 55). Kadare uses the analogy of Kosovar identity, which did not change under the Serbian rule, to that of Albanian identity that remained "European" under the Ottomans. Qosja, on the other hand, considers Kadare's thesis racist (Qosja 2006); arguing with some of those factors that Kadare proposes to prove the European identity of Albania. For example, Qosja continues to oppose Kadare, who considers the Albanian population to genetically have the "white colour of the skin"; the same as Europeans. As a result, he calls Kadare's thesis dangerous, differentiating Albanians from Asians and Africans, at a time when Europe is in the process of unifying, and adapting cultures and languages, and is not created on the basis of race or skin colour. The concept of race has changed for some time now, and European countries in their "ethnic" composition are including people with different coloured skin who share the rights of white Europeans (Frashëri 2015). Hence, Qosja deems Kadare an "Orientalist" and *Muslimanist*", in the same way that Edward Said uncovers enemies of the Orient.

While Kadare blames the Ottomans as primarily responsible

for wreaking destruction on Albania, both Kadare and Qosja are united in their criticism of the Great Powers for their damage they provided in dividing Albanian-speaking lands in 1913; Albanian neighbours for their continuous attacks on the Albanian speaking lands; of Europe for its negligence regarding the Albanian case, and in their criticism of those Albanians who work against the national interest. Moreover, both hold Albanian rilindja writers in high regard. Thus, Kadare and Qosja contemplate the same "others" in relation to Albanian identity, with one exception: The Ottoman-Turks and their religion.

Kadare viz-a-viz Qosja

It is important to remember that Qosja and Kadare—one *geg* and the other *tosk*—are writing in very different styles, attacking each other in a way that the Albanian historian and academic, Kristo Frashëri calls the Albanian "sanguine temper" (Frashëri 2015)—another known Albanian identity element. For Frashëri, Kadare is a great writer and novelist, while Qosja tries to academically probe the Albanian national identity question. However, despite the fact they are both Albanian "giants" in the field of literature and possess extensive knowledge, according to Frashëri, they both argue in "historical, sociological, philosophical and ethnological fields", in which they both lack knowledge (Frashëri 2015).

They also grew up in very different environments, which shaped their lives and ideas. Kosovo was annexed into Yugoslavia, and its economy under Tito enjoyed relative progress compared to that of the remote-centralised-communist Albania. Therefore, Kadare's and Qosja's paths were divided from the beginning. For a Kosovar such as Qosja, the Serbian-Orthodox enemy was extremely visible, and existed outside the Albanian community. Along with the Albanian language, the Kosovar-Muslim religion acted as an important bond in opposing the Serbian orthodox religion ideology, used by

Serbian nationalism against Kosovar-Albanians. On the other hand, for Kadare who was formed as a writer under Hoxha's regime, it was easy to attack Albanian easy prey enemies—the Islamic-Ottomans, Russian and Chinese "imperialists". Although things have changed in the last three decades as Kadare has lived in France since 1990, he is openly trying to revitalise the importance of Albanian identity and its Christian origins.

Albanian politicians divided between Kadare and Qosja, West and East

The onset of the twenty-first century brought about a fierce debate between Kadare and Qosja (*Lajmi.Net* 2015). In reality, it was the culmination of Albanian identity debates that increased in the post-Cold War period. Since then, bi-partisan political support for Kadare's thesis has become more apparent in Albania (Nano 2002). The post-Cold War discourse of the Albanian elite is a chorus echoing the West and its values, and Kadare is considered the spiritual leader. Albanian governments of the post-Cold War have always advanced their programs of returning Albania to the "European family", which will end the historical humiliation of the country. As a result, the majority of Albanian policy makers support Kadare's thesis, which considers Albanian identity part of European identity. At the peak of the debate, when Qosja criticised Kadare in his essay, *The racist ideas of Ismail Kadare*, the former head of the Albanian Parliament, Jozefina Topalli, was quick to state that "Albanians have European identity" (*Shekulli on line* 2006).

Former Albanian President Bamir Topi did the same, stating: "Albania must return to Europe… to which it belongs both historically and geographically…" (Topi 2008). Topi's predecessor, Alfred Moisiu went even further in one of his speeches, stating that "Albanian Muslims carry 15 centuries of Christianity in their soul" (Moisiu 2005). This emotive statement shows that after another century,

Albanian leaders are still trying to convince their audience that Albania is a Christian country. Therefore, these statements demonstrate a political willingness to follow the "Euro-Atlantic" path as the only way the Albanian state-building process "must go". However, it can be argued that these are politically motivated individual statements by Albanian leaders, but they are not supported by the policies of the Albanian government.

The Kadare-Qosja debate has divided most Albanian scholars who either side with Kadare or proclaim to be against his thesis. Frashëri suggests that both Kadare and Qosja focus too much on religious identity issues and, thus, miss the real debate about Albanian identity (Frashëri 2015). For him, Kadare's thesis needs correction, whereas all the Qosja analyses are wrong; Albanian identity should be understood outside of religious bias; other elements such as Albanian language and culture can better explain it. In their attempt to better explicate Albanian and European identity, Frashëri thinks, both Kadare and Qosja are confusing "identity" with "civilisation" (Frashëri 2015). For Frashëri identity is a property of a "nation" and cannot be changed, whereas civilisation is very dynamic and continually absorbs new elements (Frashëri 2015). It can be argued that Frashëri's "unchanged identity" sides with Kadare's thesis, and on the other hand, opposes Qosja who equalises the "religious civilisation", which for Frashëri does not exist (Frashëri 2015). Although for him Islam and Christianity are guided by their "static" policies, little changes are made to reflect continuous developments. However, Frashëri notes that "religion has no power over civilisation" (Frashëri 2015) but rather follows developments in civilisation. Hence, Islam and Christianity cannot be identified with either Eastern or Western civilisations, as "religion is different from civilisation" (Frashëri 2015).

Other Albanian scholars are divided in their analyses. Ibrahimi supports Qosja for his realistic assessment of the Albanian demographic composition and also sides with him in criticising Kadare for idealism. Ibrahimi expresses his concern over the cultural and spiritual re-orientation of Albanians who live in territories of ex-Yugoslavia, for shifting their loyalties from Tirana towards Pristina (Ibrahimi 2006). Other scholars, in the same way as Qosja, analyse the new orientation of the Kosovar-Albanian society that seems to focus on religious rights and creating a new Kosovar identity (Gorani 2011: 289). However, the new Kosovar identity issue requires more research, and as mentioned, it is not the focus of this book. Although Shala upholds Kadare's thesis of the Western-European-Christian origins of Albania, in *Qose-Kadare and the dynamic identity*, he fails, in the same way that Kadare and Frashëri do, to recognise the dynamism of Albanian identity and the fact that, historically, it has been transformed to reflect elements of both East and West.

One of Kadare's historical rivals, Agolli, supports Qosja's arguments about Albanian identity. He highlights the dynamism of the concept of identity, in stressing that Albanian identity, language, cultural and social habits have changed, and many more changes can be expected in the future (Agolli 2006). However, Agolli neglects Albanian religious identity, focusing more on the dynamics of continuous social, cultural and political change. Another Albanian writer and critic, Nano, in his analyses, does not side with either Qosja or Kadare. While for Nano, Kadare exaggerates in thinking that Balkan nations "helped" the Ottoman culture adding "desire to become more European", Qosja perceives Albanian identity to be a mix of Oriental and Occidental components (Nano 2006). Furthermore, for Nano, Qosja unjustly equates barbarian events of Eastern-Ottomans with those of Western-Europeans. According to Nano, Albania's "Eastern civilisation" is not "autochthone and authentic" and, thus, Albania has no other choice but to follow its own culture, which, is similar to that of Europe since its birth (Nano 2006); a concept that is not far, if not the same as the thesis of Kadare. Plasari, another Albanian scholar, instead criticises both Kadare and Qosja ¾ Kadare for "nonsense" in claiming that the Albanian Christian Church is older than the Orthodox one, and Qosja who is "mixing-up Istanbul with Jerusalem" (Plasari 2012). Plasari is referring to Qosja's claim with regards to freedom of religion that Christians can go for their religious rituals even to Turkey, if they wish to. The issue of Muslims traveling and participating in their religious rituals to Jerusalem might be irrelevant, while shows that often the focus of the Kadare-Qosja debate gets out of context. However, Plasari correctly notes that the debate between Kadare and Qosja is beneficial for the Albanian nation but also tells us there is much to be resolved concerning the question of Albanian national and religious identity.

Visar Zhiti, an Albanian artist who was arrested during the Albanian "Cultural Revolution" in 1979 and released in 1987, highlights the importance of plurality as part of national identity and states that both Kadare and Qosja represent Albanian identity. Indeed, this is an important issue for Albania and merits further scholarly research rather than subjective analysis by Kadare and Qosja. Zhiti also points out that Kadare, Qosja and their supporters should try to disengage in debates about a personality such as Mother Teresa. Nevertheless, the Albanian "clash of civilisations" debate between Kadare and Qosja is a clear indication of how contested the Albanian national identity is. Ultimately, recent comments by Nano that Skenderbeg was more Christian than Albanian, and that his mother was Serbian (Nano 2017), sparked outrage from Albanian scholars, historians, and even ordinary Albanians whose comments on social media reached the point of death threats. While Skenderbeg seems to be untouchable for Albanians, ordinary people need to participate in this debate and have a voice.

A pleasant conversation with Kadare

A late afternoon on 29 August 2013, I had the privilege to meet with Kadare at his *Mali i Robit* vacation home. I was hoping through our conversation to learn something in addition to his writings about Albanian identity. The end of that long conversation was, once more, the confirmation of Kadare's thesis on Albanian-European identity. Kadare has no intention to bend his thesis, nor does he open any space for speculation about Albanian identity. For him Albanians are Christians and only time will deny the "crazy" idea of Qosja that equates Albanians to be half Christian and half Muslims, which for Kadare means Turks. As he stated: "what is that Mosque doing next to Skenderbeg Square in the middle of Tirana?" (Kadare 2013c). Kadare's main "others" of this conversation were Albanian high rank politicians on all sides of Albanian politics who, according to Kadare, do not understand the danger that comes from Islamic Turkey, while positioning their own interests above Albania. Although pessimistic, Kadare insists that Albania must join Europe and farewell Turkey and has never stopped expressing his concerns regarding the future fate of Albania.

Albanian identity in the making

Albanian identity is contested by Albanians themselves. As we have seen through endless debates between Kadare and Qosja, but also other Albanian scholars, politicians and the media, an agreement is missing. The main two opposing factions are those of Kadare and Qosja who have become catalysing forces of this debate. Energies spent in these debates, and the elevated tone used by participants, shows how difficult it is for Albanians to agree on what constitutes their own identity. While Kadare's "others"—the West, Orient, Albania's neighbours and Albanians themselves are not motionless, the Ottoman-Turks have always been unchanged: aggressors, ruthless and ready to assimilate, or "swallow" Albanian identity. On the other hand, Qosja is building his claims regarding religious tolerance of the Ottoman Empire on voluntary conversions. However, forced conversions also took place, along with lack of infrastructure development, political instability, and more importantly, the Ottoman policy of stopping Albanians from developing their own language and Latin alphabet—all indications of political aims of The Porte. Qosja claims that Albanian identity is more aligned to "Islamic civilisation" as Albania's culinary culture; folk dress; songs and dances; death and birth ceremonies and their rules; gender culture; morals and laws; pop art that have Turkish and Arabic similarities; religious, illuminist, pedagogical and moral literature written in Arabic; bridges, mosques, *tekkes* and *tyrbes* built during the Ottoman occupation.

However, while there is no doubt Albanians embraced imported cultural elements such as culinary, folk, songs and dances, celebrations, morals and pop art with Turkish and Arabic similarities, they struggled to learn and practice Arabic literature, alphabet, and never detached from their Albanian language. Building of mosques, *tekkes* and *tyrbes* has little link with Albanian willingness, but rather shows Sultan's political aim to build a permanent structure in order to achieve his ends: make Albanian lands an extension of the Empire and assimilate all *Arnahut*-Albanians in Turks in order to then get physically closer to the West.

Another thing to consider is that, during the communist period, the Ottoman heritage, Turkish and Arabic culture elements were more preserved through Albanians living in ex-Yugoslavia. The reasons are known: while after 1967 Hoxha's regime sought to remove religious activity from Albania's life, Albanians of Yugoslavia continued to safeguard anything that protected their uniqueness, and practicing Islam was perceived as defending Albanian identity. Therefore, in the twenty-first century, as Yzeiri mentions, Albanian "religious identity roots" has been changed for all Albanians and this fact needs to be contemplated when defining Albanian identity. Therefore, both Qosja and Kadare have failed to correctly define Albanian identity. Kadare's Albanian identity that has resisted both the Ottoman atrocities and communist pressures is more comprehensible for Albanians who lived under the regime of Hoxha. However, for Albanians of Kosovo, Montenegro, Serbia and North Macedonia, Kadare's hate for Ottoman-Turks and Islam is challenging.

Qosja exercises his rights to oppose Kadare's racist ideas and believe that Albanian identity reflects elements of both the Western and Eastern civilisations. Frashëri, who tried to stop the debate between the two, is engaging instead in philosophical analyses of definition of "identity", which according to him is the property of the "nation" and thus cannot change and evolve unlike civilisation, which is dynamic and can absorb new elements. The Albanian national identity has changed and evolved, while Frashëri's unchanged identity (but change of civilisation) is close to Kadare's thesis. Other Albanian politicians, scholars and media are superficially "scratching" Albanian identity puzzle; focusing often on "sanguine temper" of Kadare and Qosja. Albanian identity debate does not represent Kadare and Qosja, but is rather represented by them, and the continuation of these analyses will only bring to the light benefits for Albanians and the international community to better comprehend Albanian identity.

6
FAREWELLING THE EAST?

Being in the middle of the battleground between West and East, there is no doubt that Albanian identity and its future direction reflect elements of both civilisations. The question in the twenty-fist century is whether those links with Turkey are strong enough to stop Albania from joining West? Is Albania seeking to escape its Ottoman heritage, re-orient itself towards the West and "restore" its pre-Ottoman "European identity" and reclaiming a Western-Christian aspect? Albania is developing strong links with West, but will the Albanian government quietly accommodate to the pressures, requirements, and outright requests of the Turkish state? Erdogan's Turkey has leverage over Albania and thus, is not hesitating to apply pressure on areas such as diplomacy, politics, economy, energy and regional security. Furthermore, historical factors on the close cultural ties and religion may help the Turkish government to further that pressure on Albania, but is this enough for Albanian policymakers to abandon the West?

The aim of both Albanian and Turkish governments in the twenty-first century has been that of strong support for each-other, but it is unclear whether the majority of Albanian people support the idea of increased proximity with Turkey and the Middle East. There have been indications that some Albanian citizens are not happy with the increased Turkish influence. An example is the open discussion in April 2018 between the Albanian foreign minister Ditmir Bushati and the Albanian diaspora in the United States where he was asked to explain why the Albanian government was flirting with Turkey, while awaiting to become a European member state (Ben-Meir and Xharra 2018). Another example was the vandalisation of Hasan Pasha's memorial in the city of Shkodër in July 2016 (*Top Channel* 2016b). In this incident, the Turkish flag was removed, after Turkish commentator Talha Uğurluel called Skenderbeg a "bandit" who came down from the mountains attacking women and children, in the same way that "terrorist Kurds" attack Turkey today (*Top Channel* 2016a). On another occasion, Turkish flags were removed along Prishtinë streets during Independence Day celebrations in Kosovo on 17 February 2017 (*Koha Jone* 2017), which is another indication that not all Albanians approve the Kosovar and Albanian government decisions to look to Turkey for increased international support. What is less clear is whether these are isolated acts of a small number of people, or part of a growing popular sentiment. Nevertheless, Albanian and Kosovar governments cannot ignore these incidents.

The Ottomans are bad... Turks are good...

The Albanian-Turkish relationship is multi-dimensional and complex in historical, cultural, political and other terms (Pajaziti 2011: 2). Not all Albanians have negative views about the Ottoman era. Along with Qosja, another Albanian scholar, Pajaziti, has demonstrated that the negative perception of the Ottomans represents Albanian elitist views, whereas in reality, Albanian people living in Albania, Kosovo and Macedonia have generally positive sentiments towards Turkey (Pajaziti 2011: 9). A study in this field conducted by GENAR in 2008-2009, and summarised by Pajaziti, suggests that Albanians of Macedonia are closely tied to the Ottoman-Turkish culture and language. According to Pajaziti's study, the Albanians of North Macedonia speak more Turkish than the Albanians of Kosovo and Albania, and 41.2 percent of Albanian-North-Macedonians interviewed called Turkey "fatherland" compared to 0.6 percent of Kosovars and zero percent of Albanians. According to Pajaziti, the majority, 60.6 percent of Albanians and 53.8 percent of Kosovar Albanians think Turkey is a friendly country, but Kosovar-Albanians seem to be closer "to the Turkish cultural code" (Pajaziti 2011: 12). Moreover, almost a third of Albanians considered Istanbul as the most beautiful city in the Balkans to spend their vacations—better than Tirana or Athens.

Debates on social media show a clear division between those Albanians who perceive themselves as having an Albanian-Western-European identity and others who are more sympathetic with Turkish-Oriental identity. If Turkey were a major source of influence, power and employment, we could have expected that the majority of Albanian emigrants head to Turkey. This is not, however, the case. Since 1991, the main destination for Albanian migrants are rather two European countries: Italy and Greece. While this may in part be due to geographic proximity, the perceived cultural ties with Turkey are clearly not strong enough to attract large numbers of Albanian migrants. However, acording to Mejdini, in the last ten years, Turkey remains the top touristic destination for Albanians (Mejdini 2017). It is safe to claim that at the popular level, modern Turkey is considered as a close-culturally-related country for many Albanians, but not a major player in terms of employment or offering a better future (Balaban 2015: 493-94).

Turkish television series are aiming to portray a new Turkish society that can be identified as a role model for Balkan countries. According to Pajaziti, 95.1 percent of Albanians in North Macedonia watch between one to four hours per day Turkish TV series (Pajaziti 2011: 10). Although Kosovar and Albanian viewer numbers are lower (61.2 and 38.7 percent respectively), the empathy for Turkish culture is nonetheless evident. Turkish influence in the Western Balkans, and especially in Albania, reveals geopolitical, geo-economic and geo-cultural doctrines (Lami 2017: 36). While Albanians enthusiastically watch Turkish TV programs and thus absorb Turkish culture, on the other hand, significant Albanian media pundits and public intellectuals, identify Ottoman characters with negative traits of promiscuity, polygamy, and other Turkish cultural characteristics (Sulstarova 2010: 354). This is the point where the opinions of Albanians differ. Unlike the Ottoman Empire, modern Turkey is considered by everyday Albanians to be a country with a compatible friendly culture. Yet, the damage caused by Ottomans to the Albanian speaking lands is still present in the Albanian subconscious minds.

Albanians blame the Ottoman Empire, not modern Turkey, for halting Albania's historical development. The Albanian *rilindja* writers started the process of distancing Albanian identity from Ottoman culture. In today's Albanian schoolbooks, *rilindja* writers are identified as fighting for the Albanian cause with everything they possessed, "*me pushkë dhe me penë*" [through guns and pens]. This begins with an early *rilindja* illuminist: Naum Veqilharxhi who wrote the first Albanian language schoolbook (*Abetare*) in 1846. He warned that "nations need a written language as the only way of surviving" (*Panorama on line* 2011). Other *rilindja* leaders who had a significant impact in Albanian identity formation were the Frashëri brothers. Sami Frashëri, (1850-1904) (known in Turkey as Şemseddin Sami), was a writer, linguist and playwright who played a major role not only in the creation of the Albanian alphabet in 1886, but he was also instrumental in founding the Turkish alphabet (Gawrych 1983: 523). In 1879 Sami Frashëri founded a cultural and educational organisation called the "Printing of Albanian Writings" in Constantinople (Zickel and Iwaskiw 1994: 19). He refined the grammar of the Albanian language in 1890, but also illuminated the future of Albania; revealing, in line with Veqilharxhi, that Albania one day must be an independent nation (Gawrych 1983: 523). His older brother, Naim (1846 – 1900), labelled the Ottomans as "a big beast" that came from Asia and with "cruelty in their eyes" and "a satanic heart", "killed, severed and impoverished" in a way that "grass wouldn't grow" wherever the beast stepped on the Albanian soil which had previously "flourished" (N. Frashëri 1967: 99-100). Their oldest brother, Abdyl (1839-1892), was also known as one of the first political ideologues of the Albanian Awakening who played a crucial role in the League of Prizren. Abdul was captured by Turkish troops and sentenced to jail for his anti-Turkish propaganda (Elsie 2010: 147). Therefore, Albanian rilindja leaders forged the Albanian anti-Turkish sentiment, a concept that is present in today's Albanian textbooks in Primary and Secondary schools. For example, *The History of the Albanian People* published by the Albanian Science Academy describes Ottoman Sultans as invaders of the Albanian lands; bringing ruin and destruction and taking the Albanian children hostage (Pajaziti 2011: 6).

This fact has not gone unnoticed by Turkish authorities who refuse to describe the Ottoman occupation of Albania with the term "invasion". Turkish authorities are extremely careful about how they describe the Ottoman occupation. According to the Turkish narrative, the Ottomans came to Albania to administer and protect it instead. Recent requests from Turkish authorities to the Albanian and Kosovar governments to alter the presentation of Ottoman history in Albanian schoolbooks, and to portray the Ottomans as "friendly administrators" (Rrozhani 2011) or, preferably, "protectors" who brought about political stability on the Albanian speaking lands highlight this belief, and show that this is a complex issue, which continues to cause trouble in the bilateral relations between Turkey and Albania.

During his visit to Tirana in October 2009, Turkey's foreign minister Ahmet Davutoğlu observed that Balkan countries and

Turkey share "a common history, destiny and future" (Rexha 2017: 30). This sparked debate in the Albanian media, but the Albanian government authorities were hesitant to admit whether Davutoğlu and Turkish authorities had also requested amendments to Albanian schoolbooks (Rexha 2017: 30). In 2011, the Turkish Prime Minister, the Minister of Education and the Turkish Embassy in Prishtina officially requested Kosovar authorities to review all history school texts that are related to the Ottoman ruling of Kosovo and remove words such as "'barbaric', 'wild', 'invasion', 'violence', 'murder', 'blood tribute' and 'slavery'" (Rexha 2017: 31). As a result, a commission led by Kosovo's Ministry of Education reviewed all history textbooks. The commission found that the textbooks portrayed the Ottomans as "severe conquerors" and moved to remove ninety percent of these words and phrases (Rexha 2017: 38). This ignited a real debate in Albania and Kosovo. The Kosovar-Albanian historian, Frashër Demaj, expressed his disappointment with both Albanian and Kosovar governments for interfering with historians and specialists in the field. Demaj openly refused to recognise decisions made by the commission which interfered in scholarly issues and ignored copyright policies (*Koha Net* 2013).

In March 2013, Ismail Kadare led a petition signed by 100 Albanian intellectuals (Murati 2013), sent to the Albanian and Kosovar Presidents Bujar Nishani and Ahtifete Jahjaga. This petition of Albanian intellectuals demanded that any amendment on the Albanian history needs to be analysed and implemented according to methodological principals of historical science and not the interests of the Turkish government. The petition reminded the government authorities that the Ottomans "occupied" Albanian speaking lands not in a "friendly" way, but rather by force; disconnecting Albania from Europe and causing indelible drama and tragedy to the historical memory of the Albanian nation. It continued:

The Turkish occupation for five-centuries was violent, and within this period there were continued acts of violence, killings and exterminations, whilst Albanians were the most persecuted people of the Empire...Let's remember the fact that unlike other languages of the Empire, the Albanian language was forcibly prohibited. This fact alone reveals the genocide of the Ottoman Empire against Albanians, their culture and identity...We cannot hide historical truths...The changing of history by Turkish experts represents cultural aggression, striking at the backbone of the nation; unacceptable insults for Albanians with consequences for their future and identity (*Gazeta Shqip* 2013).

The petition of course did not represent the views of the Albanian and Kosovar governments, but rather independent voices of Albanian writers, academics and artists who lived in Albania and abroad. However, each of those Albanian intellectuals who signed the petition have also a certain level of influence over Albanian thinking. Nevertheless, the Turkish government continues to use its political influence against Albanian and Kosovar government authorities and constraining them to re-interpret history in a way to depict Turks in a more positive light. Others such as the Turkish scholar, Türbedar, maintain that Turkey has not done enough to halt prejudices that associate Turks with the Ottomans. For example, Türbedar believes that Albanians are rewriting their history and portraying Turks as enemies of Albanians, despite cultural similarities and their love for Turkish television series. Türbedar stresses that even the Albanian Academy of Sciences portrays the Ottomans as "fanatic, backward and intolerant rulers, who oppressed Albanians with heavy taxes, political discrimination and the absence of the most elementary human rights, and would even resort to the massacre of the Albanian population" (Türbedar 2011: 150). While Türbedar is convinced of the Albanian-Western

Orientation, in the twenty-first century, this topic remains a thorn in bilateral relations between Turkey and Albania and it is easier to blame the Ottomans.

Borrowed words and handing them back

Another area of farewelling the Ottoman legacy is that of abandoning Turkish words, which have remained along within the Albanian language during its evolution. Although at the end of the nineteenth century *rilindja* writers began purging Turkish words from the Albanian language, the presence of these words in spoken and written Albanian continues to be another controversial topic. It can be argued that the tendency of escaping from the Ottoman heritage in Albania started at the turn of the twentieth century (*Panorama on line* 2011), a time when the Albanian *rilindja* leaders realised that religious divisions would be problematic for the establishment of a national identity, and thus, drew on language as a source of national unity.

Similar to other languages, the Albanian language has not been immune from the phenomenon of borrowing words from other languages. The Albanian language analyses require more attention regarding the Turkish-main source of borrowed words. Dizdari found that in the last few decades, the Albanian language contains 4,406 (Dizdari 2005: 4) Turkish words, and most of these words entered the Albanian spoken and written language during the eighteenth and nineteenth centuries (Derjaj 2012: 89). Turkish words entered the Albanian language through the Ottoman bureaucracy, military and religious services, the philosophic and religious education, economic links with trade centres in Turkey and other areas of the Empire and short and long-term immigration of Albanian speaking people that happened for economic, education and political reasons (Lafe 1999: 39-46). The Porte forced Albanians to learn Turkish as the only language of administration, education, religious and trade activities in the Albanian-speaking lands. Privileged Albanians who benefitted from concessions of The Porte used more and more "*Osmanlica*" as the official language, whilst many Albanian intellectuals who were educated in Turkey absorbed elements of Turkish language, which were then inevitably added to their Albanian language and culture.

Another factor that brought about more Turkish words in the Albanian-speaking language was the role of *bejtexhinj* writings that started at the end of the seventeenth and ended at the beginning of the nineteenth century. This long period of *bejtexhinj* writings is believed to have been constituted in two parts: The first period ended at the end of the eighteenth century, and in a form of "Oriental poems", emphasised beauties of nature, human spirit, and some social phenomena such as love, gender and morals; criticising Albanian poverty, whereas the second period criticised the Ottoman oppressors, while having more religious content. Writings of some *bejtexhinj* authors such as Nezim Frakulla, Sulejman Naibi, Dalip and Shahin Frashëri, Zyko Kamberi, Zenel Bastari and Tahir Gjakova spread through handwritten copies and oral tradition to then penetrate the Albanian spoken language and establish their "Orientalisms" (Derjaj 2012: 91).

There are conflicting opinions regarding the role of *bejtexhinj* in Albania. Although these writings were an infusion of moralities and philosophy, they were full of "Turkish-Orientalisms"— elements that according to Kadare, damaged the development of written Albanian. Others such as Derjaj, think that *bejtexhinj* activism saved the Albanian folk language (Derjaj 2012: 93). The high influence of the Turkish language also affected (in a different way) *rilindja* writings. An example is Naim Frashëri's poem "Qerbelaja" where religious and moral motives are similar to those of *bejtexhinj* poems; painted by the influence of the Turkish culture at the time. However, the difference from the *bejtexhinj* period is that *rilindja* created its own linguistic style based on traditions and Albanian oral spoken language that had survived over centuries, rather than overusing Turkish words to express Albanian culture and tradition. Therefore, *rilindja* writers distanced themselves from the Turkish language used by *bejtexhinj* writers. Naim Frashëri, for example, criticised all those writers who "mixed" and "disfigured" the "beautiful-Albanian" language with that of Turkish (Shkurtaj 2009: 51-74) In short, at the end of the nineteenth and the beginning of the twentieth century, Albanian *rilindja* leaders accentuated Albanian language, myths, traditions and culture; all elements that according to Smith are necessary to form a nation and its identity (Smith 1993: 130).

The process of clearing Turkish loanwords from the Albanian language intensified at the beginning of the twentieth century. Acording to Derjaj, in 1908, the Albanian language dictionary created by the Albanian *Bashkimi* association contained one Turkish word for every eight Albanian words, whereas in 1954, an Albanian dictionary (*Fjalori gjuhës shqipe*), reduced Turkish words by half, or one in sixteen. By 1980, when the Albanian contemporary dictionary (*Fjalorin e gjuhës së sotme Shqipe*) was published, the number of Turkish loanwords was reduced again to one in every twenty-three words, constituting a total number of 1,800 words (Derjaj 2012: 95).

Proper research by Albanian sociolinguistic scholars exploring real effects of Turkish loanwords is limited (Bufli 2013; Derjaj 2012; Gjoleka September 2015; Shkurtaj 2009; Thomai 2002). While some scholars argue that borrowing loanwords from another language is enriching, others argue that borrowing only causes damage to a language, and therefore, loanwords should be removed (Gjoleka 2015: 152). Whatever the scholarly arguments might be, in Albania, there "is no doubt that the language purification process ... from the Turkish borrowings in particular has been a long and complicated process" (Gjoleka 2015: 152). The controversy of completely banning Turkish words from the Albanian language continues.

Some Turkish-based words have remained in spoken Albanian even though they have a synonym, which is part of the Albanian standard language (Thomai 2002: 219). Although the Turkish word *penxhere* (window) in Albanian dictionary is replaced with *dritare*, the use of *penxhere* is still widespread. Another example is the Turkish word *xham* (glazing), which despite its replacement with qelq, is still very resilient and widely used in Albanian lexicon. This is an excellent example of how changes to language take time to come into use in the vernacular, despite being adopted at a higher and more official level. Along with Turkish loanwords borrowed by Albanian speakers to interconnect with the Ottoman bureaucracy, other elements of the Turkish lexicon and morphology are also present in the Albanian spoken language. An example is the use of the suffix –*çe* in words such as *vendçe* "in the manner of the local natives; calmly; very hard" or *kosovarçe* "in the manner of natives from Kosovo" (Bufli 2013: 30). Bufli discusses how Albanians added their own prefix such as "*madh*" (big) or "*keq*" (bad), to then create new Albanian adjectives such as *gazepmadh, qametmadh and adetkeq*; words that all originate from Turkish words such as *gazap* (anger, hate, exasperation), *kiyamet* (catastrophe, disorder, tumult) and *adet* (traditional custom, tradition, piece). However, I argue that words such as *gazep, qamet* and *adet* are replaced in Albanian language with words such as *zemërim, fatkeqësi* or *apokalips* and *qokë (in geg)* or *shkuarje (in tosk)*, and therefore the usage of Turkish words can be avoided, if Albanians want to do so. The process of using Turkish words by Albanian speakers is not a neat and tidy philological phenomenon, but rather evidence of a long and complicated cultural exchange between Turks and Albanians. Similarly, Balaban and Çağlayan think that the process of borrowing words carries marks of cultural layers (Balaban and Çağlayan 2014: 264). Bufli mentions that, according to Gusmani, "borrowing" of morphemes is not simply a process of imitation, but rather requires "active behaviour on the part of the speaker" (Bufli 2013: 30). Therefore, the process of cleansing the Albanian dictionary of Turkish words started during the Albanian *rilindja* period in the mid-nineteenth century and still continues but is not a simple exclusion of Turkish loanwords. Purifying Albanian language from Turkish loanwords may also mean "cleaning" the Albanian culture from "Oriental elements" left in Albania as a result of the Ottoman legacy. This is not a simple academic process as has been discussed. There is a great love of Turkish TV programmes in Albania and their serial movies which are bringing back more Turkish words and cultural elements to Albania. However, is this enough for Erdogan's Turkey to maintain the leverage over the Albanian government and halt Albanian Western road?

Energy and economic security

Energy security is another "tool" in the hands of Erdoğan to exercise influence over Albania. As part of recent agreements between Erdoğan and Putin, Russia rectified the agreement to deliver gas through the Turkish stream (*Top Channel* 2017d). Although this project will compete with TAP—the first pipeline that delivers gas to Europe that does not originate from Russia, Turkey will be a key player as both TANAP and Turkish Stream run through its territory. While Europe becomes more dependent on Turkey regarding both pipelines, Albania can only hope that TAP will be the preferred pipeline for European countries. Turkey, on the other hand, holds the key to gas delivery through Albania, a country that does not have a domestic gas distribution system, and thus, is hoping its economy and population will benefit from these pipelines.

Although the European Union is Albania's main trading partner, the Albanian government cannot afford to ignore economic relations with Turkey. Turkey has already invested €3 billion in Albania, which is nearly one fifth of the Albanian GDP. The level of imports from Turkey is considerable for the Albanian economy. Albania's economy would struggle without the imports from Turkey. Turkey's economic donations to Albania between 1991-1997 has not stopped in the twenty-first century. Albania's trade relationship with Turkey is growing and a further alignment will bring more support to the Albanian economy. In 2018, the Albanian government decided to build a second civil airport—the Vlorë Airport which will exceed the size of the only other airport in Albania—the Mother Teresa airport in Tirana. The 2.7 billion USD project was promoted by the Turkish Ambassador who stated that Turkey is the second biggest investor in Albania, and economic help is more important than words, in changing the perception of Turkey in Albania.

However, in December 2019, the consortium of three companies, Cengiz Construction, Kalyon Construction, and Kolin Construction that seem to have close ties to the Erdoğan regime, withdrew from the project. It is unclear whether this is happening due to financial difficulties these companies are facing as a result of Erdoğan's party losing the Istanbul elections earlier, or the increased scrutiny of the European Commission on the deal between Albanian and Turkish governments (*Exit News* 2019). Nevertheless, the Albanian authorities cannot ignore these vital projects. Inevitably, increasing involvement of Turkey in the Albanian economy will have political implications for Albania. A small country, Albania has a long history of survival and opportunistic policies crafted on basis of its own interests.

Islam—the main ally of Erdoğan in Albania

In the twenty-first century, Erdoğan and the Turkish government are trying to "play the religious card" in order to fill the gap created by the collapse of the communist regime (Anđelković 2017). An example is the money donated by the Turkish government to build the Ethem Beu Mosque next to Skenderbeg square in Tirana. Next to this Mosque, in 2017, during the celebration of *Kurban Bajram*, at the Skenderbeg square, the monument of Skenderbeg was fenced by large screen panels provided by the Albanian Islamic Community. The disappointment culminated with comments of the Albanian Imam Armand Aliu on the media, stating that Albanian Muslims should not be proud of Skenderbeg who ruthlessly fought Islam and therefore, Albanians should choose between their national hero and religious pluralism. This sparked debate in Albanian society and social media going as far as to call to arrest the Imam for placing Albanian identity second to Islam. Nevertheless, this episode and the fact that Albanian Bektashism has developed its own way beyond Sunni Islam indicates that, in the short-term, Albanians have no intention of abandoning Islam.

While "religious harmony" is an added value to the Albanian national identity, preserving Islam by a majority of the Albanian population makes it easier for Turkey to influence Albanian identity, and thus, allowing it to come closer to the Western Balkans and indeed Albania's Muslims. Religion has to some extent played a key role in building the Albanian national identity and this fact has been noticed by Turkish authorities, who in the twenty-first century are emphasising the support for their "Muslim brothers" in the Western Balkans. Although Albanians place their Albanian national identity before religion, as long as Islam continues to remain the majority religion in Albania, it will be easier for Erdoğan's Turkey to interfere, if not manipulate Albanian identity. In religious terms, Islam continues to represent the majority of Albanians.

The Turkish government is trying to express its sympathy for "Muslim brother" states. Well known for his defence of the International Muslim community, Erdoğan is warning the West to avoid

Islamophobia, which, not surprisingly he thinks has become a serious problem. After the terrorist attack on the French journal *Charlie Hebdo* on 9 January 2015, Erdoğan agreed with the Turkish Parliamentary speaker Cemil Çiçek, that the international community must "stand together against Islamophobic incidents which would create clashes among religions, civilisations and sects". While the Turkish government, including its president, are using Turkish influence to protect Muslim rights and fight stereotypes against Islam, some think there is now a slow drift towards Islam. For others, the Turkish government's reactions can also be interpreted as an "increasingly punitive and xenophobic" approach embraced by President Erdoğan of recent, doing more harm to the fight against Islamophobia (Tekdal 2015).

Turkey's political pressure in Albanian domestic affairs

In a recent interview for *Top Channel*, in June 2017, Erdoğan stated that "we [Turks and Albanians] have been strong together for five centuries" (Balla 2017), avoiding words such as "occupation" and "invasion". The next day, the Kosovar-Albanian journalist and politician Arbana Xharra wrote a letter to the Turkish Ambassador in Prishtina; to dispute the statement issued by the Turkish President. She stated that the reason for Erdoğan's comment is to "convince us that we were not occupied [by the Ottoman-Turks], but rather we were lovers". As Xharra continues:

> We do not share the same culture. However, we do share the history of being part of the Ottoman Empire. You must take on your shoulders occupation and crimes against the Albanian language, culture and humanity, which you exercised for five centuries in Albanian speaking lands… we learn from facts and history, except that of Turkey and neo-Ottomanism that you are trying to impose (*Panorama on line* 2017b).

In a similar way, Shala, thinks that the physical occupation of Albanian lands by the Ottoman Empire is replaced in the twenty-first century by a spiritual, moral and cultural invasion of Turkey—a model that offers an alternative to Europe, the neo-Ottomanism, which is based on the superiority of the "Islamic morality" (Shala 2018).

Erdoğan's Turkey has repeatedly requested the closure of all Turkish schools in Albania, which are supposedly financed by the Turkish religious leader in exile, Gülen, who Erdoğan accuses of trying to break down Albanian culture and religious pluralism. Erdoğan's controversial request also included the closure of the Turgut Özal College, the elementary school that he himself inaugurated in February 2005, at a time when the AKP and the movement of Gülen were allies. It is argued that Turkish authorities are persecuting those organisations and individuals who uncovered the corruption of Erdoğan's cabinet in December 2013. A similar request to close Gülen's schools was rejected by other African countries in 2014. In an article published on 14 May 2015, Zaman noticed that Erdoğan's request to close Turkish schools in Albania disappointed some Albanian politicians (*Lapsi lajme* 2015). The same article cited the Albanian Socialist deputy, Ben Blushi, who stated that "Albania is not a Turkish colony" and then "our father is not Erdoğan, but Ismail Qemali". According to the Albanian former finance and economy minister, Arben Malaj, the request to close Turkish schools, are politically driven and contain a danger for Albanian democracy. *Zaman* also cites an Albanian media analyst, Mero Baze, who thinks that Turkey as the Oriental partner of Albania, will need more Albania – its Western partner (*Lapsi lajme* 2015). Although all these attempts of Xharra, Blushi, Baze, and indeed Kadare, are but individual opinions, they also apply pressure on the Albanian government that is very cautious on these sensitive issues and often refuse to argue with these authoritative voices; keeping a neutral position, or better said, working hard to not jeopardise the bilateral relations with Turkey—its "strategical" ally in the region. Not only Albania's ambiguous position on these issues can have ramifications with its Euro-Atlantic partners, it may also encourage Erdoğan to go a step further; increasing the Turkish pressure on Albania's decision to join the Europe and the West.

In his attempt to renew his request to close schools "financed" by Gülen in Albania, Erdoğan and the Turkish Ambassador in Albania, "suggested" Albanian parents send their children to "safe" Turkish schools; managed by the Maarif Foundation and financed by the Turkish government. It is the Maarif Foundation that in a secret deal with the Albanian government, in August 2018, bought the first Albanian private University—the New York University of Albania and all its sister institutions (Aliju 2018). Although existing Turkish schools in Albania have a good reputation in preparing quality students, on the other hand, using its influence, the Turkish government is interfering in Albanian domestic affairs on issues such as education of future generations that for a small and poor country such as Albania is crucial. More importantly, the Albanian government is allowing Turkey to do so.

After the end of the Cold War, bilateral relations between Turkey and Albania have increased and Turkish government has tried to influence, if not manipulate, decisions made by the Albanian government in the international arena. This became clear when Turkey forced Berisha's government to join the Organisation of Islamic Cooperation (OIC) in 1992 (Vickers and Pettifer 1997: 105), as it did when Erdoğan pressured the same Berisha to vote in favour of the Palestine Resolution 67/19 on 29 November 2012. On the other hand, Berisha was pressured by the US administration to side with Israel. Under such pressure Albania abstained. The Albanian media, *Top Channel*, in paraphrasing the Turkish *Hürriyet*, described the Albanian vote as "conditioned by Erdoğan" (*Top Channel* 2012a).

Albania's abstention shows once more the difficulty of the Albanian position and the pull between West or East, acknowledging the complications of Turkish influence over Albania. In 2017, the Albanian government sided again with Palestine, and thus, voting on the UN resolution against the US decision to recognise Jerusalem as the capital of Israel—a project sponsored by Turkey. The reaction of the Albanian President Ilir Meta was immediate. He wrote a letter of regret to US President Trump; promising he will request an explanation and clarification from the Albanian government for this disappointing vote. In his letter, Meta reassured Trump that this vote does not reflect the will of the Albanian nation. In concert with Meta, opposition political parties such as the Democratic Party (PD) and the Socialist Movement for Integration (LSI) and different leaders from both sides of Albanian politics disagreed with this vote, which questions Albania's strategic Partnership with the US. Recently, Kosovar PM, Hoti, pressured by Trump administration signed the recognition of Israel and its capital, Jerusalem, in a three-party agreement between Kosovo, Serbia and the US on 4 October 2020 (Markovic and Xhaferi 2020). Albania may do the same in a near future. The US leverage over Albania and Kosovo can easily replace that of Turkey. Vickers and Pettifer believe on lack of a strong political influence of Turkey over Albania (Vickers and Pettifer 1997: 108). Of course, Turkish influence cannot compare with that of the US over Albania.

Turkey, EU and Albanian politics

In June 2020, the European Parliament voted 15 conditions for Albania to meet in order to further European Union (EU) membership negotiations. It would seem the EU has been cautious for some time to open negotiations with Western Balkan countries, especially Albania. The EU Parliament member for the National Rally, Thierry Mariani, made it clear he is against Albanian membership;

believing that "Albania is the centre of Turkish influence in the region" (*Exit News* 2020). While Mariani is a right-wing exponent of the French Le Pen Republican Rally, the question many Albanians ask is if this is the real reason why the EU is "delaying" in welcoming membership to a Muslim majority country in the Balkans such as Albania?[8]

The Albanian Euro-Atlantic Orientation is overarching theme for Albania. Its political direction and strategic partnership with both, Europe and the US, are unquestionable. However, Turkey is also a strategic partner for Albania. Turkey's optimism on joining Europe is coming to an end. Erdoğan has continuously threatened the European Union to scrap the refugee agreement signed in March 2016, and it seems that Turkey has also tried to "say goodbye" to Europe since then. In July 2017, he stated that Turkey can do without the EU (*Top Channel* 2017b)—a statement that in October 2017 was strengthened even more, mentioning that Turkey does not need Europe anymore, but rather it will soon be the other way around. According to Erdoğan, "Europe has died in Bosnia and buried in Syria" (*Panorama on line* 2017c). The more the Turkish government distances itself from the EU, the more complicated the Albanian position becomes with regard to relations with both Europe and Turkey.

Erdoğan's decision to get closer to Putin in the twenty-first century, generates challenges, if not threats for the EU and Balkan's region. The tip of the iceberg was in 2015, when Russia decided to re-route the South Stream natural gas pipeline from Bulgaria through to Turkey (Reed and Arsu 2015). Since then, despite differences over the Syrian civil war, Istanbul and Moscow have become closer. Turkey is also strengthening ties with Russia's main partner in the Balkans, Serbia. In October 2017, Erdoğan visited Serbia with a large delegation of 180 businessmen. Twelve new trade agreements between them demonstrates a developing closeness for

Serbia and Turkey, as well as Turkey's desire to become more closely aligned with the Western Balkans in a way that Bechev defines as "a neo-Ottoman quest" (Bechev 2017). Serbian Minister of Commerce, Rasim Lajic, believed that while this was positive for Serbia, it also represented a shift in Turkey's foreign policy regarding relations with Kosovo and Albania. According to Lajic, relations between Turkey and Albania are not the same as two years ago and the shift is due to the 2016 attempted coup. Lajic's optimism stating that "now Erdoğan is with us" was complemented by Serbian foreign minister Ivica Dačić who entertained Erdoğan; singing a Turkish-Balkan-known-old-song that relates to the Ottoman era: the "*Osman Aga*" (*Top Channel* 2017c). In October 2020, the Serbian government has seriously expressed its interest to consider purchasing of the effective Turkish "Bayraktar TB2" war drones.

These recent shifts in Turkish foreign policy constitute a concern, especially for Kosovar Albanians who are eagerly hoping for Serbia to recognise the Republic of Kosovo. Under pressure from Erdoğan, in March 2018, Kosovar intelligence in coordination with their Turkish equivalents arrested six Turkish citizens—five of them teachers—who were residing and working in Kosovo. The Turkish government claimed that they were all members of the Gülistan Educational Institution in Gjakova and Prizren with links to the Gülen movement. They were all immediately deported to Turkey in a secret operation praised by Erdoğan. Under US pressure, Kosovar President Hashim Thaci, the Prime Minister Ramush Haradinaj and the Head of Parliament Kadri Veseli, all stated they had no information about this secret operation and denied the deportation of these six Turkish citizens. As part of this campaign, the Turkish Ambassador in Albania, in 2018, urged Albanian authorities that they also deport all Turkish political opponents from Albania. Previously, Greek authorities had halted the deportation of Turkish soldiers, amidst fears that deported Turkish citizens would face unfair trials in Turkey. However, the Kosovar and Albanian governments are siding with Turkish authorities rather than with European concern for the respect of human rights of all individuals. One of Kadare's greatest fears is that the Albanian political elites may decide to ally themselves with Turkey, as this case of the Kosovar government clearly shows. In line with Kadare and his supporters, Yzeiri also believes that both political elites of Kosovo and Albania are not pushing enough to restore European-Albanian-identity, but rather they downplay the Turkish cultural and religious influences; allowing, for example, Turkish TV programmes and activities of "…black mosques where jihad is preached…" (Yzeiri 2015) to be free in Albania and Kosovo. As a result, Yzeiri believes, both elites of Albania and Kosovo are showing their preference for the East (Yzeiri 2013). Motivations for this are clear: in the last decades they have seen Turkey as a "big brother" not only to finalise unfinished business of recognising the Republic of Kosovo, but also to protect the rights of all Albanians in the region. Therefore, security implications are paramount and will determine the future foreign policies and political shifts of both Kosovar and Albanian governments. While getting closer to Moscow and Belgrade, Ankara is also increasing pressure over Tirana and Prishtina promising them the renaissance of Albanians within the new pan-Islamic Empire run by its new Sultan, Erdoğan (Shala 2018). In the twenty-first century, economic, security, energy and political challenges, combined with divisions between Albanians regarding their culture, religion and identity are all tools in the hands of Erdoğan to impede Albanians from abandoning the East, but also their march on the rocky Western road.

Under the present conditions, Albania is unlikely to abandon the East. This periodical "flirting" with Turkey, will have ramifications for the Albanian government in the years to come, as mentioned by Phillips. Interviewed by the *Voice of America* in April 2018, he highlighted Turkey's aim was to utilise Albania to impose its neo-Ottoman platform in the Western Balkans (David Phillips 2018). Phillips asked Albanian government authorities to clarify whether they are choosing to side with West or with the East, as the current level of support for Erdoğan's Turkey orients Albania strongly toward the Islamic East (David Phillips 2018). The silence of the Albanian government on this issue speaks volumes and shows how resilient Albanian needs are.

Turkey's controversial role in regional security

Territorial ambitions of both Serbia and Greece in the twentieth century have forced Albania to trust Turkey more than its direct neighbours, Serbia and Greece. This trust is continuing in the twenty-first century as Turkey has been allowed to train the Albanian Army, police forces and the Republican Guard. Thus, we see that the precariousness of security for the Albanian speaking lands is the driver for this trust and makes it indispensable for Albanians. In the twenty-first century, Albanians have not placed their security fears to rest, despite NATO, EU and Turkish involvement in Albania and Kosovo.

However, Turkish military engagement in the region needs careful attention. In September 2017, Erdoğan announced a deal to purchase surface-to-air missile systems—S-400s from Russia— "in the clearest sign of his pivot toward Russia and away from NATO and the West" (Gall and Higgins 2017). This is not the first time that Turkey has attempted to buy arms from non-NATO countries. Earlier plans to buy missiles from China, were abandoned under pressure from the United States. According to Gall and Higgins, Erdoğan's:

> preference for the Russian model, with its sense of restoring a lost empire, returning Turkey to a more independent place in the world and rejecting Western democracy (Gall and Higgins 2017).

Russia also sold weapons to Greece, another NATO member and to Cyprus, however, Turkey is a military power in the region and this deal may change the balance of power in the Balkans. Along with Russia and some NATO countries such as Germany and United States, Turkey is also competing in the Balkans (Ademovic 2016). After the Cold War, it is often argued that the disengagement of NATO and EU in Serbia, Montenegro, Kosovo, Albania and North Macedonia will be quickly replaced not only by Russia, but also China, military superpowers that have interests in the region. Turkey's advancement in the Balkans as pro-Russian and anti-European, may shift the geo-political agendas of Western Balkan countries; challenging self-perception identities of countries with large Muslim populations such as Albania, Kosovo, and Bosnia.

On the other hand, while Putin is drawing closer to Erdoğan, the anxiety of Kosovar Albanians is increasing, as they see the US and Turkey as their protectors against Serbian plans to regain Kosovo. Albanians believe that Putin will return Kosovo to Serbia. On 5 February 2017, the Serbian defence minister declared that Serbia ordered 30 tanks, and as many armored vehicles from Russia, six MIG 29s fire jets and was still negotiating for another eight (*Boston Globe* 2017). Former Kosovar Prime Minister Ramush Haradinaj was arrested in France under a Serbian Interpol order for war crimes while being dismissed twice by the Hague's court; a train with posters "Kosovo is Serbia" written in 21 different languages attempted to enter Kosovo and was stopped at the last minute, and the illegal wall built by Serbians in Mitrovica was pulled down after peaceful negotiations between Serbian and Albanian authorities in February 2017 (*Deutsche Welle* 2017). While Albanians welcome Turkey to soften Russian ambitions in the Western Balkans, on the other hand, they still hope for Turkey to be the barrier for historical encroachment against Albanians in the region. Albanians of North Macedonia are no less concerned about Turkey's latest shifts, after Russia openly accused the West of supporting a pro-Albanian agenda in North Macedonia, which for Russia means nurturing the Greater Albania concept (McLaughlin 2017). Ultimately, Albanians don't want to see Turkey's military presence diminished in the region, but, more importantly, they fear a Russo-Turkish alliance. Erdoğan's Turkey is also exercising the new alliance with Russia to thwart the West, the EU, and of course, maintaining its pressure on Albania.

Unexpected findings

While the findings detailed above were the deliberate focus of the book, there is a point to which I wish to draw attention—political and military agreements between Putin's Russia and Erdoğan's Turkey in the twenty-first century. The long war-campaigns between the Ottoman and Russian Empires commenced in the second half of the sixteenth century and ended with the victory of the Russians in the nineteenth century. Strong competition between these two Empires, has also shaped Balkan identities and the way Balkan states have interacted with the East. This fact was painted with religious colours by Balkan nationalism; creating a sort of historical competition between Orthodox-Christians and Muslims. This approach of religious categorisation directly affected Albanians who were considered as Muslims and thus, enemies of Orthodox neighbours. I have shown in this book that at the end of the Ottoman Empire, Albanians were trapped between the Balkan Orthodox allies that were supported by Russia, and the Ottoman Turks. Towards the end of 2015, signs of a new era in bilateral relations between Turkey and Russia started to emerge after plans that a Russian company would build a 20 billion USD nuclear power plant in Southern Turkey. The implementation of the project was officially celebrated by both Erdoğan and Putin in April 2018. In addition, Erdoğan's recent decision to buy Russian armaments is another surprise for NATO and the EU, considering that Turkey is one of the biggest militaries of NATO in the region. The EU is a strong economic partner for Turkey, however, Erdoğan's frustration with the EU due to the endless process on EU membership is evident. He is using this fact to achieve his ends in becoming a powerful authoritarian leader in the region, a new Caliph, or Sultan, who is aiming to rule a new Turkish-Islamic Empire. An alliance with Putin, can help him to use this relationship as a leverage vis-à-vis its European and NATO partners in the region.

These latest developments somewhat at odds with historical disagreements between Russia and Turkey, are creating a new opportunity for both Turkey and Russia to extend their influence in the Western Balkans, and thus, halt the Euro-Atlantic perspective of these countries. Although it is not clear whether these new agreements with Putin are a façade for Erdoğan, the reality is that Turkey is moving away from Europe and the West. Turkey's latest shift is a bigger challenge for Albanian diplomacy in the twenty-first century. Albania is committed to its Euro-Atlantic path, which means Europe, United States, NATO and Western civilisation, but it does not want to lose its regional strategic partner, Turkey. As Turkey is moving away from the West, NATO and Europe, Albania's paranoia that Turkey will join up with the Orthodox axis of Russia and Serbia will increase.

What to take away from this book?

Albania continues to be one of the poorest countries in the Balkans and this is a reason why any kind of help in economy, education and especially regional security is welcomed. Not only are Albanians still closely linked to the Turkish culture, religion, language and history, many (including the Albanian government) believe Turkish military power will protect them from "others" in the region. The reluctance of Albanian political elite to implement democratic reforms, and also delays of the EU in accepting Albania as a member state, are in line with Turkish interests.

Firstly, it is worth noting that the Albanian national identity is constructed in the context of many ideological influences, while defined as a product of interaction between domestic and international forces. Factors such as Albanian and Balkan nationalism, ethnicity, religion, language, interests of regional and Great Powers, and domestic-political competition for leadership have played a role in defining Albanian identity. None of these factors can be underrated, and only a holistic analysis in an historical context will fully explain the Albanian national identity. Most of the above elements are contested, along with the Ottoman influence and legacy that have impacted Albanian identity. This book has shown that the Ottomans affected Albanian-speaking lands; allowing a further deterioration and keeping the country underdeveloped. During the Ottoman rule, Albanian identity inevitably absorbed elements of Turkish culture. Therefore, the question is whether these links are strong enough to force Albanian policy makers to side with Turkey and abandon the West.

Secondly, the book finds that the Albanian policies in the twentieth and the twenty-first centuries have been opportunistic and forced upon it in order to survive. The claim that Albanians are attempting to regain their dignity caused by the Ottomans who conquered Albanian-speaking lands for more than five centuries is not accurate. While Albanian humiliation is linked to the Ottoman occupation and not that of modern Turkey, a structured and methodological approach from the Albanian government is missing, and more importantly, the willingness to do so is questionable. On the other hand, the Turkish government is constantly offering help in areas such as economy, defence and security, but is also implementing cultural and religious projects, which promote the Turkish influence in Albania. The advancement of Turkish policies in Albania is portraying the "Turkish way of life" as a role model for Albanians, who are considering Turkey a friendlier country than their direct neighbours, Serbia and Greece. As a result, Turkish policies aim to bring them closer to Albania and the Western Balkans. Thus, throughout the twentieth century, Albanian foreign policies have shifted between the West to East. The West offers prosperity and security for Albanians in the twenty-first century, and the East also seeks to offer the same benefits.

Ultimately, the Albanian government has made the Euro-Atlantic orientation its strategic priority in the twenty-first century. This trajectory is not without difficulty for Albanian speaking people who live in the region. The majority of Albanians are hoping that Albania, Kosovo and North Macedonia will all become EU member states, and thus, Albanians can all unite under the EU banner. In the absence of an EU army, NATO then becomes Albania's protector, but the US will need to craft a more active foreign policy engagement in Western Balkans in order to balance the influence of Turkey and Russia in the region. The second option will be for the Albanian government to maintain the Euro-Atlantic orientation while not abandoning Turkey and thus, the East, which is in effect the current Albanian policy. If continuing to do so, Albania will make the same mistake as Serbia; aspiring to be with the EU while seeking support from Russia. Albania cannot afford to continue accommodating to Turkey's pressures, and at the same time, proceed on the Euro-Atlantic route.

And there is a third option, which is less likely to happen. The case if Albania decides to abandon the Euro-Atlantic way and side with Turkey. This decision will have bigger ramifications for Albanians in both the short and long-term. This places Albania in direct disagreement with the US, which will cause considerable difficulty, as the last thing Kosovar Albanians wish is to abandon their perceived shield, the US. The Republic of Kosovo could not have existed without the NATO military campaign led by the US. On the other hand, the American government has invested a significant amount of resources and energy in the Albanian democratic process and cannot afford to abandon their key ally in the Western Balkans. In reality, in the first two decades of the twenty-first century, the Albanian government is continuing to dream the West, while *mutatis mutandis* is not abandoning their old friend, Turkey. Erdoğan's Turkey, on the other hand, is using all of its influence and legacy to halt Albania's Western road and thus, pull Albania once more, back towards the "Ottomans" of today. It is time for Albanian policymakers to better value benefits from both West and East, which seems to be obvious. They may help to farewell Turkey, implement some radical political and social changes and embrace the Euro-Atlantic way of democracy and prosperity.

Concluding remarks

Albanian identity is little known to Western civilisation. Since the middle ages Albanians were described by subjective and stereotypical ways by European travellers. It is not embellishment to state that still in the twenty-first century, Europeans know little to nothing about Albanians. Europeans need to better understand where Albania is located and why Albanians are scattered in the Western Balkans. Albanians never invaded other lands, but rather were themselves invaded by neighbours, who carved up parts of Albanian speaking lands.

Albanian identity is a contested theme. Albanians have developed an idiosyncratic and syncretic "identity" over the centuries, reflecting the layered elements of the nation's past. Of the Roman, Byzantine, Ottoman and Communist periods, it is the long centuries of Ottoman rule that inevitably left the greatest impact on Albanian culture and society. Communist leader, Enver Hoxha attempted to shift Albanian identity to another dimension, but the short-term impact of communism paled in comparison to the long-term, deep-seated effects of the Ottoman period.

As the Ottoman Empire was coming to an end at the beginning of the twentieth century, the Great Powers at the time led the redistribution of the Albanian speaking territories and redesigned borders of nation-states in the Balkans. Although the decision made by the Great Powers did not fully accommodate all requests of the emerging Balkan states, the greatest impact of this decision would be faced by Albania. The new Balkan borders decided at the London Conference in 1913 led to the incorporation of territories with a majority of Albanian-speaking population into Montenegro, Serbia and Greece—a situation which remained unchanged into the twenty-first century. The feasibility of reversing the decision of the Great Powers and the re-establishment of an Albanian nation-state in the twenty-first century, despite its attraction for Albanians, seemed unlikely to happen. Albanians were humiliated by Great Powers decision to divide Albanian-speaking lands, but also the Ottoman-Turks who not only failed to protect Albanian lands from their partition, they also opposed the independence of Albania. The project of uniting Albanians in the same nation-state does not have strong political support in Albania, but rather is fuelled by Albanian and Balkan nationalism. The Albanian government today is reluctant to speak about "Greater Albania" and claims that this is not on their agenda, at least not until EU membership is obtained, when Albanians might then be under the same political umbrella.

The book has analysed the controversies surrounding Albanian identity by presenting the two main counterposing theories about Albanian identity. The first one sustained by Kadare sees Albanian identity as historically determined and Western. Kadare claims that Albania belongs to the European family, and the Ottoman barbarians removed Albania from Europe. In opposition to Kadare's theory, the Kosovar scholar, Qosja has formulated his own theory, which emphases the hybridity developed through the Ottoman occupation and thus, considers Albanian identity to be more oriented towards the East than the West. Such counterposed theories demonstrate the unresolved nature of the question of the Albanian national identity. Their debate circles around the role of religion and the Ottoman heritage in shaping Albanian identity. Thus, debates about Albanian identity and its belonging to the Ottoman heritage are far from resolved and in the current Albanian environment, scholars and writers, politicians and media commentators, are divided in their perceptions. Many support Kadare's argument in favour of a still-extant European identity underpinning Albanian culture. For Kadare this "frozen" identity survived the Ottoman centuries and must be freed from the remnants of the Ottoman heritage. Others position themselves with Qosja—the leader of the opposing camp who argues that Albanian identity is different from that of Europe, that Albanian civilisation draws on both East and West, in particular, that Albanians lost their Christian origins, becoming deeply influenced by Muslim culture during the past centuries, and hence belong to the East rather than the West.

Tensions remain high in the Western Balkans, Turkey is now a powerful state, and Turkish influence has been strongly directed towards the Albanian, Kosovar and Bosnian governments, as well as to local Muslim populations, many of whom are Albanians. Turkish foreign policy has been aggressively promoted in Albania and Kosovo, on the basis that deep-seated cultural similarities, geo-political, economic, regional and energy security matters bind their futures together.

From the outset, the aim of this book was to shed new light on the nuances of Albanian identity and its political direction in relation to the impact of its Ottoman heritage and to gauge the extent to which this Turkish influence on Albanian identity has continued into the twenty-first century. There is no doubt that at this moment allying itself with the West appears more attractive and the desire of Albanian policy makers to follow this Euro-Atlantic road seems comprehensible. Whether this will provide certainty for Albania's survival and political independence is less convincing thereby "Escaping the East and aspiring for the West" continues to remain a major crossroad for Albania.

Bibliography

Abazi, Enika (2008), 'Kosovo Independence: An Albanian Perspective', *Seta, Policy Brief*, 11, 1-5.

Abazi, Enika and Doja, Albert (2013), 'Further Considerations on the Politics of Religious Discourse: Naim Frashëri and his Pantheism in the Course of Nineteenth-Century Albanian Nationalism', *Middle Eastern Studies*, 49 (6), 859-79.

Ademovic, Jasmin (2016), 'Great Power Competition in the Balkans Heating Up', *Geopolitical Monitor*, <https://www.geopoliticalmonitor.com/great-power-competition-in-the-balkans-heating-up/>, accessed 13 March 2018.

Agolli, Dritëro (2006), 'Intervistë për debatin e identitetit kombëtar Shqiptar' [An interview over the debate of the Albanian identity], author's translation, *Shqip*, <http://gazeta-shqip.com/lajme/>, accessed 11 November 2011.

Agoston, Gabor and Masters, Bruce (2009), *Encyclopedia of the Ottoman Empire*. New York: Facts on File Library of World History.

Aksoy, Murat (2015), 'Turkish economy declines from 17th to 19th place in ranking of biggest economies', http://mobile.todayszaman.com/op-ed_turkish-economy-declines-from-17th-to-19th-place-in-ranking-of-biggest-economies_368579.html, accessed 5 February 2016.

--- (2015), 'Erdoğan's Atatürkian visions', *Today's Zaman on line*, <http://www.todays-zaman.com/op-ed_erdogans-ataturkian-visions_403887.html>, accessed 12 November 2015.

Albanian Council of Ministers, 'Albania', <http://arkiva.km.gov.al/?fq=brenda&r=&gj=gj1&kid=54>, accessed 4 July 2020.

Aliju, Dzihat (2018), 'Turkey takes over Albania's first private university', *Anadolu Agency*, <https://www.aa.com.tr/en/europe/turkey-takes-over-albanias-first-private-university/1233554>, accessed 18 August 2018.

Alpion, Gezim (2011), *Encounters with Civilizations: From Alexander the Great to Mother Teresa*. New Brunswick and London: Transaction publishers.

Anđelković, Katarina (2017), 'Turkey playing on the card of Islam in Albania?', *Western European Balkans*, < https://europeanwesternbalkans.com/2017/10/04/turkey-playing-card-islam-albania/>, accessed 11 May 2018.

Albanian Ministry of Foreign Affairs (2015), '60 vjet Shqiperi ne OKB' [60 Years in United Nations], author's translation, <http://www.punetejashtme.gov.al/-files/userfiles/press_brochure_minfor_(2).pdf>, accessed 12 May 2018.

Anscombe, Frederick F. (2006), 'Albanians and "Mountain Bandits"', in *The Ottoman Balkans: 1750-1830* ed. Frederick Anscombe. Princeton: Markus Wiener Publishers, 87-114.

Balaban, Adem (2015), 'The Impacts of Turkish TV Serials Broadcasted in Albania on Albanian and Turkish Relations', *European Journal of Social Sciences, Education and Research*, 5 (1).

Balaban, Adem and Çağlayan, Bünyamin (2014), 'Common Cultural Turkish words in Albanian and Greek languages', *Journal of Educational and Social Research*, 4 (2), 262-70.

Balla, Sokol (2017, 'Erdogan: Gyleni rrezikon Shqipërinë. Shqetësim për sherrin Rama-Meta' [Erdogan: Gullen places Albania at risk. Concerns regarding disagreements between Rama-Meta], author's translation, an interview with the Turkish President Erdogan, *Top Channel*, <http://top-channel.tv/video/erdogan-gyleni-rrezikon-shqiperine-shqetesim-per-sherrin-rama-meta/>, accessed 10 May 2018.

Barkey, Karen (2008), *Empire of Difference: The Ottomans in Comparative Perspective* (Cambridge Cambridge University Press).

Barleti, Marin (2012), *The Siege of Shkodra: Albania's Courageous Stand Against Ottoman Conquest, 1478.* , ed. Translated and edited by David Hosaflook. Originally published as *De obsidione Scodrensi, 1504*; Tirana: Onufri.

BIBLIOGRAPHY

Beaumont, Peter (2016), 'Fethullah Gülen: who is the man Turkey's president blames for coup attempt?', *The Guardian*, <https://www.theguardian.com/world/2016/jul/16/fethullah-gulen-who-is-the-man-blamed-by-turkeys-president-for-coup-attempt>, accessed 13 March 2017.

Bechev, Dimitar (2017), 'Erdogan in the Balkans: A neo-Ottoman quest?', *Aljazeera*, < http://www.aljazeera.com/indepth/opinion/erdogan-balkans-neo-ottoman-quest-171011094904064.html>, accessed 15 January 2018.

Bego, Ingrid (2017), 'Why are the Western Balkans in crisis? These are the three primary tensions', *The Washington Post*, <https://www.washingtonpost.com/news/monkey-cage/wp/2017/06/26/why-are-the-western-balkans-in-crisis-these-are-the-three-primary-tensions/?utm_term=.a52a7f984eb5>, accessed 10 October 2017.

Bellos, David (2012), 'On Translating Ismail Kadare', *Translation Review*, 1 (76), 17-22.

Bethell, Nicholas (1984), *The Great Betrayal: The Untold Story of Kim Philby's Biggest Coup*. London: Hodder & Stoughton.

Ben-Meir, Alon and Xharra, Arbana (2018), 'Albania Must Choose Between the EU and Turkey', *Alon Ben-Meir online website*, <http://alonben-meir.com/writing/albania-must-choose-eu-turkey/>, accessed 3 May 2018.

Bianchi, Viviana (2018) 'Carlo Sforza and Diplomatic Europe1896-1922', unpublished PhD Thesis, Universita di Sapienza, (matricola 1143248).

Bieber, Florian (2000), 'Muslim identity in the Balkans before the establishment of nation states', *Nationalities Papers: The Journal of Nationalism and Ethnicity*, 28 (1), 13-28.

Baltsiotis, Lambros (2011), 'The Muslim Chams of Northwestern Greece: The grounds for exclusion of a "non-existent" minority', *European Journal of Turkish Studies*, 2. http://journals.openedition.org/ejts/4444, accessed 18 July 2020.

Binder, David (1988), 'Rivalry Aside, 6 Balkan Lands Meet and Agree', *The New York Times*, <http://www.nytimes.com/1988/03/06/world/rivalry-aside-6-balkan-lands-meet-and-agree.html>, accessed 14 April 2016.

--- (1991), 'U.S. Diplomats Prepare for Return to Albania', *The New York Times*, accessed 14 March 2012.

--- (1999), 'Greater albania?', *Washington Times*, <http://0-proquest.umi.com.alpha2.-latrobe.edu.au/pqdlink?did=39024982-&Fmt=3&clientId=20828&RQT=309&VName=PQD>, accessed 17 May 2012.

Birge, John K. (1937; reprint, 1994), *The Bektashi order of dervishes*. London: Luzac Oriental.

Blumi, Isa (2002), 'The role of education in the formation of Albanian identity and its myths', in Stephanie Schwandner-Sievers and Bernd Jurgen Fischer (eds.), *Albanian Identities: Myth and History*. Bloomington: Indiana University Press, 49-59.

Bogdani, Mirela and Loughlin, John (2007), *Albania and the European Union: The Tumultuous Journey Towards Integration and Accession*. London, New York: I.B. Tauris , Palgrave Macmillan.

Boston Globe (2017), 'Serbia set to get Russian fighter jets', <https://www.bostonglobe.-com/news/world/2017/02/12/serbia-set-get-russian-fighterjets/htPAH1KOI5IKO55R95k6cK/story.html>, accessed 12 March 2018.

Brown, James (September, 1995), 'The Turkish Imbroglio: Its Kurds', *The Annals of the American Academy of Political and Social Science: Small Wars*, 541, 116-29.

Bufli, Gjorgji (2013), 'Interlinguistic phenomena in Albanian Turkisms', *Rivista Internazionale di Tecnica della Traduzione* [*International Journal of Translation*],(15), 29-43.

Bulut, Mehmet and Idriz, Mesut (2012), *Turkish Albanian Macedonian Relations: Past, Present and Future*. Ankara: Adam-Actor.

Butler, Daren (2017), 'Recep Tayyip Erdogan threatens to say 'goodbye' to the EU unless they move Turkey's accession forward', *Independent*, <http://www.independent.co.uk/-/news/world/europe/receptayyip-erdogan-turkey-joining-eu-european-union-member-bloc-accession-talks-ankara-a7714691.html>, accessed 2 May 2018.

Bushi, Skënder (2016), 'Amforat e Antikitetit të Vonë në Shqipëri (shek. IV – VII m. Kr.)' [Amphorae of late antiquity in Albania (IV – VII AD)], author's translation, unpublished PhD thesis, *Qendra e Studimeve Albanologjike* [Center of Albanological Studies], Tiranë.

Bushi-Xhaferaj, Era (2016), 'Piktura murale në monumentet e kultit të krishterë në Shqipëri (shek. XII-XIV)' [Mural pictures of Christian cult monuments in Albania (XII – XIV AD)], author's translation, unpublished PhD thesis, *Qendra e Studimeve Albanologjike* [Center of Albanological Studies], Tiranë.

Byron, Janet (1976), *Selection among alternates in language standartization: The case of Albanian* (Netherlands: Mouton &Co).

Caliceti, Giuseppe (2010), *Italiani per esempio: L'Italia vista dai bambini immigrati* [*Italians for example: Italy seen by immigrant children*]. Milano, Bergamo: Feltrinelli Editore Milano.

Ceka, Neritan (2000), *Ilirët*, Tiranë: Shtëpia Botuese e Librit Universitar.

Clayer, Nathalie (2012), 'The Bektashi Institutions in Southeastern Europe: Alternative Muslim Official Structures and their Limits', *Die Welt des Islam*, (52), 183-203.

Cohen, Philip J. (2013), 'Ending the war and securing peace in former Yugoslavia', in Stjepan Mestrovic (ed.), *Genocide after emotion: The postemotional Balkan War*. New York: Routledge.

Cornell, Svante E. (2012), 'Erdogan's speech at Turkish electorate June 2011 in "Changes in Turkey: What Drives Turkish Foreign Policy?"', *Middle East Forum*, <https://www.-meforum.org/articles/2011/what-drives-turkish-foreign-policy>, accessed 12 May 2018.

--- (2011), 'Changes in Turkey: What Drives Turkish Foreign Policy?', *MIDDLE EAST QUARTERLY* Winter 2012, published in *Hürriyet* 13-24.

Crampton, R. J. (1997), *Eastern Europe in the Twentieth Century – And After*. 2nd edn.; London, New York: Routledge.

Crone, Patricia (2003), *Pre-industrial societies: Anatomy of the pre-modern world*. Oxford: One World Publications.

Daily News (2014), 'Turkey to build Balkans' largest mosque in Tirana', Hürriyet, http://www.hurriyetdailynews.com/turkey-to-build-balkans-largest-mosque-in-tirana-73512, accessed 23 March 2018.

Davutoğlu, Ahmet (2010), 'Turkey's Zero-Problems Foreign Policy', *Foreign Policy*. <http://foreignpolicy.com/2010/05/20/turkeys-zero-problems-foreign-policy/>, accessed 11 November 2015.

Deliso, Christopher (2007), *The Coming Balkan Caliphate: The Threat of Radical Islam to Europe and the West*. Westport, Connecticut and London: Praeger Security International.

Demetriou, Olga (2013), *Capricious Borders: Minority, Population, and Counter-Conduct Between Greece and Turkey*. United States: Berghahnbooks.

Denzin, Norman K. and Lincoln, Yvonna S. (2005), *Handbook of Qualitative Research*. Thousand Oaks, Calif: Sage Publications.

Department of State, *Papers Relating to the Foreign Relations of the United States, The Paris Peace Conference, 1919*, vol. IV, 111-116, <https://history.state.gov/historical-documents/frus1919Parisv04/pg_116>, accessed 25 October 2020.

Derjaj, Adriatik (2012), 'Mendimi i brendshëm dhe i jashtëm në gjuhë: Mbështetur në frazeologjizmat orientale' [Internal and external thoughts regarding language: Based on Oriental phraseologies], author's translation, Tirana University.

Deutsche Welle (2017), 'Kosovo fears for US ties under Trump', <http://www.dw.com/-en/kosovo-fears-for-us-ties-under-trump/a-37186938>, accessed 7 February 2017.

Deutsche Welle (2018), 'From ally to scapegoat: Fethullah Gulen, the man behind the myth', <https://www.dw.com/en/from-ally-to-scapegoat-fethullah-gulen-the-man-behind-the-myth/a-37055485>, accessed 16 September 2018.

BIBLIOGRAPHY

Dizdari, Tahir N. (2005), *Fjalor i orientalizmave në gjuhën Shqipe* [Dictionary of orientalism phrases in the Albanian language]. Tiranë: AIITC.

Doja, Albert (2006), 'A Political History of Bektashism in Albania', *Totalitarian Movements and Political Religions*, 7 (1), 83-107.

--- (2000), 'The Politics of Religion in the Reconstruction of Identities: The Albanian Situation', *Critique of Anthropology*, 20 (4), 421-38.

Duijzings, Ger (2000), *Religion and the Politics of Identity in Kosovo*. London: Hurst.

--- (2002), 'Religion and the politics of "Albanianism": Naim Frasheri's bektashi writings', in Stephanie Schwandner-Sievers and Bernd Jurgen Fischer (eds.), *Albanian Identities: Myth and History*. Bloomington: Indiana University Press, 60-9.

Durham, Mary Edith ([1909], 1985), *High Albania*, new edn.; Boston: Beacon.

--- (July/December 1919), 'Albania and Powers', *Contemporary Review*, (119).

Duka, Valentina (2007), *Histori e Shqipërisë 1912-2000* [Albanian History 1912-2000], author's translation. Tiranë: SHBLU.

Elsie, Robert (2010), *Historical Dictionary of Albania*, 2; Lanham, Toronto, Plymouth, UK: The Scarecrow Press, Inc.

--- '1945 Final Report of the German Wehrmacht in Albania', *Texts and documents of Albanian history*, <http://www.albanianhistory.net/1945_German-Wehrmacht/index.html>, accessed 15 October 2020.

Elshani, Milazim (2016), 'Shteti Shqiptar dhe Kosova 1920-1939' [Albanian State and Kosova 1920-1939]', author's translation, unpublished PhD Thesis, Tirana University.

Erickson, Edward J. (2004), 'Turkey as regional hegemon - 2014: strategic implications for the United States', *Turkish Studies*, 5 (3), 25-45.

Exit News (2019), 'After Erdoğan's Defeat, Turkish Consortium Withdraws from Vlora Airport Project', <https://exit.al/en/2019/04/22/

after-erdogans-defeat-turkish-consortium-withdraw-from-vlora-airport-project/>, accessed 22 August 2020.

Exit News (2020), 'MEPs Raise Concerns Over Turkish Influence in Albania', 24 June 2020, <https://exit.al/en/2020/06/24/meps-raise-concerns-over-turkish-influence-in-albania/>, accessed 29 June 2020.

European Commision: Directorate – General for Trade (2020), 'European Union, Trade in goods with Albania', <https://webgate.ec.europa.eu/-isdb_results/factsheets/country/details_albania_en.pdf>, accessed 4 September 2018.

Fischer, Bernd Jürgen (1984), *King Zog and the Struggle for Stability in Albania*. New York: Columbia University Press.

Foster, Peter (2016), 'Behind the murky world of Albanian blood feuds', *The Telegraph*, <http://www.telegraph.co.uk/news/2016/04/16/behind-the-murky-world-of-albanian-blood-feuds/>, accessed 16 November 2017.

Fox, Leonard (1989), *Kanuni i Lekë Dukagjinit [The Kanun of Lekë Dukagjini], Albanian text collected and arranged by Shtjefën Gjeçov*. New York: Gjonlekaj.

Frashëri, Kristo (2015), 'Identiteti i shqiptarëve dhe të metat e debatit Qose-Kadare' [Albanian identity and shortcomings of Qosja-Kadare debate], *Alba Soul*, author's translation, <http://www.albasoul.com/vjeter/modules.php?op=modload-&name=News&file=article&sid=1970>, accessed 25 October 2018.

Frashëri, Naim (1967), *Historia e Skënderbeut [The History of Skenderbeg]*. Tiranë: Instituti i Historisë dhe Gjuhësisë.

Frashëri, Sami (1999), *Shqipëria: ç'ka qenë, ç'është dhe ç'do të bëhetë? [Albania: what it was, what it is and what it will become]*, author's translation. Tirana: Mesonjetorja e pare.

Gall, Carlotta and Higgins, Andrew (2017), 'Turkey Signs Russian Missile Deal, Pivoting From NATO', *The New York Times*, <https://www.nytimes.com/-2017/09/12/world/europe/turkey-russia-missile-deal.html>, accessed 23 October 2017.

Garbuz, Mustafa (2014), *The long winter: Turkish politics after the corruption scandal*. Rethink Paper 15: Institute Washington DC.

Gazeta Dita (2020), '15 kushtet e BE, reporteri për Shqipërinë: Rama është më i ashpër me gazetarët se sa me trafikantët, kështu nuk hapen negociatat!' [15 conditions from EU, Albanian reporter: Rama is tougher with journalists than trafficants, thus no way to open negotiations], author's translation, <http://www.gazetadita.al/video-15-kushtet-e-be-reporteri-per-shqiperine-rama-eshte-me-i-ashper-me-gazetaret-se-sa-me-trafikantet-keshtu-nuk-hapen-negociatat/>

Gazeta Shqip (2013), 'Intelektualët, peticion kundër rishikimit të historisë nga autoritetet turke' [Scholars, petition against the review of history by Turkish authorities], author's translation, <http://gazeta-shqip.com/lajme/2013/03/27/intelektualet-peticion-kunder-rishikimit-te-historise-nga-autoritetet-turke/>, accessed 13 May 2018.

Gawrych, George W. (1983), 'Tolerant Dimensions of Cultural Pluralism in the Ottoman Empire: The Albanian Community, 1800-1912', *International Journal of Middle East Studies*, 15 (4), 519-36.

Gingeras, Ryan (2016), *Fall of the Sultanate: the Great War and the End of the Ottoman Empire, 1908-1922*. New York: Oxford University Press.

Gjoleka, Meri (2015), 'The Albanian language in the face of globalization Challanges: The issue of borrowings', *European Scientific Journal* 11 (25), 146-64.

Gorani, Dukagjin (2011), 'Orientalist Ethnonationalism: From Irredentism to Independentism Discourse analysis of the Albanian ethnonationalist narrative about the National Rebirth (1870-1930) and Kosovo Independence (1980-2000)'. School of Jurnalism, Cardiff University, unpublished PhD thesis.

Gow, James (2005), *Defending the West* (Cambridge: Polity).

Graf, Tobias P. (2017), *The Sultan's Renegades: Christian-European Converts to Islam and the Making of the Ottoman Elite, 1575-1610*. New York: Oxford University Press.

Guy, Nicola (2008), 'Ethnic nationalism, the Great powers and the question of Albanian independence, 1912-1921'. Durham University.

Hall, Derek (1994), *Albania and the Albanians*. London: Pinter Reference.

Hall, Richard C. (2000), *The Balkan Wars 1912–1913: Prelude to the First World War*. London & New York: Routledge.

Hamm, Harry (1963), *Albania-China's Beachhead in Europe*. New York: Frederick Praeger.

Heper, Metin (2004), 'Turkey "between East and West", Working Paper AY0405-16'. Institute of European Studies, University of California Berkeley.

Hodgkinson, Harry (2004, reprinted 2017), *Scanderbeg*, ed. Bejtullah Destani and Westrow Cooper. London and New York: I.B.Taurus in association with The Centre for Albanian Studies.

--- (1999), *Scanderbeg*, ed. Bejtullah D. Destani and Westrow Cooper. Centre for Albanian Studies.

Hoxha, Enver (1979), *Reflections on China*. 2; Toronto: Norman Bethune Institute.

--- (1980), *The Khrushchevites*. Tirana: 8 Nëntor.

--- (1982), *The Anglo-American Threat to Albania*. Tirana: 8 Nëntor.

--- (1983), *Vepra 19* [Volume 19], author's translation, Tiranë: Mihal Duri.

Hoxha Ibrahim D. (2000), *Viset kombëtare shqiptare në shtetin grek* [Albanian lands in Greece], author's translation, Tiranë: Dituria.

Huntington, Samuel P (1993), 'The clash of civilizations?', *Foreign Affairs*, 72 (3), 22-49.

Hürriyet Daily News (2016), 'Turkey's exports drop 14.4 pct in first month of 2016', <http://www.hurriyetdailynews.com/Default.aspx?pageID=238&nID=94596&NewsCatID=344>, accessed 5 February 2016.

Ibrahimi, Zekerija (2006), 'Bregovici dhe Tatlisesi' [The Bregovic and Tatlises], *Shekulli*, <http://www.shekulli.com.al/index.php?page=shownews&newsID=94100>, accessed 3 November 2010.

BIBLIOGRAPHY

İnalcik, Halil (1998), 'Turkey between Europe and Middle East', *Perceptions: Journal of International Affairs* 3(1).

(1915), 'Agreement between France, Russia, Great Britain and Italy, signed at London', *Internet archive*, https://archive.org/details/agreementbetween00franrich/page/6/mode/2up>, accessed 5 July 2020.

INSTAT - Albanian Republic, Statistics Institute (2016), 'Femra dhe Meshkuj në Shqipëri 2016' [Women and Men in Albania 2016].

Institute of Political Studies, Pamflet, 'Albanian State and Society 1944-1990', accessed 11 August 2020.

Jacques, Edwin E (2009), *The Albanians: An Ethnic History from Prehistoric Times to the Present*. 1; Jefferson, North Carolina and London: McFarland & Company, Inc.,.

Jarvis, Chris (1999), 'The Rise and Fall of the Pyramid Schemes in Albania', *International Monetary Fund*, <https://www.imf.org/external/pubs/ft/wp/1999/wp9998.pdf>, accessed 17 May 2018.

Jelavich, Barbara (1973), *The Ottoman Empire, the Great Powers, and the Straits Question: 1870-1887*. Bloomington and London: Indiana University Press.

Jelavich, Charles and Barbara (1977), 'The Establishment of the Balkan National States, 1804-1920', in Peter F. Sugar and Donald W. Treadgold (eds.), *A History of East Central Europe*. VIII; Seattle and London: University of Washington Press.

Jenkins, Richard (2008), *Rithinking Ethnicity: Arguments and explorations*, second edn.; London: SAGE Publications.

Jing, Ke (2013), 'The four others in I. Kadare's works: a study of the Albanian national identity', unpublished PhD thesis. ThinkIR: The University of Louisville's Institutional Repository, Electronic Theses and Dissertations.

Judah, Tim (2001), 'Greater albania?', *Survival: Global Politics and Strategy*, 43 (2), 7-18.

--- (2019), The clock ticks for Albania's "demographic dividend", published at Balkan Inside, <https://balkaninsight.com/2019/11/14/the-clock-ticks-for-albanias-demographic-dividend/>, accessed 4 July 2020.

Kadare, Ismail (2006), *Identiteti evropian i shqiptarëve* [*The European identity of the Albanians*], author's translation, Tirana: Onufri.

--- (2011), *Mosmarrëveshja: Mbi raportet e Shqipërisë me vetveten* [*Disagrement: On relations of Albania with itself*], author's translation, Tirana: Onufri.

--- (2013a), *Bisedë për brilantët në pasditen e dhjetorit* [*Conversation about brilliants on a December afternoon*]. Tirana: Onufri.

--- (2013b), 'Relacioni sekret' [Secret relation], *Bisedë për brilantet në pasditen e dhjetorit* [*Conversation for brilliants on a December afternoon*] author's translation, Tirana: Onufri.

--- (2013c), an interview with Ismail Kadare by the author, Mali i Robit, 29 August 2013.

Karalis, Vrasidas (2010), 'Greek Christianity after 1453', in Ken Parry (ed.), *The blackwell companion to Eastern Chritianity*. Malden and Oxford: Wiley-Blackwell.

Kaser, Karl (2012), 'Serfdom in Eastern Europe', in Karl Kaser (ed.), *Household and Family in the Balkans: Two decades of historical family research at the University of Graz*. Berlin: Lit Verlag.

Kilford, Chris (2016), 'Turkey's international reputation in free-fall', *Today's Zaman*, <http://mobile.todayszaman.com/op-ed_turkeys-international-reputation-in-free-fall_411147.html>, accessed 5 February 2016.

Koha Net (2013), Turqia interesohet për trajtimin e Perandorisë Osmane në Kosovë' [Turkey interested to protect the Ottoman Empire in Kosovo], <http://koha.net/?page=1,13,138186,>, accessed 13 March 2013.

Koha Jone (2017), 'Hiqet flamuri turk në Prizren. Reagon Ministria e Jashtme e Kosovës' [Turkish flag removed in Prizren. Reacts Kosovar foreign Affairs Ministry], author's translation, <http://www.

BIBLIOGRAPHY

kohajone.com/2017/02/17/hiqet-flamuri-turk-ne-prizren-reagon-ministria-e-jashtme-e-kosoves/>, accessed 12 May 2018.

Kola, Paulin (2003), *The Search for Greater Albania*. London: C.Hurst & Co. Ltd.

Krauthamer, Ky, 'In Albania, Madrasas Even the Secular Love', *Transitions Online: Regional Intelligence*, <http://www.tol.org/client/article/23425-albania-islam-turkey-education.html>, accessed 20 February 2015.

Kressing, Frank (2002), 'A Preliminary Account of Research Regarding the Albanian Bektashis: Myths and Unresolved Questions', in F. Kressing and K. Kaser (eds.), *Albania, A Country in Transition: Aspects of Changing Identities in a South-East European Country* (Baden-Baden: Nomos), 65-91.

Kucukgocmen, Ali (2018), 'Erdogan's AKP says to ally with nationalists for 2019 elections', *Reuters*, <https://www.reuters.com/article/us-turkey-election-regulation/erdogans-akp-says-to-ally-with-nationalists-for-2019-elections-idUSKCN1G52DP>, accessed 6 October 2018.

Lafe, Emil (1999), *Persizmat në kuadrin e orientalizmave të Fjalorit të gjuhës së sotme shqipe* [Persian within Oriental components in the current Albanian distionary] author's translation, Perla.

Lami, Blendi (2017), 'Geo-culture as a Turkish foreign policy tool for influence in Albania', *International Journal of Academic Research and Reflection*, 5 (1).

Lajmi.Net (2015), "Rikthehet polemika mes Qosjës dhe Kadaresë" [Polemics between Qosja and Kadare return], author's translation, <https://lajmi.net/rikthehet-polemika-mes-qosjes-dhe-kadarese/>, accessed 22 August 2020.

Lapsi lajme (2015), 'Zaman: "Kërkesa e Erdogan për të mbyllur shkollat turke inatos politikanët shqiptarë"' [Zaman: "Erdogan's request to close Turkish schools upset Albanian politicians], author's translation, <http://www.lapsi.al/lajme/2015/05/14/zaman-%E2%80%9Ck%C3%ABrkesa-e-erdogan-p%C3%ABr-

t%C3%AB-mbyllur-shkollat-turke-inatos-politikan%C3%ABt-shqiptar%C3%AB>, accessed 17 November 2015.

Licursi, Emiddio Pietro (2011), 'Empire of Nations: The Consolidation of Albanian and Turkish National Identities in the Late Ottoman Empire, 1878 – 1913', unpublished thesis. Department of History, Columbia University.

Limaj, Hajro M. (2012), *Midis Ankarasë dhe Tiranës: 1990-2000. Nga ditari i një atasheu ushtarak* [*Between Ankara and Tirana: 1990-2000. From the diary of a military attaché*], author's translation, Tirana: Emal.

Logoreci, Anton (1977), *The Albanians : Europe's forgotten survivors*. London: Gollancz 230 p., [4] leaves of plates.

Marcovic-Khaze, Nina and Xhaferi, Perparim (2020), "Trump's gambit in the Balkans", *Lowy Institute*, <https://www.lowyinstitute.org/the-interpreter/trump-s-gambit-balkans>, accessed 15 October 2020.

Malcolm, Noel (1999), *Kosovo: A Short History* (London: Harper Perennial/HarperCollins).

--- (2002), 'Myths of Albanian National Identity', in Stephanie Schwandner-Sievers and Bernd J Fischer (Eds.), *Albanian Identities: Myth and History*. Bloomington: Indiana University Press.

Mango, Andrew (2004), *The Turks Today*. Great Britain: John Murray.

Mapo (2013), 'Turqit "pushtimi i dytë" i Shqipërisë nga biznesi' [Turks "the second invasion" of Albania from the business], author's translation, <http://www.mapo.al/-2013/02/turqit-pushtimi-i-dyte-i-shqiperise-nga-biznesi>, accessed 11 November 2015.

Mapo (2018), "Tri esetë në anglisht: 'Bota' e Kadaresë , 'drama e pamundur' e Shqipërisë" [Three essays in English: Kadare's 'world, Albania's 'impossible drama'], author's translation, <http://www.mapo.al/tri-esete-ne-anglisht-bota-e-kadarese-drama-e-pamundur-e-shqiperise/>, accessed 29 August 2018.

Mascitelli, Bruno and De Lazzari, Chiara (2016), 'Interculturalism, multiculturalism and Italianess: the case of Italy', *Australia and New Zealand Journal of European Studies*, 8 (2), 49-63.

McLaughlin, Daniel (2017), 'Russia accuses West of pushing pro-Albanian agenda in Macedonia', *Irish Times*, <https://www.irishtimes.com/news/world/us/russia-accuses-west-of-pushing-pro-albanian-agenda-in-macedonia-1.2995811>, accessed 15 April 2017.

McNabb, David E. (2015), *Research approaches for political science: Quantitative and qualitative approaches*. 2 edn.; London and New York: Routledge.

Mehmeti, Leandrit I. (2017), 'Kosovar Identity: Challenging Albanian National Identity', *Australia and New Zealand Journal of European Studies,* 9 (1), 16-25.

Mejdini, Fatjona (2017), 'Turqia mbetet në krye të destinacioneve të preferuara të shqiptarëve për pushime' [Turkey remains the favourite top turistic destination for Albanians], author's translation, <https://www.reporter.al/turqia-mbetet-ne-krye-te-destinacioneve-te-preferuara-te-shqiptareve-per-pushime/>, accessed 27 August 2018.

--- (2014), 'Shqipëria refuzon Organizatën Islamike, jo pjesë e aktivitetit në Teheran' [Albania Refuses the Islamic Organisation, no part of its activity in Teheran], author's translation, *Shqip*, <http://gazeta-shqip.com/lajme/2014/02/17/shqiperia-refuzon-organizaten-islamike-jo-pjese-e-aktivitetit-ne-teheran/>, accessed 14 February 2015.

Mesi, Herion (2014), 'Turqia, marrëveshje të fshehtë me Shqipërinë për modernizimin e FA-ve' [Secret agreement between Turkey and Albania to modernise military forces], author's translation, *Gazeta Shqip*, <http://gazeta-shqip.com/lajme/2014/02/17/turqia-marreveshje-te-fshehte-shqiperine-per-modernizimin-e-fa-ve/>, accessed 10 May 2018.

Misha, Glenny (1999), *The Ballkans 1804-1999: Nationalism, War, and the Great Powers*. London: Granta Books.

Mlloja, Genc (2015), 'Relations between Turkey and Albania are at an excellent level. An interview with the Turkish Ambassador to Albania, Hidayet Bayraktar', *Albanian Daily News*, http://www.albanian-news.com/index.php?idm=3244&mod=2, accessed 12 May 2018.

Moisiu, Alfred (2005), 'Toleranca ndërfetare në traditën e popullit shqiptar' [The tolerance of Albanian Inter-religious tradition], author's translation, lecture at Oxford Forum, *Koha Jonë*, <http://www.kohajone.com/lexo.php?id=42679>, accessed 11 November 2011.

Morgan, Peter (2018), 'The Three Worlds of Ismail Kadare'. Unpublished manuscript authorised by the author.

--- (2010), *Ismail Kadare: The Writer and the Dictatorship 1957-1990*. Oxon and NY: Modern Humanities Research Association and Routledge.

--- (2011), *Shkrimtari dhe Diktatura:1957-1990* [*The Writer and the Dictatorship:1957-1990*], author's translation, Tirane: Maney Publishing & Modern Humanities Research Association: Shtepia Botuese 55.

--- (2015), '"Strange commerce of memory and forgetting': Albania, Kosovo and Europe in Ismail Kadare's File on H...". Manuscript, authorised by the author.

Murati, Violeta (2013), '100 intelektualë dhe Kadare kundër: Jo politikë turke në historinë tonë!' [100 intelectuals and Kadare against: No Turkish politics in our history!], author's translation, *Standard*,<http://www.standard.al/2013/03/28/100-intelektuale-dhe-kadare-kunder-jo-politike-turke-ne-historine-tone/>, accessed 10 May 2018.

Myrdal, Jane and Gun Kessle (1976), *Albania Defiant*, translated by Paul Britten Austin, United States of America: Monthly Review Press.

Nano, Fatos (2002), 'Nuk u Globalizua Terrorizmi, por Lufta kunder tij' [No globalisation of terrorism, but the war against it], author's translation, *Shekulli Online*, <http://www.shekulli-.com.al/shekulli/?s=Nano%3A+Nuk+u+Globalizua+Terrorizmi%2C+por+Lufta+kunder+tij>, accessed 11 September 2011.

Nano, Mustafa (2017), 'Skënderbeu ka qenë më shumë i krishterë se shqiptar, nënën e kishte sllave' [Skenderbeg was more Christian than Albanian and his mother was Sllav], author's translation, *Telegrafi*.

com, <http://telegrafi.com/skenderbeu-ka-qene-shume-krishtere-se-shqiptar-nenen-e-kishte-sllave/>, accessed 18 July 2017.

--- (2006), 'Kultura Perëndimore dhe Qytetërimi Lindor i Shqiptarëve' [The Western Culture and Albania's Oriental Civilization], author's translation, *Shqip*, <http://albanur.eu/show-thread.php?t=282>, accessed 17 July 2015.

Norris, Harry Thirwall (1993), *Islam in the Balkans: Religion and Society between Europe and the Arab World*. London: Hurst & Company.

--- (2006), *Popular Sufism in Eastern Europe: Sufi brotherhoods and the dialogue with Christianity and 'Heterodoxy'*. New York and Canada: Routledge.

Norton, John (2001), 'The Bektashi in the Balkans', in C. Hawkesworth, M. Heppell, and H.T. Norris (eds.), *Religious Quest and National Identity in the Balkans*. New York: Palgrave, 168-200.

O'Donnell, James (1995), 'Albania's Sigurimi: The Ultimate Agents of Social Control', *Problems of Post-Communism*, 42 (6).

Ora News (2018), 'Ambasadori turk: Nga historia e kaluar mes Shqipërisë dhe Turqisë të marrim më të mirën' [The Turkish Ambassador: Let's extract the best from the history between Albania and Turkey], author's translation, <https://www.youtube.com/watch?v=-lQ_yRU4qN5Q>, accessed 17 March 2018.

Özel, Soli (2007), 'Turkey Faces West', *The Wilson Quarterly*, 31 (1), 18-25.

Pajaziti, Ali (2011), 'Turk and Turkey perception at Albanians in the beginning of 21st century', *Past, Present and Future of Turkish-Albanian-Macedonian Relations*, International Symposium, Skopje, Macedonia-Prishtinë, Kosovo. Ankara Center For Thought And Research and International Balkan University.

Parllaku, Azem (2016), 'Shqipëria "rreshqitje e butë" poshtë sqetullës së Turqisë' [Albania "soft slide" under the thumb of Turkey], author's translation, *Focus News*, <http://fjalajone.-com/shqiperia-rreshqitje-e-bute-poshte-sqetulles-se-turqise/>, accessed 10 May 2018.

Pano, Nicholas C (1997), 'The Process of Democratisation in Albania', in K Dawisha and B Parrot (ed.), *Politics, Power, and the Struggle for Democracy in South-East Europe*. Cambridge: Cambridge University Press, 285-352.

Panorama on line. (2017), 'Vlora 20 vjet me parë: Si e priti Zani Caushi me armë Prodin' [Vlora 20 years ago: How armed Zani Caushi received Prodi], author's translation, <http://www.panorama.com.al/fotolajm-vlora-20-vjet-me-pare-si-e-priti-zani-caushi-me-arme-prodin/>, accessed 23 February 2017.

Panorama online. (2017a), 'Putin dhe Erdogan armiq të betuar? Marrëveshja e madhe e bashkëpunimit' [Putin and Erdogan sworn enemies? The big friendship agreement], author's translation, <http://www.panorama.com.al/putin-dhe-erdogan-armiq-te-betuar-marreveshja-e-madhe-e-bashkepunimit/>, accessed 12 May 2018.

Panorama on line (2017b), "'S'paskemi qenë të pushtuar, por dashnorë", përgjigjja e gazetares shqiptare për Erdogan'" [You were not oppressors, but rather we were lovers, the answer of the Albanian media for Erdogan], author's translation, <http://www.panorama.com.al/spaskemi-qene-te-pushtuar-por-dashnore-pergjigjja-e-gazetares-shqiptare-per-erdogan/>, accessed 10 March 2018.

Panorama on line (2017c), 'Tensionet/Erdogan kërcënon sërish, tregon se çfarë e pret Europën' [Tensions/Erdogan threatens again, explaining what will happen to Europe], author's translation, <http://www.panorama.com.al/tensionet-erdogan-kercenon-serish-tregon-se-cfare-e-pret-evropen/>, accessed 24 October 2017.

Panorama on line (2011), 'Veqilharxhi, babai i Alfabetit dhe Abetares Shqiptare' [Veqilharxhi, the father of the Albanian alphabet and the Abetare], author's translation, <http://www.panorama.com.al/veqilharxhi-babai-i-alfabetit-dhe-abetares-shqiptare/>, accessed 10 May 2018.

Panorama on line (2018), David Phillips interviewed by The Voice of America, 'Eksperti amerikan: Rama të mos kërcejë nëpër dasmat e Ankarasë, lidhja me Erdogan nuk i shërben Shqipërisë' [The American expert: Rama should not dance in Ancara's weedings, Albania does not benefit from the relationship with Erdogan], author's translation, <http://www.-panorama.com.al/eksperti-amerikan-rama-te-mos-kerceje-neper-dasmat-e-ankarase-lidhja-me-erdogan-nuk-i-sherben-shqiperise/>, accessed 30 April 2018.

Patton, Michael Quinn (1985), *Quality in qualitative research: Methodological principles and recent developments*. Chicago: Invited address to Division J of the American Educational Research Association.

Payton, Jr James R. (2006), 'Ottoman Millet, Religious Nationalism, and Civil Society: Focus on Kosovo', *Religion in Eastern Europe*, XXVI (1), 11-23.

Pearson, Owen (2004), *Albania and King Zog: Independence, Republic and Monarchy, 1908-1939*, III vols. Albania in the Twentieth Century: A History, I; London: The Centre for Albanian Studies in Association with I. B. Tauris.

--- (2005), *Albania in Occupation and War: From Fascism to Communism, 1940-1945*, III vols. Albania in the Twentieth Century: A History, II; London: The Centre for Albanian Studies in Association with I. B. Tauris.

--- (2006), *Albania as Dictatorship and Democracy, From Isolation to Kosovo War 1946-1998*, III vols. Albania in the Twentieth Century: A History, III; London: The Centre for Albanian Studies in Association with I. B. Tauris.

Petrović, Žarko and Reljić, Dušan (2011), 'Turkish Interests and Involvement in the Western Balkans: A Score-Card', *Insight Turkey* 13 (3), 159-72.

Pettifer, James (2001), 'Greater Albania', *The World Today*, 57 (7), 18-20.

Plasari, Aurel (2012), 'An interview with Aurel Plasari, "Debati për identitetin? Kadare ka nonsens, Qosja ngatërron Stambollin me Jeruzalemin"' [Arguing about identity? Kadare has no-sense, Qose is mixing up Istanbul with Jerusalem], author's translation, *Shekulli*, <http://shekulli.com.al/web/p.php?id=2847&kat=104>, accessed 26 August 2012.

Psilos, Christophoros (2006), 'Albanian Nationalism and Unionist Ottomanization 1908 to 1912', *Mediterranean Quarterly*, 17 (3), 26-42.

Qosja, Rexhep (2006), 'Idetë raciste të Ismail Kadaresë' [The racist ideas of Ismail Kadare], author's translation, *Shqip*, accessed 12 August 2011.

--- (2006), Page created by AlbaNur for Dr. Rexhep Qosja, 'Premisa të gabuara' [Wrong premises], *Takimi i Madh* [*The Great Meeting*], author's translation, <http://www.-macedonianguide.com/rexhep_qosja/rexhep_qosja.html>, accessed 5 May 2015.

Rabasa, Angel and Larrabee, F. Stephen (2008), *The Rise of Political Islam in Turkey*. Santa Monica, Arlington, Pittsburg: Rand Corporation.

Reed, Stanley and Arsu, Sebnem (2015), 'Russia Presses Ahead With Plan for Gas Pipeline to Turkey', *The New York Times*, https://www.nytimes.com/2015/01/22/business-/inter-national/russia-presses-ahead-with-plan-for-gas-pipeline-to-turkey.html, accessed 11 May 2018.

Rexha, Blerina (2015), 'Greater Albania – The next step for Kosovo?', The University of Sydney.

--- (2017), 'The Influence of Pan-Slavic Ideologies on Kosovar Schooltexts: Implications for Diplomatic Relations with Turkey', *Australia and New Zeland Journal of European Studies*, 9 (1), 26-42.

Reuters (2018), 'Turkish opposition parties say election alliance no longer necessary', <https://www.reuters.com/article/us-turkey-politics-opposition/turkish-opposition-parties-say-election-alliance-no-longer-necessary-idUSKBN1JU1X4>, accessed 5 October 2018.

Rredhi, Gëzim 'Epika historike kushtuar Lidhjes Shqiptare të Prizrenit' [Historical Epics dedicated to The Albanian Prizren League], author's translation, in Aktet (ed.). II; Gjirokaster: Universiteti 'Eqerem Çabej', 133-38.

Rrozhani, Arben (2011), 'Qeveria e Shqiperise ka firmosur per ndryshimin e historise : Osmanet jo pushtues por "administratore miqesore"' [Albanian government signed for changing the history:

Ottomans not as invaders, but "friendly administrators"], author's translation, *24 Ore*, <http://24-ore.com/index.php/kronika/7464-qeveria-e-shqiperise-ka-firmosur-per-ndryshimin-e-historise-osmanet-jo-pushtues-por-administratore-miqesore.html>, accessed 6 October 2011.

Rustow, Dankwart (1987), *Turkey: America's Forgotten Ally*. New York: Council for Foreign Relations.

Said, Edward W (1995), *Orientalism: Western Conceptions of the Orient*. New York & London: Penguin Books.

--- (1985), 'Orientalism Reconsidered', *Cultural Critique*, (1), 89-107.

Sayari, Sabri (2000), 'Turkish foreign policy in the post-Cold War era: The challenges of multi-regionalism', *Journal of International Affairs*, 54 (1), 169-82.

Schoon, Eric W. (2015), 'The Paradox of Legitimacy: Resilience, Successes, and the Multiple Identities of the Kurdistan Worker's Party in Turkey', *Social Problems Advance Access*, 1-20.

Schwandner-Sievers, Stephanie (2008), 'Albanians, Albanianism and the strategic subversion of stereotypes', *Slovene Anthropological Society*, 14 (2), 47-64.

Security Council Report: Special Research Report, (2008), 'Cyprus: New hope after 45 years on the Security Council agenda', (3), 1-24.

Seton-Watson, Hugh (2019), *The East European Revolution*. New York: Routledge.

Shala, Azdren (2018), 'Pushtimi i ri Turk [Turkish neo-invasion]', author's translation, *Gazeta Tema*. <http://www.gazetatema.net/2018/02/15/pushtimi-i-ri-turk/>, accessed 12 May 2018.

Shehu, Fatmir (2011), 'The Influence of Islam on Albanian Culture', *Journal of Islam In Asia*, Special Issue, 1, 389-407.

Shekulli Online (2006), 'Topalli mbështet Kadarenë: Kemi Identitet Evropian' [Topalli's support for Kadare: We have European Identity], author's translation, <http://www.shekulli.-com.al/shekulli/?s=%E2%80%98Topalli+mbeshtet+Kadarene%3A+Kemi+Identitet+Evropian%E2%80%99>, accessed 11 January 2011.

Shkurtaj, Gjovalin (2009), *Pesha e fjalës shqipe* [*The wieght of the Albanian word*], author's translation, Tiranë: Shtëpia Botuese Ufo Press.

Skendi, Stavro (1957), *Albania*. London: Atlantic Press for the Mid-European Studies Center of the Free Europe Committee.

--- (1967), *The Albanian National Awakening, 1878-1912*. Princetown, New Jersey: Princeton University Press.

Smith, Anthony D. (1993), 'A Europe of Nations. Or the Nation of Europe?', *Journal of Peace Research*, 30 (2), 129-35.

Squires, Nick (2014), 'Pope Francis hails Albania as model of religious harmony in attack on religious extremism', *The Telegraph*, <http://www.telegraph.co.uk/news/-worldnews/europe/albania/11111600/Pope-Francis-says-Albania-is-a-model-of-religious-harmony-during-first-visit-to-Muslim-majority-nation.html>, accessed 16 February 2015.

Stafa, Florenc (2014), 'Turqi, çdo universitet do të ketë xhami' [Turkey, every university will have a mosque], author's translation, *Shekulli*, http://www.shekulli.com.al/p.php?id=60939-, accessed 21 February 2015.

Stavrianos, Leften Stavros ([1965] 2000), *The Balkans since 1453*. New York: New York University Press.

Steed, H Wickham (1927), 'Italy, Yugoslavia and Albania', *Journal of the Royal Institute of International Affairs*, 6 (3), 172-3.

Stenning, Alison (2005), 'Out there and in here: studying Eastern Europe in the West', *Royal Geographical Society*, 37 (4), 378-83.

Stocker, Sharon R. and Davis, Jack L. (2006), 'The earliest history of Apolonia: Heroic reflections from beyond the acropolis', in Lorenc Bejko and Richard Hodges (eds.), *New Directions in Albanian Archaeology*. Tirana: International Centre for Albanian Archeology.

Sugar, Peter F. (1977), *Southeastern Europe under Ottoman Rule, 1354-1804*. Seattle: University of Washington Press.

Sullivan, Kevin (2013), 'Those Nasty Stereotypes', *BalkanInsight*, <http://www.-balkaninsight.com/en/blog/those-nasty-stereotypes>, accessed 12 December 2014.

Sulstarova, Enis (2010), *Në pasqyrën e Oksidentit: Studime dhe artikuj* [In the mirror of Occident: Studies and articles], author's translation, Skopje: Logos-A.

Tanner, Marcus (2015), 'The Ghost of Greater Albania Won't go Away', *BalkanInsight*. <http://www.balkaninsight.com/en/article/the-ghost-of-greater-albania-won-t-go-away>, accessed 14 July 2015.

Tase, Peter (2014a), 'Albania And Turkey: Two Nations With Common Vision To Strengthen Bilateral Cooperation, 1990-2000', *Foreign Policy News*, < http://foreign-policynews.org/2014/01/25/albania-turkey-two-nations-common-vision-strengthen-bilateral-cooperation-1990-2000/>, accessed 14 April 2016.

--- (2014b), 'Turkey and Albania establish a dynamic agenda of bilateral relations', *Foreign Policy News*, < http://foreignpolicynews.org/2014/05/02/turkey-albania-establish-dynamic-agenda-bilateral-relations/>, accessed 12 January 2016.

Taspinar, Ömer (2008), 'Turkey's Middle East Policies: Between Neo-Ottomanism and Kemalism', *Carnegie Endowment for International Peace.*, 10.

Tekdal, Arif (2015), 'Erdoğan's harsh, xenophobic rhetoric damages fight against Islamophobia', *Sunday's Zaman*, <http://www.todayszaman.com/national_erdogans-harsh-xenophobic-rhetoric-damages-fight-against-islamophobia_369946.html>, accessed 15 February 2015.

Telegrafi (2015), 'Ambasadori i Shqipërisë në Turqi: Feja e shqiptarit është shqiptaria, në Turqi janë pesë milionë shqiptarë' [The Albanian Ambassador in Turkey: The Albanian religion is Albanianism, in Turkey live five million Albanians], author's translation, <http://m.telegrafi.com/lajme/ambasadori-i-shqiperise-ne-turqi-feja-e-shqiptarit-eshte-shqiptaria-ne-turqi-jane-pese-milione-shqiptare-2-67961.html>, accessed 17 November 2015.

Tema on line (2018), 'Punonjësit e huaj në Shqipëri, Turqit mbajnë vendin e parë, kinezët të dytin' [Foreign workers in Albania, Turks in the first place, Chinese second], author's translation, <http://www.

gazetatema.net/2018/09/01/punonjesit-e-huaj-ne-shqiperi-turqit-mbajne-vendin-e-pare-kinezet-te-dytin/>, accessed 2 September 2018.

Tretiak, Daniel (1962), 'The Founding of the Sino-Albanian Entente', *The China Quarterly*, 10, 123-43.

'The Treaty of London 1913' (2011), <http://www.mtholyoke.edu/acad/intrel/-boshtml/bos145.htm>, accessed 26 May 2014.

The Economist (2016), 'Turkey's religious diplomacy. Mosqued objectives. Turkey is sponsoring Islam abroad to extend its prestige and power', <https://www.economist.-com/news/europe/21688926-turkey-sponsoring-islam-abroad-extend-its-prestige-and-power-mosqued-objectives>, accessed 3 May 2018.

Thomai, Jani (2002), *Leksikologjia e gjuhës shqipe* [*The Lexicology of the Albanian Language*]. Tiranë: Toena.

Todorova, Maria (2009), *Imagining the Balkans*. New York: Oxford University Press.

Top Channel (2012a), 'Berisha: US role in Israel-Palestine, decisive', <http://top-channel.tv/english/artikull.php?id=7722>, accessed 15 February 2015.

Top Channel (2012b), 'Basha: Vota kundër SHBA, gabim. Shqipëria abstenoi në 2012' [Vote against the US, wrong. Albania abstained in 2012], author's translation, <http://top-channel.tv/2017/12/22/basha-vota-kunder-shba-gabim-shqiperia-abstenoi-ne-2012/>, accessed 12 May 2018.

Top Channel (2016a), 'Historiani turk fyen Skënderbeun, reagime të forta kundër tij' [Turkish Historian offends Skenderbeg, strong reactions against him], author's translation, <http://m.top-channel.tv/lajme/artikull.php?id=330492&homepage>, accessed 8 July 2016.

Top Channel (2016b), Shkodër, dëmtohet memoriali i Riza Pashës. Hiqet flamuri turk' [Shkodër, damage of the Riza Pasha memorial. Turkish flag disapeared], author's translation, <http://m.top-channel.tv/lajme/artikull.php?id=330659&homepage>, accessed 11 May 2018.

BIBLIOGRAPHY

Top Channel (2017), Pelegrinazhi në Malin e Tomorrit, Meta mes besimtarëve bektashinj' [Pilgrimage at Tomorri mountain, Meta between Bektashi belivers], author's translation, <http://top-channel.tv/lajme/artikull.php?id=362072>, accessed 20 September 2018.

Top Channel. (2017a), Erdogan: "I wish Edi Rama good luck with his projects"', http://top-channel.tv/english/erdogan-i-wish-edi-rama-good-luck-with-his-projects/, accessed 3 May 2018.

Top Channel. (2017b), 'Erdogan: Turqia bën edhe pa BE-në' [Erdogan: Turkey can do without EU], author's translation, <http://m.top-channel.tv/lajme/-artikull.php?id=359400&homepage>, accessed 2 May 2018.

Top Channel (2017c), 'Daçiç argëton Erdoganin me këngën e Osman Agës' [Dacic entertains Erdogan with the song of Osman aga], author's translation, <http://top-channel.tv/2017/-10/11/dacic-argeton-erdoganin-me-kengen-e-osman-ages-video/>, accessed 23 October 2017.

Top Channel (2017d), 'Drejtori i Tokave: Problemin zgjidheni me Kanun' [Land's director: You must resolve the issue with kanun], author's translation, <http://m.top-channel.tv/lajme/artikull.php?id=350023&kryesore>, accessed 15 March 2017.

Topi, Bamir (2008), 'Albania's Domestic and Foreign Policy 2008 Agenda', *AIIS*. <http://www.aiis-albania.org/>, accessed 23 February 2011.

Türbedar, Erhan (2011), 'Turkey's New Activism in the Western Balkans: Ambitions and Obstacles', *Insight Turkey* 13 (3), 139-58.

Uras, Umut (2016), 'Turkey: Coup plotters 'acted early' in fear of arrests', *Aljazeera*. <https://www.aljazeera.com/news/2016/07/turkish-putschists-acted-early-fear-arrests-160718131344577.html>, accessed 28 July 2020.

Vasa, Pashko (2005), 'Oh Albania, poor Albania', in R. Elsie trans first published in English (ed.), *Albanian Literature: a Short History*. New York: I.B. Tauris.

Vickers, Miranda ([1995] 2001), *The Albanians: A Modern History*. London: I.B. Taurus.

Vickers, Miranda and Pettifer, James (1997), *Albania: From Anarchy to a Balkan Identity*. New York: New York University Press.

Vickers, Miranda (1998), *Between Serb and Albanian: A History of Kosovo*. London: Hurst & Company.

Vryonis, Jr Speros (1969-1970), 'The Byzantine Legacy and Ottoman Forms', *Dumbarton Oaks Papers*, 23 (24), 251-308.

Vullnetari, Julie (2007), 'Albanian Migration and Development: State of the Art Review', *IMISCOE Working Paper 18*. Amsterdam: Institute for Migration and Ethnic Studies (IMES).

Vullnetari, Julie and King, Russell (2016), 'From Shortage Economy to Second Economy: An Historical Ethnography of Rural Life in Communist Albania', *Journal of Rural Studies*, 44, 198-207.

Wagner, Alina (2016), *Musine Kokalari and Social Democracy in Albania*. Tirana: Friedrich Ebert Foundation.

Wasti, Syed Tanvir (2016), 'Three Ottoman Pashas at the Congress of Berlin,1878', *Middle Eastern Studies* 52 (6), 938-52.

Weiker, Walter F. (1968), 'The Ottoman Bureaucracy: Modernization and Reform', *Administrative Science Quarterly*, 13 (3), 451-70.

Winnifrith, Tom (1992), *Perspectives on Albania*. New York: St.Martin's Press, Inc.

World Bulletin (2013), 'PM Erdogan: Turkey is Kosovo and Kosovo is Turkey', <http://www.worldbulletin.net/haber/121375/pm-erdogan-turkey-is-kosovo-and-kosovo-is-turkey>, accessed 24 August 2018.

Woodard, Rodger (2008), 'Language in ancient Europe: an introduction', in Rodger Woodard (ed.), *The Ancient Languages of Europe*. New York: Cambridge University Press, 7-8.

Wright, Sue (2000), *Community and Communication: The role of language in nation state building and European integration*, ed. John Edwards. Multilingual Matters LTD; Clevedon, Buffalo, Toronto and Sydney: Library of Congress Cataloging in Publication Data.

Xhaferi, Perparim (2017a), 'The Political Contribution of Albanian Writers in Defining Albanian Identity: the Debate between Ismail Kadare and Rexhep Qosja', *European Journal of Language and Literature*, 7 (1), 121-28.

--- (2017b), 'The Post-Ottoman Era: A Fresh Start for Bilateral Relations between Albania and Turkey?', *Australia and New Zealand Journal of European Studies*, 9 (1), 42-62.

Yapp, Malcolm Edward and Shaw, Stanford Jay (2018), 'Ottoman Empire: Historical Empire, Eurasia and Africa', *Encyclopaedia Britannica*. <https://www.britannica.com/place/Ottoman-Empire>, accessed 27 July 2018.

Yavuz, M. Hakan (1998), 'Turkish identity and foreign policy in flux: The rise of Neo-Ottomanism', *Critique: Critical Middle Eastern Studies*, 7 (12), 19-41.

--- (2020), *Nostalgia for the Empire: The Politics of Neo-Ottomanism*. New York: Oxford University Press.

Young, Antonia (1999), 'Religion and society in present-day Albania', *Journal of Contemporary Religion*, 14 (1), 5-16.

Yzeiri, Ilir (2015), 'Identiteti ynë në rrezik' [Our identity is in danger], author's translation, *Top Channel*, <http://top-channel.tv/mobile/artikull.php?id=313199>, accessed 29 November 2015.

--- (2013), 'Albanofobia e Berishës dhe islamofobia e Erdoganit' [Berisha's Albanophobia and Ergogan's lsamophobia], author's translation, *Gazeta Shqip*, <http://gazeta-shqip.com/-lajme/2013/02/28/albanofobia-e-berishes-dhe-islamofobia-e-erdoganit/>, accessed 12 May 2018.

Zhiti, Visar, 'Kadare dhe Qose së bashku krijojnë identitetin tonë' [Kadare and Qose together create our identity], author's translation, *Albanur*, <http://albanur.eu/showthread.php?t=277>, accessed 23 February 2011.

Zickel, Raymond E. and Iwaskiw, Walter R. (eds.) (1994), *Albania: A Country Study*. 2 edn., Washington, D. C.: Library of congress.

Appendix

The Albanian delegation statement at The Paris Peace Conference, 1919.

THE COUNCIL OF TEN

Secretary-General not later than Saturday, March 8th. This will not apply to Commissions set up after February 15th which may be unable to render their final reports at so early a date, but it is requested that in these cases interim reports may be presented dealing with all matters affecting the preliminaries of peace with Turkey.

PARIS, 22nd February, 1919.

Addendum

ALBANIAN CLAIMS

Statement by Touran Pasha

Refer to Page 8,[4] BC-38, Report for February 24, 1919

The Albanians base all their hopes on the justice of this High Assembly, on whom they rely utterly. They trust that the principle of nationality so clearly and solemnly proclaimed by President Wilson and his great Associates will not have been proclaimed in vain, and that their rights—which have, up to now, been trampled underfoot—will be respected by the Congress whose noble mission it is to dower humanity with a peace which, to be durable, must be based on right and justice.

It was the Congress of Berlin which first of all denied the rights of the Albanian nation. The reasons therefor are explained by the fact that Albania, unlike other Balkan nations, has never had any protectors, and also by Albania's very advantageous geographical position, which has from time immemorial excited the cupidity of her neighbours.

The Treaty of Berlin[5] deprived Albania of the territories of Antivari, Hoti, Grouda, Triopchi, Kichi, Podgoritza, Plava and Goussigne, to the benefit of Montenegro; and of a part of Southern Albania (Epirus) between the Gulf of Proveza and the Kalamas River, to the benefit of Greece. This flagrant injustice led the Albanians to form the Prizrend Patriotic League, which opposed the handing over of the territories of Plava, Goussigne, Hoti, and Grouda by force of arms. The Great Powers thereupon gave Montenegro the port of Dulcigne in compensation for those territories, which the Albanians retained. This compensation was carried out by means of a naval demonstration, well known under the name of "Dulcigne Naval Demonstration".

In the south, the Prizrend League made the same energetic resistance. The International Commission which came to Preveza to

---

[4] See minute 3, p. 104.
[5] *Foreign Relations*, 1878, p. 895.

carry out the transfer of Albanian territory to Greece met with popular resistance, and had to leave the country without fulfilling its ungrateful task. On the strength of its report, the Powers who had signed the Treaty of Berlin were obliged to acknowledge as Albanian the region which they had decided to cede to Greece, and fixed the Greek frontier at the Arta River.

The Treaty of Berlin has justly been called "Albania's Funeral Treaty". Nevertheless, the mutilations made by it might be called scratches, when compared with those later inflicted on Albania by the Conference of London of 1913. This Conference not only settled the Kalamas line (repudiated by the Albanians, as stated above), but also gave Greece the whole region from Arta to Cape Stilos. This region, which is known as the Chameria and is between 30 and 40 kilometres long, had a population of 63,000 before the Balkan War—40,000 being Albanians, 14,000 Christian Albanians, and 9,000 Greeks (or speaking Greek among themselves).

To the North, the Conference gave Montenegro and Serbia the territories of Kraya and Anamalit and the clans of Hoti and Grouda, the districts of Plava, Goussigne and Ipek, the Eastern part of the Mitrovitza district, the districts of Prichina, Guilan, Ferizovitch and Kachanik, part of the Uskub district, and the districts of Prizrend, Kalkandelen, Gostivar, Karcheva, Dibra, Strouga and Ochrida. The Albanian population of these districts, which are situated in the ancient vilayets of Kossova and Monastir, forms an 80% majority over the Slav elements. We therefore claim all these territories, which were torn from us by the Treaty of Berlin and the Conference of London of 1913.

Kossovo, also known as Old Serbia, has been inhabited by Albanians from time immemorial. The Serbs only appeared there in the 7th century, but could never establish their mastery owing to continual insurrections by the Albanians and to Bulgar rivalry.

Serbian preponderance in the Kossovo region has always been transitory, and in spite of Serbian oppression and persecution the large majority of its population has always been Albanian. The Serbian population which has penetrated there forms a minority of only 15%.

During the last few years and especially in 1910, 1911, and 1912, the Albanians attempted to regain their independence by insurrections. In 1912, 18,000 Albanians of Kossovo captured the town of Uskub after a desperate struggle against the Turkish Army, and compelled Turkey to grant them certain concessions.

The Ottoman Government was about to own the justice of Albanian aspirations by granting autonomous administration to part of Albania comprising the vilayets of Kossovo, Scutari and Yaninia, and part of the vilayet of Monastir. The Balkan States realised the weakness of a Turkey unable to subdue the Albanians, and feared the creation of an autonomous Albanian state in territory which they had long desired to possess. They therefore hastened to declare war against Turkey, and so the Albanians were unable to benefit by the concessions which they had won by armed force.

At the time of the territorial readjustment of the Balkans in 1913, our country was sacrificed for the sake of its neighbours, because the imminent danger of a European conflagration had to be averted at all costs. But now that the conflagration is over and the questions connected therewith are being settled by the triumph of the rights of nationalities, we are fully convinced that the rich districts which are wholly Albanian and as such necessary to the existence of Albania, will in justice be restored to their mother country.

Even though small foreign minorities must inevitably be included within the boundaries of the State of Albania, large groups of Albanians will, on the other hand, remain outside its boundaries.

The Conference is certain to appreciate the difference between our own legitimate desire for the return of brother Albanians to the Albanian family and the unjust claims of our neighbours, who, not content with having snatched from us so much wholly Albanian territory by force, now ask permission from the Congress to take yet more away.

Thus Greece claims the part of Southern Albania called Northern Epirus, arguing that it has a population of 120,000 Greeks and 80,000 Albanians. We dispute these figures, and maintain that the pro-Greek population of that region does not exceed 20,000 inhabitants. These 20,000 inhabitants live in the valley of Drinopoli and the plain (Vource) of Delvino; they are farmers who possess neither fields nor houses, but cultivate the land belonging to the Albanians.

It is also argued that all orthodox Albanians should be considered Greeks, regardless of nationality. This empty claim has naturally induced the Greek clergy to make their religion an instrument of oppression and tyranny.

The League of Prizrend had wrung from Turkey permission to open an Albanian school at Koritza; but the Greek clergy excommunicated orthodox parents who sent their children to this school, and denounced them to the Ottoman Government as conspirators against the State.

By this means they procured the deportation and imprisonment of many heads of Albanian families and led to the said school being closed.

As the Ottoman Government, for its part, brought the same pressure to bear on Mussulman parents to prevent them from sending their children to the Albanian school, the Greek clergy were in this instance allies of the Ottoman Government against patriotic Albanians.

Those who consider orthodox Albanians as Greeks urge that it would be unjust to attempt to subject a Christian majority, with a superior civilisation, to a Mussulman minority with an inferior civilisation.

There can be no question of a difference of civilisation between children of the same race who live together under the same conditions, speak the same language, and have the same customs. If orthodox Albanians have attended Greek schools, Mussulman and Catholic Albanians denied the right to be taught in their native tongue have, on the other hand, attended Turkish, French, Italian, English and American schools.

Much emphasis is laid on the Greek sympathies of orthodox Albanians. In contradiction to this we bring forward the opinion of Lord Hobhouse, who accompanied Lord Byron to Albania and at the beginning of the 19th century wrote as follows concerning the populations forming the Ottoman Empire:—

"Only the Albanians are conscious of nationality; all the other peoples of the Empire are grouped according to religion".

Monsieur Aubaret, French delegate on the Commission for Eastern Roumelia, says in a Memorandum presented to the said Commission on August 13th, 1880:—

"They (the Albanians) live in complete unity; they are Albanian before everything else. If it is true that the Catholics are warmly attached to their religion, it is not less true that both they and their Mussulman fellow-countrymen value national consciousness, love of the soil and respect for old customs very highly, and put them before all other considerations."

In "L'Illustration" of 7th April, 1917, M. Vaucher writes concerning the Koritza district:—

"Albania for the Albanians is the motto of all the inhabitants of this rich plain of Koritza . . .

"For two months (as a Republic) the Albanians have . . . shown that they are capable of living on good terms with one another. There are no more religious quarrels, for the excellent reason that there is nobody now to stir them up."

Our opponents claim precisely that part of Albania which was burnt out by the Cretan bands of Zographos and disguised Greek soldiers under the command of Greek officers. This is clearly shown by the sketch which I have the honour to submit to you,[6] and which gives the names of the villages concerned.

It is a curious fact that the Greeks set fire to precisely those villages which they considered and still consider Greek. On this subject M. Vaucher, correspondent of "L'Illustration," writes:—

"The whole region of Kolonia has been laid waste since Greek bands passed through it in 1913. Names marked on the map are

---

[6] Not filed with the minutes.

merely memories, for in reality they are only represented by shapeless ruins marking the site of Mussulman villages."

The Greeks are probably claiming Northern Epirus in order to intimidate the Albanians and make them renounce their just claim to Southern Epirus and especially to the Chameria district, which is essentially Albanian.

At a time when our opponents maintain that the orthodox Albanians of Northern Epirus desire to be united to Greece, the Vlachs of Pindus (who, nevertheless, have experienced Greek rule) are asking for union with Albania. How can these two desires be reconciled?

How can one admit that the Albanians wish to disown their fellow-countrymen, when a foreign community like the Vlachs, which has lived under Greek rule, asks nothing better than to be united to Albania?

Taught by suffering, Albania in her reconstituted form will feel it incumbent upon her to live in perfect unity, in a spirit of wide tolerance, and she will allow foreign minorities all rights granted to them by the most civilised countries.

The southern boundary line of Albania seems to have been drawn by nature; it is the chain of the Gramos and Pindus mountains. This is the only boundary corresponding to the defensive and economic requirements of a country as weak as Albania.

If Albania had been free to act, she would certainly have offered to help the Allies by every means in her power. Until the country was invaded by the enemy she put all available resources at the disposal of the Allies, by helping and feeding Serbian troops during their retreat through Albanian territory.

This help given to Serbian troops gains a new significance in view of the atrocities and systematic massacres perpetrated on the Albanian population of Kossovo by those same Serbian troops during and after the Balkan wars. They also burnt numerous Albanian villages, as all European press correspondents reported at the time.

The Albanians were of the greatest assistance to the Italian and French troops after their arrival in Albania, and furthermore refused to form auxiliary Albanian corps in Southern Albania, in spite of all the promises made them by Austria and a Balkan State.

The Conference desires to lay the foundations of a lasting peace. There can be no such peace in the Balkans unless the rights of nationalities are respected.

If, for instance, the Congress, contrary to this principle, were to confirm the dismemberment so unfortunately effected in 1878 and 1913, the country would never enjoy the peace which is essential to its economic development. Such a proceeding would, moreover, give rise to periodical crises in Greece and Serbia, neither of which could absorb an Albanian majority so proud of its independence and so deeply attached to its national traditions. Such a situation would stir up continual disturbances along the frontiers of the Albanian State.

The excesses and massacres suffered by the Albanian populations inhabiting districts annexed by the above-named States give just cause to fear the fate in store for them, and their only hope of peace would be emigration or death.

The probable fate recalls the words of Tacitus: "Ubi solitudinem faciunt pacem appellant".

Source: Department of State, *Papers Relating to the Foreign Relations of the United States, The Paris Peace Conference, 1919*, vol. IV, 111-116 <https://history.state.gov/historicaldocuments/frus1919Parisv04/pg_116>, accesed 25 October 2020.

INDEX

Agolli, Dritero, 158

Ali Pasha, 7, 42, 45, 46, 48, 49, 53, 56

Ankara, 94, 105, 113, 119, 124, 183

Atatürk, Kemal, 87-89, 94, 95, 112, 115, 126, 195

Austro-Hungary, 39, 73-78, 81-84

Balkan, 3, 4, 6, 7, 15, 16, 18, 21, 26, 30, 35, 49, 65, 71-6, 83, 84, 94-6, 118, 120, 121, 124, 125, 135, 143, 149, 158, 176, 181, 182, 184-6, 190, 192

Berisha, Sali, 18, 123-5, 128, 179

Berlin Congress, 28, 67, 84, 220

Bektashi, 46, 54-7, 64, 86, 137, 138, 176, 198, 199, 201, 207, 211, 219

Bulgaria, 14, 42, 63, 65-7, 70, 72, 74, 76, 88, 106, 146

China, 15, 104-6, 184, 204, 218

Congress of Lushnje, 86

Dervish, 54, 55

Devşirme, 52, 53

Durres, 23, 33, 43, 44, 47, 70, 72, 81, 82, 84, 131, 134, 135, 144

East, 8, 13, 14, 15, 16, 18, 20, 21, 25, 30, 31, 38, 39, 42, 45, 53, 58, 62, 72, 78, 81, 100, 102, 103, 106, 107, 111, 112, 115, 116, 118-23, 125, 136, 138, 141, 144, 151, 152, 156, 158, 162, 163, 180, 183, 184, 186, 189, 190, 192, 193

EU, 10, 14, 15, 17-20, 30, 113, 115, 119-22, 129, 131, 136, 137, 180, 181, 183, 185-7, 189, 191, 197, 199, 202, 203, 219

Erdoğan, Tayyip, 114-9, 121, 122, 128, 131-3, 163, 174-9, 181-7, 190

Euro-Atlantic, 18, 20, 30, 31, 139

Frashëri, Abdyl, 60, 66

Frashëri, Mit'hat Bey, 60, 97

Frashëri, Kristo, 11, 154, 155, 157, 158, 162

Frashëri, Naim, 56, 57, 59, 167, 171, 172

Frashëri Sami, 49, 50, 166

Geg, 28, 36, 38, 58, 61, 155, 173

Greece, xi, xiii, 2, 12, 13, 16, 17, 19, 21, 22, 24, 25, 42, 58, 64, 67, 70, 72, 74, 76-8, 80, 81, 83, 84, 88-91, 94-6, 99, 101, 102, 106, 124, 125, 128, 129, 136, 137, 144, 165, 184, 185, 189, 191, 197, 200, 204

Greater Albania, 15, 16, 19, 128, 186, 191, 198, 205, 207, 213, 214, 217

Grey, Edward, 75, 76, 78, 81

Hoxha, Enver, xi, 2, 12, 16, 17, 95-109, 151, 156, 161, 162, 190, 204

Illyria, 23-26, 39, 90, 92, 142-4, 146, 149

Italy, xi, 1, 2, 12-14, 21, 22, 43, 47, 64, 71, 75-7, 80, 82-4, 86, 87, 95-8, 100, 101, 129, 130, 136, 165, 199, 205, 208, 216

Janine, 47, 56, 60, 63, 66, 70, 73, 76
Jeniçeri, 52, 54, 55

Kadare, Ismail, ix, 7-11, 20, 31, 94, 95, 108, 141-62, 168, 171, 178, 183, 191, 192, 197, 202, 205-8, 210, 213-5, 221

Kanuni, 28, 29, 86, 94, 144, 145, 202, 219

Kokalari, Musine, 98, 100, 220

Kosovo, 5, 6, 8, 12, 14, 16-20, 34, 53, 56, 60, 66, 70, 76-8, 95, 98, 99, 118, 121, 125-9, 132, 133, 141, 149-51, 153-6, 158, 162, 164, 165, 167-9, 173, 177, 180, 182-5, 189, 191, 192, 195, 200, 201, 203, 206-11, 213, 214, 220

London Conference, 75-9, 82, 84, 86.
Lushnje, 73, 86
Luzaj, Isuf, 96-8, 100, 101

Macedonia and North Macedonia, 5, 12, 14, 17, 20, 67, 70, 72, 74, 77, 78, 88, 124, 129, 144, 162, 164, 165, 185, 186, 189, 198, 209, 211, 214

Manastir, 66, 68, 72, 76

Megali Idea, 16, 90, 91

Milosevic, Slobodan, 6, 127

Montenegro, 12, 14, 16, 20, 21, 42, 65-7, 69, 72, 73, 77, 78, 83, 95, 162, 185, 191

Mosque, 46, 123, 125, 133, 140, 146, 150, 152, 160, 161, 176, 183

Ottoman, xi, xii, 3-6, 8, 11, 12, 15, 16, 18, 20, 26, 29, 30, 33-53, 55-67, 69-73, 75-7, 81, 83, 84, 87, 89, 90, 112-6, 118-21, 133, 140-56, 158, 160-4, 166-71, 173, 174, 177, 178, 182, 184, 186, 188, 190-2, 196, 197, 203, 205, 206, 208, 213, 215-7, 220, 221

Paris Peace Treaty, 84, 86

Qosja, Rexhep, 8, 20, 31, 141, 151-62, 164, 191, 192

Religion, 13, 29, 30, 34-6, 38, 51, 53-9, 62, 68, 89, 94, 112, 113, 120, 133, 137, 138, 140, 146, 147, 152, 153, 155, 157, 159, 163, 176, 177, 183, 187, 188, 192

Romania, 17, 42, 74, 106

INDEX

Russia, xi, 15, 17, 42, 56, 65, 67, 70, 74-7, 82, 118, 136, 137, 156, 174, 181, 184-7, 189, 198, 202, 205, 209, 214

Serbia, xi, 4-6, 12, 14-17, 19, 21, 34, 35, 42, 57, 65-7, 70, 72-4, 76, 77, 78, 81, 83, 84, 95, 124-8, 143, 148-50, 153-6, 159, 162, 180-2, 184, 185, 187, 189, 198

Skenderbeg, 6, 11, 43, 47, 48, 50, 52, 56, 58, 71, 90, 94, 142, 144-6, 148, 151, 159, 160, 164, 176, 210, 218

Shkoder, 23, 44, 46, 60, 66, 70, 73, 77, 96, 97, 144, 164, 218

Stalin, Joseph, 4, 16, 102, 103, 104, 107

Tanzimat, 39, 41, 42, 45

Timar, 39, 40, 42

Tirane, 24, 25, 27, 37, 46, 94-7, 102, 104-7, 153, 158, 160, 165, 167, 175, 176, 183, 196, 199-202, 204, 206, 208, 210, 216, 218, 220

The Porte, 4, 30, 33, 38-41, 44-9, 51-3, 56, 58, 60-6, 68-70, 72, 146, 150, 161, 170, 171

The Prizren League, 56, 66, 167

Tito, 4, 16, 102, 106, 155

Toptani, Esat Pasha 72, 73, 81, 82

Tosk, 28, 36, 38, 46, 58, 61, 155, 173

US, 12, 18, 21, 22, 83, 100, 102, 103, 105, 113, 117, 119, 122-4, 130, 133, 138, 180-2, 185, 186, 189, 190, 200, 207, 214, 218

Vilayet, 56, 60, 66, 70, 72, 76, 78

Vlore, 21, 43, 44, 46, 47, 77, 78, 83, 84, 95-7, 125, 135, 175

Western, xii, 3-5, 13, 14-17, 20, 21, 24, 31, 40-2, 55, 78, 86-8, 95, 100, 106, 111-3, 117, 118, 119-21, 130, 132, 135, 157, 158, 163, 165, 169, 174, 176, 178, 180, 182, 184, 185, 187, 189, 190-2, 196, 197, 211, 213, 215

Zogu, Ahmet, 86, 87, 88, 94-9

www.ingramcontent.com/pod-product-compliance
Lightning Source LLC
Chambersburg PA
CBHW061441300426
44114CB00014B/1780